ALL SOLDIERS RUN AWAY

Alano's War: The Story of a British Deserter

By
Andy Owen

Lammi
Publishing Inc.

Published by Lammi Publishing, Inc., headquartered in Coaldale, Alberta, Canada.
http://lammipublishing.ca

North African Campaign Map produced and (c) 2017 by Paul Hewitt, Battlefield Design.
www.battlefield-design.co.uk

Italian Campaign Map produced and (c) 2017 by Paul Hewitt, Battlefield Design.
www.battlefield-design.co.uk

Library and Archives Canada Cataloguing in Publication
Owen, Andy, 1977-, author
All soldiers run away : Alano's war : the story of a British deserter / by Andy Owen.

Includes bibliographical references.
Issued in print and electronic formats.
ISBN 978-1-988932-01-9 (softcover).—ISBN 978-1-988932-02-6 (Kindle).—
ISBN 978-1-988932-03-3 (EPUB)

1. Juniper, Alan, 1918-2016. 2. Military deserters—Great Britain—Biography. 3. Soldiers—Great Britain—Biography. 4. Desertion, Military—Great Britain—History—20th century. 5. World War, 1939-1945—Desertions—Great Britain. I. Title.

D810.D57O94 2017   940.54'8   C2017-905580-1
                                             C2017-905581-X

Text editing by Karen Hann
Cover design by Paul Hewitt, Battlefield Design

For Katie, Max, and Lawrence

Table of Contents

Alan Juniper Timeline

1918	22 May	London	Alan Juniper born
1939	3 Sep	London and Paris	Britain and France declare war on Germany
	15 Dec	Winchester	Alan called up and posted to the London Rifle Brigade
1940	15 May		Posted to 1st Battalion Tower Hamlets Rifles later to be known as 9th Rifles Battalion (9RB)
	26 May–4 Jun	Dunkirk	The evacuation of Allied soldiers from mainland Europe
	22 Jun	Paris	France surrenders
	Sep	Egypt	Italian forces push into British-held Egypt
	15 Nov–31 Dec	Duchess of Athol	9RB sail to Egypt
1941	Jan	North Africa	Operation COMPASS retakes Tobruk for the Allies and pushes the Italians west
	22 Mar	Mersa Brega	After keeping peace between Arabs and Italian small holders in Cyrenaica 9RB arrive in Mersa Brega
	31 Mar	Mersa Brega	Germans launched their first offensive of the North Africa Campaign
	11 Apr	North Africa	Tobruk garrison surrounded by Axis forces. Over next two weeks 9RB continue to retreat to Cairo.
	15 May	North Africa	Operation BREVITY launches and ends shortly after in defeat for the Allied Forces

	15 Jun	North Africa	Operation BATTLEAXE launches and ends shortly after in defeat for the Allied Forces
	19 Jun	North Africa	Appointed Lance Corporal
	22 Jun	Soviet Union	Germany invades Russia
	18 Nov	North Africa	Operation CRUSADER launched relieving the siege of Tobruk and pushing Axis troops back past Mersa Brega.
	7 Dec	Hawaii	Japan attacks the US Fleet at Pearl Harbour
	11 Dec	Washington, DC	The United States declares war on Germany, Italy, and Japan.
1942	21 Jan	North Africa	The Axis launch counter-attack recapturing Benghazi by 28 January
	6 Feb	Gazala	Allied Forces have fallen back to a line from Gazala to Bir Hakeim, west of Tobruk
	9–11 May	North Africa	Goes Absent Without Leave (AWOL) for which he forfeits two days' pay and is confined to barracks
	26 May	Gazala	Axis launches attack which becomes Battle of Gazala
	13 Jun	Gazala	'Black Saturday' as Allies suffer heavy defeats. Followed the next day by a withdrawal from the Gazala line.
	21 Jun	Tobruk	The fall of Tobruk to Axis forces
	1–27 Jul	Alamein	Allies falls back to Alamein and attempt to halt the Axis advance
	5–29 Jul	North Africa	AWOL
	2 Sep	Cairo	Pleads 'not guilty' at Field General Court Martial (FGCM) but found 'guilty'.
	13 Oct	Cairo	Posted to 51st Military Provost Detention Barracks (MPDB) & then on to 50th MPDB

	23 Oct–11 Nov	Alamein	The Second Battle of Alamein, which results in Allied victory and turns the campaign in their favour
	7 May	Tunis	The fall of Tunis followed six days later by the surrender of the remaining North African Axis forces
1943	20 Jul	Cairo	Released from 50 MPDB having served 322 days and posted to 2nd Battalion Rifle Brigade (2RB)
	24 Jul	Rome	Mussolini arrested
	3 Sep	Italy	Allied invasion of Italy
1944	17 Jan–18 May	Gustav Line, Italy	The Battle of Monte Cassino
	4 May	Taranto, Italy	2RB land in Italy
	30 May	Cassino	2RB pass through Cassino on move on to the front
	4 Jun	Rome	US Forces enter Rome
	11 Jun	Cantelupo	2RB secure Cantelupo
	6 Jun	Northern France	D-Day, Allied invasion of mainland Europe
	18–22 Jun	Perugia	The Battle of Perugia, in which 2RB take part in a significant night attack to take an overlooking peak
	5 Jul	Italy	Alan Juniper is declared deserter
	Aug	Lacugnano	Alan arrives in Lacugnano
1945	2 May	Germany	Germany surrenders
	24 Oct	Italy	Alan Juniper is apprehended and held in close arrest
	28 Nov	Italy	At FGCM pleads guilty & found guilty. Sentenced to 2 years plus the rest of previous sentence not served. Sent to MPDB32 and then The Glasshouse, Colchester

1947	14 Jan	UK	Sentence suspended posted to the Rifle Brigade
	4 Aug	UK	Demobbed in to Reserves
1959	30 Jun	UK	Discharged from Reserve Liability

Maps

North African Campaign

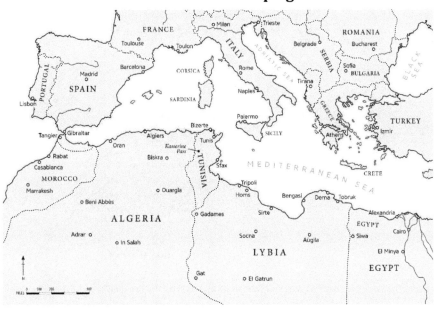

© 2017 Paul Hewitt, Battlefield Design

Italian Campaign (with Lacugnano)

© 2017 Paul Hewitt, Battlefield Design

Introduction
Trying to Forget

When we dwell on the enormity of the Second World War and its victims, we try to absorb all those statistics of national and ethnic tragedy. But, as a result, there is a tendency to overlook the way the war changed even the survivors' lives in ways impossible to predict.

Europe's Long Shadow, Antony Beevor

It is difficult not to dwell on the enormity of the statistics. The Second World War was the deadliest military conflict in history in terms of total lives lost. The statistics vary, with estimates of deaths ranging from fifty million to more than eighty million. Estimates for the number of civilians killed vary from twenty-nine to fifty-five million. The figures for total military dead vary from twenty-one to twenty-five million.[1]

The first Armistice Day was in 1919, after King George V on 7 November that year, had issued a proclamation which called for a two-minute silence: "All locomotion should cease, so that, in perfect stillness, the thoughts of everyone may be concentrated on reverent remembrance of the glorious dead."[2]

After the end of the Second World War in 1945, Armistice Day became Remembrance Day to include all those who had fallen in both world wars and other conflicts. Over the years, across the globe, hundreds of thousands, more likely millions, of people have stood solemnly, heads bowed, some in front of monuments of stone covered with the names of some of those glorious dead observing the silence. But in all those minutes of silence every November, what are we remembering? For many of us now, are we remembering the personal connections to those who fought in these conflicts are being lost. This time is rapidly disappearing from living memory. How many of those fifty to eighty million stories do we know? Is it now just imagined heroes running at machine gun posts with no fear, who then moved on unaffected by what they did or saw that we remember?

We are not even sure of the bare statistics; the estimates disagree in magnitudes of millions. The conflicts in which I have personal experience in Iraq and Afghanistan have resulted in indescribable suffering for hundreds of thousands, but the totals would fit in to the margins of disagreement. For every individual affected by war, though, it is irrelevant as to the size of the statistic that their experience belongs. True tragedies are intimate—restricted to those involved and those close to them, the rest is limited to imaginations of the sympathetic. But to many of the millions, we cannot even extend to them that sympathy. We don't know the stories of many of the people, just the myths of nations. Some of those myths should be challenged. Since the end of the Second World War there may have been enough minutes of silence to remember each one of those victims, civilian and military, but maybe not to remember the survivors whose lives were changed "in ways impossible to predict".[3] And it is not just those that survive—it is their families, too. Lives that had not yet begun as the war ended would be impacted.

One such life was that of Stephenie Stockley. We met on social media in August 2015 seventy years after the end of the war that her father, Alan Juniper, had fought in. In her bio she claimed that; "My father's story deserves to be told." She was looking for someone to help write up the story of his wartime experience. I had just published a novel, and I was looking for a new project. There was a link to an interview with BBC Radio Solent, which I clicked. The journalist told listeners that Stephenie's family had kept Alan's tale a secret for many years, but now, at the age of 60, she was planning to tell her story through a book. An emotional voice that I didn't yet recognise told the sympathetic interviewer; "I had never ever said out loud that my dad was a deserter until a couple of years ago."[4] It seemed like it could be a fascinating story.

It is becoming increasingly important to capture stories like Alan's as many such stories are now lost forever, and more and more are lost every year. The United States National World War Two Museum in New Orleans estimates that approximately 430 American veterans of that war currently pass away every day, or one every three minutes—with only 700,000 remaining of the original 16,000,000.[5] The museum estimates that in twenty years, none will be left. Memories that do not get laid down by the telling, to be compressed over time, aren't found by the fossil hunters of future generations. They will instead just find the rusting bullets and bones that generated those statistics. The North African desert, where Alan first saw the war, has the ordnance of two great armies is buried within its bowels. Some of the stories from this theatre of operations are part of our national consciousness. Others, though, have already been lost in the sands of time.

The first battle that Alan's battalion was involved in, the Battle of Mersa Brega, is one of those lost stories. It was a small battle by Second World War standards. However, when the pursuit back across the Libyan desert is included, it resulted in a comparable number of deaths of soldiers to the total losses suffered by British troops in the Iraq War, 2003 -2010 (179 UK troops killed—138 of which were classified as having been killed in hostile circumstances).[6]

Alan has now passed away. In his final years, he suffered from dementia. He can no longer tell us any more of his story. Everything he did not share has now gone, and, like most of those in his generation, he did not share much. His daughter Stephenie described it as like "pulling teeth" trying to get him to talk about the war. As the guns fell silent, about much that happened to him, he also fell silent.

There were some things the family had always known, some things that others may have tried to hide. Alan's family had always known that he deserted in Italy in 1944. They also knew that while on the run in the chaos of post-occupation Italy after deserting, he found solace in a village, with people with whom he could not converse, and who had been until very recently been the enemy. Here Alan became "Alano," member of the community, friend, and adopted family member, rather than Rifleman Juniper deserter from Her Majesty's Armed Forces. Alan's family visited the village regularly after the war, and they remain in touch with the community to this day. The solace and the friendships the village offered Alan seemed to outweigh any shame he felt regarding his decision to desert.

The onset of dementia, however, took Alan back to memories he had tried to suppress for most of his life and had never shared with his family. It became obvious that there was much of his story that the family did not know. After requesting his war record, the family learned that Alan had also briefly gone AWOL and then a few months later deserted in 1942 in the desert of North Africa. His record showed that he had spent time in a military prison before being released to fight again in Italy. Even Alan's wife of fifty years had not known this.

At the age of eighty-five, Alan eventually received a diagnosis, from psychologists at Combat Stress, the UK's leading veterans' mental health charity. He was diagnosed with what used to be known as shell shock in the First World War, battle fatigue in the Second World War, but is now known as Post Traumatic Stress Disorder (PTSD). The French essayist Michel de Montaigne noted that "Nothing fixes a thing so intensely in the memory as the wish to forget it." As the dementia worsened, his ability to suppress these memories lessened. In his last years, he feared the Royal Military Police were coming to take him away as they had done before all those years ago.

There was one incident from that time that he kept returning to again and again, before eventually the memory dissolved, that could have been the reason he deserted and the cause of his PTSD. It was an incident that suddenly explained to his family his fear of being in confined spaces, a fear so great that he could not even bear to be inside his own house for extended periods and sought out a career that would keep him outdoors. That career led him from the parks of East London to the Aga Khan's golf course in Sardinia and to golf courses in Abidjan and Yamoussoukro in the Ivory Coast at the request of the then-president. Alan's family members are only now beginning to understand the effects of his time in war had on him.

This is a search for the causes of those effects. It is a search for an incident in a desert filled with violence, confusion and loss many years ago; it is the search for one grain of sand in a dune sea. The search will hopefully help Alan's family better understand what he went through, but it will hopefully also better help us, the public, understand how we generally think about desertion and serve as a starting point to understand the ethics of this rarely discussed act. For me as an ex-soldier, his story may raise some awkward questions.

In December 2015, the second series of *Serial* began. *Serial* was an investigative journalism podcast hosted by Sarah Koenig, where she narrated a nonfiction story over multiple episodes. In this series, it chose as its subject matter the most high-profile desertion by a soldier from a NATO force on operations in recent years: Sergeant Bowe Bergdahl. Bergdahl, a US soldier, was held for five years by the Taliban and then arrested for desertion after his negotiated release. The podcasts addressed some very wide-ranging issues from the failure of the strategic mission in Afghanistan, the politics of the peace process, to the what the military and other US government agencies did to try and recover him, but at the heart of the story were the questions: who is Bergdahl and why did he leave his post—did he desert, and what was his motivation for what he did?

Much uncertainty still lurks around the case, and questions remain unanswered. In one version of events reported in the media, Bergdahl deserted to join the Taliban, in another he converted to Islam during his captivity. There are numerous versions from Taliban sources of how they came to hold him. Bergdahl himself claimed that he was attempting to highlight command failures within his battalion by going missing and then turning up at the main base in the area, having made his own way there from the forward operating base he was stationed at. At the time of writing, the court martial has yet to sit on his case.

The reaction to how Bergdahl's release was secured, particularly the fact that the US traded five Taliban prisoners for his release, and the way in which congress was side stepped in the process, also became a political one (so much so that during his campaign to become the Republican nomination for the US presidential election in 2016, Donald Trump saw fit to highlight the case and say that he thought that the US shot deserters rather than cut deals for their release). Bergdahl's defence team filed a motion for dismissal, shortly after Trump was sworn in as president, citing more than forty instances of Trump's criticism at public appearances and media interviews through August 2016.[7] However, the reaction to the case from both within the military and outside is illustrative to how much of a controversial issue desertion still is today.

Koenig interviewed some of Bergdahl's company for the show and was shocked by some of the comments. One member of his company, Daryl Hanson, said he would have shot him if he had found him.[8] Another, John Thurman, had himself received counselling to deal with aftermath of conflict, so Koenig felt he would be more sympathetic to Bergdahl, particularly when he learned that Thurman had had a breakdown two years previously during coast guard basic training and had been diagnosed with Schizotypal personality disorder, said; "we all experienced the same thing but we didn't walk off." Thurman claimed to try hard to see it from Bergdahl's side and noted that we all have different mental abilities to cope with situations— but said he could not ever forgive him on principle. For Thurman, and others Koenig spoke to, Bergdahl broke that intimate bond that they all shared: "that is not something you can ever come back from—I don't care where your head was Bowe you still fucking did it. You walked off and you betrayed us. It stops there. That is the infantry man in me taking over."[9]

My first reaction upon hearing from his family that Alan was a deserter was not positive. I was initially unsure of whether to agree to write his story. As a former soldier who served alongside US forces, my initial reaction to Bergdahl's desertion was also not a positive one. I understood that sense of betrayal that Thurman spoke of. On my first hearing that Alan was a deserter, that sense of betrayal pricked in me.

But my reaction was not the same towards all cases of desertion. When I read of the 306 British soldiers who were shot at dawn for cowardice or desertion in the First World War, my feelings were much more ambiguous. Families of some of these soldiers took the Ministry of Defence to court, claiming they were suffering from what was then called "shell shock." In 2006, all 306 received posthumous pardons.[10] This included a Private Harry Farr, who was executed during the Battle of the Somme in 1916 for cowardice in the face of the enemy. Speaking after the announcement by the Ministry of Defence that a pardon would be issued, Mrs Harris, Farr's daughter, said;

> I have always argued that my father's refusal to re-join the front line, described in the court martial as resulting from cowardice, was in fact the result of shell-shock. And I believe that many other soldiers suffered from this too, not just my father.[11]

John Dickinson, the lawyer representing Mrs Harris, went on to state offer explanation:

> This is complete common sense and acknowledges that Pte Farr was not a coward but an extremely brave man. Having fought for two years practically without respite in the trenches, he was very obviously suffering from a condition we now would have no problem in diagnosing as post-traumatic stress disorder, or shell-shock, as it was known in 1916.[12]

It now seems clear that a significant proportion of those 306 were suffering from a psychological injury that would now receive a clinical diagnosis, if not from the physical damage their brains had received from the repeated exposure to high explosives, from the psychological trauma those such as 16-year-old Herbert Burden experienced after seeing his friends massacred at the battlefield of Bellwarde Ridge. Burden had lied about his age so he could join the Northumberland Fusiliers before he was officially old enough to. Instead of receiving support and treatment, he was court-martialled for fleeing after the battle, and when he was killed by firing squad he was still officially too young to be in his regiment.[13] In Alan's case, there is cause to examine what we know about the psychological trauma he endured, the impact this had on him (just as everyone's body has different physical limits, everyone's brain has different psychological limits), and the medical support he was offered at the time.

Examining Alan's story, or that of any deserter, is not just a case of establishing if the desertion is caused by psychological injury or not. When I heard about the soldiers from neutral Ireland who deserted the Irish army (that had remained out of action), to go and fight in what few would argue was not a just war with the British Army against the Axis forces, my reaction, however, was different. During the course of the war, one in six of the 42,000 members of the Irish armed forces deserted. Almost 5,000 were found guilty in their absence by court-martial of going absent without leave or simply dismissed.[14] It was only in 2012 that the Irish soldiers that did this received and apology and then an official pardon the year later through a bill introduced to the *Dail*. When they returned from the Second World War, often having fought bravely for many years, their names were added to a formal blacklist by the government, barring them from employment and refusing them military pensions. Many were ostracised in their local communities. The pardoning of these deserters was controversial even all those years later. The wider history between the Irish and British peoples no doubt added to and confused that controversy. To me, these Irish deserters were doing what they had to do to join a just war to protect the freedom of all countries in Europe from fascism. To others, these men were traitors whose actions left their own country vulnerable to foreign invasion.

After hearing of the desertion of the author and journalist Arthur Koestler, who signed up with the intention of deserting at the first opportunity of deployment, I again felt less negative than when I had hearing of Bergdahl's case. After the outbreak of the Second World War, Koestler, an Austrian and a Jew, was arrested in late 1939 (after attempting to turn himself in to the authorities as a foreign national a number of times). He was eventually moved to an internment camp among other "undesirable aliens." He was released in early 1940, but was not given an exit permit, which would have allowed him to leave France before the German invasion. So Koestler joined the French Foreign Legion in order to get out of the country. He then deserted in North Africa and headed to the UK. Koestler signed up to join the legion with the intention of deserting as soon as he was out of France.[15] Arriving in the UK without an entry permit, he was briefly detained again. Immediately after release, however, he volunteered for service with the British Army. He served twelve months in the Pioneer Corps before he was assigned to the Ministry of Information, where he worked as a scriptwriter for propaganda broadcasts and films.[16]

When I thought about German, Italian, or other Axis soldiers deserting in that same conflict, I felt none of the same emotions. Should conscripted Axis soldiers, who believed that by refusing orders and remaining in their unit they would be executed, have felt morally obliged to desert due to the unjust nature of the war they were fighting? In *Killing in War,* moral philosopher Jeff McMahan claims that "just war theory" refers to both a tradition of thought and a doctrine that has emerged from that tradition.[17] Although there is "no one canonical statement of the doctrine" there is a core set of principles that appear, with only minor variations, in many books and articles that discuss the ethics of war. *Just and Unjust Wars* by American political theorist Michael Walzer is seen as one of the most influential of such books.[18] Walzer lays out the two sets of principles that together are the foundation of traditional theories. One principle covers the resort to war (*jus ad bellum*) and the other covers the conduct of war (*jus in bello*). Traditional theories have it that the two principles are independent of each other. So, it is possible for a just war to be fought unjustly and for an unjust war to be fought in strict accordance with the rules. Therefore, unjust combatants do not do wrong merely by participating in an unjust war. The decision to go to war is made by a smaller group of those in power.

Soldiers bear no responsibility for these decisions by others who they have a *prima facie* duty to obey. Individual soldiers do wrong only if they violate the principles of *jus in bello*.[19] This usually requires them to discriminate between combatants and non-combatants, intentionally attacking only the former and not the latter. Even though Axis troops were taking part in an unjust war in terms of *jus ad bellum* as long as they conducted themselves within the international laws of armed conflict they were not behaving unethically.

This has been the view for several centuries, but the relationship between these principles have been challenged in more recent years and a revisionist account has been put forward by philosophers such as McMahan. They argue that war is morally continuous with other forms of violent conflict and therefore reject the idea that a different morality comes into effect in war—such as those created by a *prima facie* duty for soldiers to obey those above them in the command chain (Cecile Fabre, for example, compares soldiers following orders in war to Mafioso following the orders of a Godfather).[20] Crucially, they believe that *jus in bello* cannot be independent of *jus ad bellum*.[21] [22] They assert that the principles of *jus ad bellum* apply not only to governments, but also to individual soldiers, who in general ought not to fight in wars that are unjust. If they do, the acts of violence they commit can be considered morally wrong even if those acts fall within existing laws of armed conflict and are comparable to acts committed morally by those fighting a just war (often the enemy in the same conflict). For some this extends to acts of self-defence (others like Fabre make distinctions, for example, believing soldiers fighting an unjust war can be justified when they protect their compatriots from unjustified killings as carried out by *ad bellum* just combatants).[23] Some would therefore see a German soldier who was part of the invading German Army and was confronted with a French soldier (most likely a civilian conscripted into the army due to the German aggression) as morally in the wrong if he inflicted violence on the French soldier even if in their tactical engagement he was defending himself or his comrades (not all revisionists would agree on this, as we will see later). These revisionist arguments suggest to me that in cases such as those in the German military in the Second World War a case could be made that the most ethical thing to do may have been deserting.

Before being faced with the outline of Alan's story, when considering desertion, I made an assumption that there was something inherently unethical in the act itself, but clearly like other moral and legal offenses context is important. My initial negative response was shaped by the context I know. I served in a volunteer army with modern logistic support, with limited operation tour dates, alongside the army that Bergdahl served with and for a time in the same conflict. Understanding the context around Alan's desertion forced me to challenge some of my beliefs about how a soldier should be and why I thought the way I thought. It may also, I hope, provoke others more qualified than I to look more widely at the ethics of desertion.

Before Alan stopped being able to recall events from his past, he had spent a lifetime trying to forget some of the key events in his story. For most of his life, Alan did not want to be associated with aspects of his own story and certainly not the associations others would make if they heard the word "deserter." This was and is the case for many who have been affected by war. For differing reasons they feel uncomfortable with the labels they've received and the assumptions others have made about their experiences. There is a resistance by many veterans, even when less affected later generations want to know all the long-buried details, to revisit those memories.

His story as presented here has had to be pieced together from the limited amount that people were able to prise from him, from the memories of others, from the dusty and impersonal records and diaries that still exist, and from the grand narratives in the history books to which he was not even a footnote. Therefore, I need to make that claim that Hollywood makes and say that Alan's story as presented in this narrative is 'based on actual events.' It is close to his story as I can get it. As well as being Alan's story, it is his family's story too, and is also the story of many of his generation and could again be the story of many in my generation, which is why there is a need to tell it. I believe that Stephenie was right—it is a story that deserves to be told. So here it is; here is Alan's story. This is the book Stephenie sought to have written.

Alan Arthur Juniper.
His family believe this would have been taken around 1940

Chapter One
Foreign Shores

The most shocking fact about war is that its victims and its instruments are individual human beings, and that these individual beings are condemned by the monstrous conventions of politics to murder or be murdered in quarrels not their own.

Words of Wisdom: Aldous Huxley, Aldous Huxley

Twenty-two-year-old Alan Juniper boarded the 28,000 ton P&O liner the Duchess of Athol in Liverpool in November of 1940 with the rest (minus two soldiers who deserted while the battalion was still in the UK before the ship set sail) of the 1 Tower Hamlets' Rifles (1TH), later to be known as 9 Rifle Brigade (9RB),.[24] He would have looked similar to how he did in the photograph on the previous page.

How he was as a person back then before he had been to war, we don't entirely know. We do know he was a gentle and humble man by the time he met his wife after the war, and, later from his children, we know that he was a protective dad who never shouted and had a silly sense of humour with a laugh that often sounded more like a giggle to accompany it. We know that later still he became a grandpa who loved being with his grandchildren, spending hours playing football outside with them. We also know he never wanted sons, as he thought daughters would not get called up to war.

The Tower Hamlets' Rifles was a Territorial Army battalion that took the majority of its fighting men from London's East End. The young men who made up the battalion were mostly the product of the harsh environment of cramped basic housing with eighteenth-century facilities that made up that area of the city. For the most part they were tough, resourceful and used to hardship. The East End of London in the 1930s and early 1940s was not as it is today, with the trendy dockside developments inhabited by those who work in the new financial centres to the east of the City. The soldiers of the battalion were described as "highly motivated" by their commanding officer Lieutenant-Colonel E. A. Shipton, as many of their families and loved ones were nightly being subjected to the Blitz by the Luftwaffe and they were keen for revenge.[25] Alan is listed in the Battalion War Diary as a 6915504 Rfn [Rifleman] A Juniper of D Company (D Company).[26]

Alan had been living in Chingford just to the north of the East End, before joining up, but he had spent a good part of his childhood in the countryside. When he was in his early teens, his father—who had had been sacked from the Metropolitan Police (after reaching the rank of sergeant) for going on strike after many years of exemplary service—became a pub landlord. According to Stephenie, Alan's father was a very quiet, stern man who maintained the air of a police sergeant rather than that of a publican. She describes Alan's mother as a "tiny, soft lady." Alan's parents died within six months of each other when he would have been forty-four; his mother passed away first, then his father six months later.

When Alan's parents moved to the pub, Alan, the youngest of four brothers, was not old enough to legally live in the pub. Therefore, his parents sent him to live with his aunt and uncle. Whilst this disrupted his schooling (something he regretted that also ensured that later on he never wrote letters back home from the front), it was the beginning of his life-long love of the outdoors. Alan was not the only one of the family to sail off to war; his second eldest brother Ken also went, and despite being conscripted into a different regiment (The Hampshire Regiment) the brothers' paths would come tantalising close to crossing later in Italy. One of the other brothers, Charles, was spared from conscription for medical reasons. The last brother, Frank, was not called up until later in the war and did not get posted overseas. After the war, Alan and Ken would remain very close, much more so than with their other brothers, until Ken's death in 1969, probably bonded by their experiences in war as much as their natural affinity to each other.

The Duchess of Atholl, 1940

Alan had only recently completed basic training, which was significantly more basic than the training troops in the British Army receive today. First, he trained in the depot in Winchester for six weeks and then trained as a specialist driver (though he did not actually have a driving license when he was selected as a driver) at Tidworth. Alan would only have fired his rifle a handful of times in training. From his records, we can see that he was described as "a reliable worker who will take on any job he is asked to and do it well" and "honest and hardworking."[27] Alan also had the unusual honour of receiving some of his training from a Hollywood star.

At the outbreak of the war, David Niven was the only British Hollywood star who returned from the US to sign up. He was commissioned as a lieutenant into the Rifle Brigade on 25 February 1940,[28] and was assigned to a motor training battalion. Alan told Stephenie with pride that he was there when he went through his training that same year.

Shortly after Alan went through training, Niven decided he wanted something more exciting, however, and transferred into the Commandos. He then went on to command 'A' or 'Phantom' Squadron GHQ Liaison Regiment and also worked with the Army Film Unit. He acted in two films made during the war, both intended to help win support for the British war effort. Niven's Film Unit work included a small part in the deception operation that used minor actor Private Clifton James to impersonate General Montgomery, after MI5 (the UK's Security Service) decided to exploit Clifton James' resemblance to him to confuse German intelligence. He travelled to the Mediterranean in role to talk about a plan to invade the south of France at a reception in Gibraltar and then in Cairo. Later, Niven took part in the invasion of Normandy, although he arrived several days after the D-Day landings. Despite being awarded the Legion of Merit (a US military decoration honouring his work in setting up the BBC Allied Expeditionary Forces Programme for the Allied forces), he refused to discuss the war on his return to Hollywood. This was despite public interest in celebrities in combat and his own well-earnt reputation for storytelling. He is believed to have once confided the following:

> I will, however, tell you just one thing about the war, my first story and my last. I was asked by some American friends to search out the grave of their son near Bastogne. I found it where they told me I would, but it was among 27,000 others, and I told myself that here, Niven, were 27,000 reasons why you should keep your mouth shut after the war.[29]

There were a few stories that have surfaced about Niven's wartime adventures. One story has him about to lead his men into action, when Niven eased their nervousness by telling them, "Look, you chaps only have to do this once. But I'll have to do it all over again in Hollywood with Errol Flynn!" On another occasion, asked how he felt about serving with the British Army in Europe, he allegedly said, "Well, on the whole, I would rather be tickling Ginger Rogers's tits!"[30]

It was in the same town that Alan underwent the first phase of his basic training that I first met his daughter Stephenie in person. When she saw his name in black and white expressed in the cold precision of military writing and record keeping at the Hampshire Records Office, she struggled not to cry. It was only a few months before Alan's death. What had made Alan himself was slowly being eroded by the thieving disease that is dementia; however, there on the page in black and white was proof of his existence.

That same afternoon we found a photo of the Duchess of Athol (above) taken from a South African beach, when Alan would have been on it heading round the continent to the Suez Canal. Stephenie looked at a picture that her father was in. Although we could not see him staring back, a young Alan Juniper was in that photo, maybe even sitting in one of the many doorways staring back at the camera trying to take his mind of his sea-sickness. Tears welled up in Stephenie's eyes. Many of the men staring back from that photo would never make it home again. None of them knew what the next few years would hold for them. Nobody in his company aboard the ship as that photo was taken would have even known exactly where they were destined for. Captain Robert Frisk in his account of his time in the desert contained as an attachment to the war diary claims that most people thought they knew for certain what the destination was. There was a lot of betting on it and "bets were laid on such widely separated spots as Norway, Italy, India, Singapore and naturally Egypt."[31] Frisk also noted that the first few days saw everyone keen to "get cracking," but on the third day out rough seas started and many of the troops went down with sea sickness. This prompted another round of betting amongst the officers who had a sweepstake on who would be the first in their number to go down.

Alan had never been on a boat before and did not take to the rough seas well. He was undoubtedly one of those to 'go down.' Many years later, he confided to Stephenie, who was suffering from seasickness on a Dover to Calais crossing, that his sickness had been awful. They would sit up on deck and eat dried crackers and apple, as it seemed to be the only thing they could keep down. He talked about the throb of the engines and the diesel smell inside the boat, which was wretch inducing. They used to sit in a corner of doorways to keep out of the wind and watch the horizon to try and keep from being sick. He sat Stephenie in a doorway just like he had done and told her to focus on the horizon. At the time, it was another two years before the Allied Forces would cross the channel on D-Day in June 1944 as part of Operation Overlord. The war in Europe was not going well for the Allies.

Alan lost a lot of weight on the six-week journey down the west coast of Africa, docking at Freetown in Sierra Leone on 29 November, and then Durban, which was the first stop where the troops could disembark. This was the safer route to take due to enemy activity in the Mediterranean Sea. It is likely they were told in advance that they would be able to disembark in Durban as Alan told Stephenie of the relief of catching sight of the stunning Table Mountain as they passed Cape Town, which would have indicated to him there was not much longer to go.

In Durban, according to the Battalion War Diaries, the battalion lost another four deserters, to go with the two who had deserted in Liverpool before setting sail. They eventually landed at Port Said Egypt on 31 December 1940. It would have been the first time Alan had set foot on foreign soil and everything would have felt disorientating and alien. Nobel Prize winner Naguib Mahfouz's novel *Midaq Alley* set in 1940s Cairo revolves around the people living and working in an old, narrow alley, which gives its name to the book. In it he describes the coffee shops as having "walls decorated with multi-coloured arabesques, now crumbling, give off strong odours from the medicines of olden times, smells which have now become the spices and folk-cures of today and tomorrow."[32] Mahfouz tells us that the alley is an "ancient relic" and "one of the gems of times gone by." Cairo is described as a city that oozes ancient and exotic history from every pore, and while society endures, its residents are only ever temporary witness to a grander show. For Alan, it would not have just been landing on strange shores, but landing in strange times. R L Crimp, who served in the sister battalion of Alan's, the 2nd Battalion, the Rifles, described his feelings on arriving in Egypt a few months later in his diary, *The Diary of a Desert Rat* as he is driven out of Suez, saying "[m]y feelings, which started sinking with the first step on Egyptian soil, are now down to zero. Never has home seemed so far away. The utter sterility of everything visible induces sensations hopeless, helpless and heartsore."[33]

The battalion spent the next five weeks in the Nile Delta preparing for active duty before being deployed to the desert. This would have been their first experience of training for desert warfare. On 11 January, D Company spent thirty-six hours on exercise in the desert. On 27 February, a sandstorm interrupted the ranges. On 17 February, the battalion received orders to go to Cyrenaica. Lieutenant Colonel Shipton writes that their first task was "policing a large area around Cyrene in Cyrenaica—that is keeping the peace between the Italian smallholders and the Arabs, who flocked back immediately the Italian Army had been driven from the area."[34] It is likely that this was the first time Alan met an Italian. He would not at this point have had any idea of the role that Italy and the Italian people would play in his later life.

The battalion had arrived after the successful Operation COMPASS. In September 1940, the Italian Army had pushed, with relative ease due to their superior numbers, sixty miles into what was then the British colony of Egypt. Commander-in-Chief Middle East, General Wavell, despite planning for impending campaigns in East Africa and the Balkans, had given instructions to Lieutenant-General Henry Maitland Wilson and Major-General Richard O'Connor to plan for an attack on these Italian forces. Wavell had many competing higher priorities so he hoped for a successful, but short-lived campaign; "a short and swift one, lasting four or five days at most."[35] He gave O'Connor no clear objective other than forcing the Italians back in as short a space of time as possible.

O'Connor developed an unorthodox plan that would involve attacking from the rear of the Italian forces and included plans to exploit the success he predicted for himself. It was not a plan for a five-day raid, but a plan for a longer campaign. The plan was executed to great success. It achieved surprise and resulted in victory after victory. By 22 January, when Tobruk, in modern day Libya, had fallen, despite being preoccupied with his forthcoming offensives in East Africa and about Prime Minister Winston Churchill's intentions with regard to the Balkans, Wavell now gave Benghazi, further west, as O'Connor's ultimate objective.

In *The Battle for North Africa*, the military historian General John Strawson (retd) notes that what followed next was "the first great left hook of the battles for North Africa."[36] A small British Force comprising the 11th Hussars, with 2nd Rifle Battalion and three artillery batteries commanded by Colonel John Combe managed to cut off the retreating Italian 10th Army by cutting inland into the desert, away from the coastal roads that were the only reliable roads in the region and the main arteries right across North Africa- from Egypt in the east to Tunisia in the west. The force got into place only hours before the leading elements of the Italian force fleeing Benghazi reached them. They managed to hold the Italian force, without any tanks, until reinforcements arrived. Strawson describes O'Connor's victories as "the one bright star in a sky almost everywhere dimmed by twilight"[37] referring to poor situation the across the other post-Dunkirk theatres of war at that time.

By 28 February Alan and D Company arrived in newly taken Benghazi and spent another three weeks performing another similar role of keeping the peace, which would have in no way prepared them for what was to happen next. Late on 22 March, after leaving D Company at Agedabia to prepare reserve positions, the three remaining companies of The Tower Hamlets' Rifles arrived at Mersa Brega some one hundred and fifty miles south of Benghazi and to the west of El Agheila. We can only presume that Alan remained in D Company at this point, but this is an assumption; it is possible he had by this stage been attached to one of the other companies in the battalion. No records exist that can confirm this; however, there is no record of his transfer to another company and some records do show such transfers. It is also the case that when Alan deserted later on in the campaign D Company was in a rear area and he deserted the day before they were due to re-join the frontline. The other companies of the battalion were already at the frontline. This supports the assumption that Alan was still in D Company at the time, but it is an assumption.

The Battle of Mersa Brega has received very little attention from British historians, who have tended to focus on the later epic battles which led to the ultimate victory of General Montgomerie's Eighth Army at El Alamein and to a lesser extent those of O'Connor before. It does not also help that the war diaries of the battalion covering the months March and April 1941 are also missing from the National Archives at Kew, as the truck which contained the diarist and the diaries was blown up at some point during the battle. When checked in 2016 it only had two lines on Wikipedia the on-line encyclopaedia—in general more is written about battles we have won than have lost:

> Battle of Brega (1941) - Brega was the location of a brief but important battle in the Western Desert Campaign of the Second World War. On 31 March 1941, during the opening phase of Rommel's first offensive, the German Afrika Korps expelled the British from their partially pre-pared positions at Mersa Brega. This opened the way for Rommel's drive to the Egyptian border and encirclement of Tobruk.[38]

Already in tracing Alan's journey I found myself searching for lost memories in a lost battle. The lack of attention doesn't however seem to fairly reflect its level of significance and importance. The defeat at Mersa left the way to Cairo open exposing to rapid loss what had taken months to gain in Operation COMPASS. To regain the land lost would take the loss of many lives on both sides, and would not be won back conclusively without one of the most significant conflicts of the war at the Second Battle of El Alamein. Once this easterly bastion was lost there was no natural or man-made obstacle to impede the enemy's progression west to Benghazi and then if the attacker had the intent and the resources the fear was they could move onwards, to Cairo, the Suez Canal and the oil fields at the heart of Mesopotamia (modern day Iraq).

General Wavell had realised the importance of holding the Brega position, even so he had given General Philip Neame (the only Victoria Cross recipient who has won an Olympic Gold Medal), who was responsible for holding the large area of ground in eastern Cyrenacia that included Mersa, no specific instructions to hold the position. He had also given Neame very few resources. Wavell's orders were in fact to abandon Mersa if pressed, after inflicting as much damage as possible on the enemy whilst keeping his forces intact.[39] Wavell had too many commitments for the resources he had. Greece was his main priority at this time, and he was knowingly taking a risk in North Africa, by also prioritising an attempt at a quick victory in East Africa (which he believed he had time for before sending troops used for this back to North Africa) over holding Cyrenacia.[40] It was an order that Neame, even though he also must have known the potential dire consequences which would result if he did withdraw, accepted. In *The North African Campaign, 1940-43*, British Army officer and military historian General Sir William Jackson notes: "Neame was following Wavell's instructions to trade space for time, but in abandoning the Mersa Brega position he uncorked the Cyrenaica bottle."[41]

Having found little detail in the most well know histories of the conflict I found a dissertation online on the battle.[42] The author put me in touch with the military historian Julian Shales, who had helped him. Shales very generously donated a copy of his account of the events between February and May, which covers in great detail the fighting at Mersa Brega and the following retreat.[43] He also took the time to answer many of my questions. Anyone wishing to read a detailed account of the Battle of Mersa Brega, told from both sides, covering all of the units involved is recommended to read Shales' work. The description of the first combat that Alan and his battalion experienced that follows use his work extensively as well as the few first-hand accounts in existence found at Kew and the Imperial War Museum.

One such first-hand account is Lieutenant Colonel Shipton's reflections held at the National Archives. It is just a few typed pages of summary on the battle from his point of view, but it does give a much-understated insight in to what Alan's battalion experienced. Lieutenant Colonel Shipton notes that it was only after they had been in these new positions for a matter of days that due to the "aggressive patrolling of the enemy, it became obvious that he meant to attack." Shipton notes that it was known that, in addition to Italian Divisions that had been forced back by O'Connor's offensive, there was one German armoured division and a good proportion of a second German armoured division on his immediate front. His orders therefore were to withdraw delaying the enemy as long as possible if they attacked as "higher command recognised that he could not hold such a force with the resources he and the wider division charged with the defence of Mersa."[44]

On 31 March, the Germans launched their first offensive of the North Africa Campaign and the Battle of Mersa Brega began. D Company was not in action on this first day[45], although they would have no doubt been able to hear the fighting that their fellow companies in the battalion were engaged in. It began soon after 0800, with armoured cars, tanks, and motorcycle combinations attacking battalion positions.[46] Lieutenant Colonel Shipton notes that his carrier patrols, which were operating about a mile and a half in front of his advance company (C Company), were in a "stiff fight, during which most valuable information was sent back."[47]

The carriers were the only armoured vehicles in the battalion. They were lightly armoured people carriers, armed with a Bren machine gun and grouped together on forward patrols carrying troops in the back. These were the first significant contacts of General Erwin Rommel's Afrika Corps in North Africa. The battalion carrier patrols were forced to withdraw to the C Company positions on Cemetery Hill which the company managed to hold until approximately 1015 that morning, when one platoon and the carriers of the company were left behind to hold the enemy as long as they could. The rest of the company was pulled back to join the battalion reserve. The small number left behind managed to hold for another thirty minutes, which must have seemed to be significantly longer, due to what Shipton described as "very heavy dive-bombing."[48] The four words do not acutely describe the horrific violence; the ear-splitting scream of the bombers diving, the physical jarring of the blast wave as the bombs detonated, the disorientation of the previously solid ground trembling.

After Cemetery Hill was lost some fifteen enemy tanks came to a halt just in front of the main position held by A Company and were then forced to withdraw by indirect fire from the accompanying Royal Horse Artillery. At the same time, enemy infantry and guns occupied the high ground of Cemetery Hill and in the words of Lieutenant Colonel Shipton "caused us consider-able trouble"[49] by firing on the battalion main positions. At about 1430 the main positions were dived bombed by sixteen German planes causing casualties. During the afternoon, a force of four enemy tanks and a company of infantry attempted to break through the right flank, but were valiantly held by a small force from A Company, C Company and a machine gun section of the Northumberland Fusiliers. Shipton describes their stand as a magnificent piece of work and notes that this would have been the first time that the soldiers of the battalion had seen action.[50] LE Tutt was with a gun battery near Mersa Brega, and he reflected the following:

> The men of Tower Hamlets went forward to face them
> [German tanks] in Bren carriers and were virtually de-
> stroyed in a matter of minutes; their bravery was
> unquestioned, but they should never have been asked to
> face such odds.[51]

The War Diary of Y Company, the 1st Northumberland Fusiliers, notes that at 1800, 1 Section, 11 Platoon, was in action until all their ammunition had finished. It goes on to note that a Corporal Harrison was killed three others were wounded. It makes no mention of whether Harrison had any dependents, what lives were forever impacted by this event, and what impact this had on the rest of the section or platoon who witnessed it. The entry ends by noting that the section destroyed its guns to prevent their falling into enemy hands. By the end of the day, both A Company and C Company from Alan's battalion had suffered casualties. It is likely that friends he had shared ship doorways with and passed on tips of how to feel less sick sea, were killed that day. They continued to hold the position until dusk. That night the front-line was stabilised twenty-five miles to the rear.

The following day, the men of D Company were brought up into the line, and the enemy continued to use dive bombers against the battalion,[52] however no ground offensive was launched and physical casualties were relatively light. The main German aircraft that was used in the ground-attack role at this point was the Junkers Ju 87 or Stuka (from *Sturzkampfflugzeug*, 'dive bomber'). Upon the leading edges of its faired main gear legs were mounted the *Jericho-Trompete* ('Jericho trumpet') wailing sirens. These sirens were designed to instil fear in those below. They worked.

Many years later, Alan told Stephenie of his experience of being dive bombed. He used the phrase "shit scared" in reference to another occasion when the convoy he was in was dive bombed, forcing him to jump from the cab of the vehicle and run for his life over the sapping desert sands. Alan would have heard a low-pitched wail which would have quickly built up to a high pitch shriek. He would have wanted the noise to stop as the unbearable shriek grew louder and louder, but he would have known what was at the end of the noise. The Stukas filled the air with their terrifying music, before then filling the air with bullets from their twin heavy machine guns mounted in the wings or the blast wave, shrapnel, and damaged fragments of men and machine caused by the heavy bomb it would drop at the nadir of its dive.

The vehicle of which Alan was a driver, a Bedford QLD troop carrier (known in the war diary as a 15 CWT), would have offered no protection whatsoever from high explosive ordinance. It is described in the military as being "soft skinned" meaning that it has little or no armour— in essence anything hitting it would do damage to it and anyone inside it. During an attack, it would be Alan's job to drive the vehicle forward towards the enemy (often over the coming months this would mean highly armoured German Panzer tanks). He would drive towards danger, through the chaos of war in a slow moving, badly protected, truck. He would bounce to a halt to allow the infantry in the back to debus and then run forward one tactical bound (ten to twenty metres depending on the terrain) fanning out into a line as they did so, before taking up firing positions most likely lying down in the prone. He would most likely see some of those who had moments before been in his truck, fellow platoon members who he had shared meals, jokes, and maybe even ship doorways, killed as they tried to advance into a hail of bullets and shells.

Alan would then, if still able, reverse his vehicle back hopefully out of range of at least direct enemy fire (but probably not indirect fire from artillery, and he would still vulnerable to attack from the air and land mines). He would then be on hand to resupply the troops with ammunition including anti-tank weapons and also extract them.

And then he would do it again, and again, and again.

During this time, he would have been in, what I heard a senior non-commissioned officer (NCO) describe our soft skinned vehicles many years later in training before deploying to Iraq as, a "bullet magnet." In the general area they were operating, there was very little cover provided by the terrain. The slow, cumbersome truck would have been an obvious and easy target drawing significant incoming fire. When in convoy, as he would be on many epic journeys to come, this was especially true, when the equally spaced out long lines of trucks and other vehicles provided easy target practice for the Luftwaffe. In an attack, the safest place to be would be as far from the vehicle as possible, definitely not the driver's seat where Alan would have to sit.

On 2 April, the battalions' scout platoons engaged with the enemy again and managed to report back that German infantry was debussing astride the main road that ran through the main positions. By 1030 infantry accompanied by tanks was attacking and the battalion was ordered to withdraw by the support group headquarters (HQ). In an interview given to the Imperial War Museum in 1996 Rifleman Albert Edward Handscombe from HQ Company noted the speed of the German advance, claiming that they "came through us like a dose of salts."[53] Eight enemy tanks managed to right flank the battalion and cut off B Company's withdrawal route forcing them to withdraw across some treacherous salt pans to their rear. The going was tough and only "some half dozen" men managed to get clear. The rest of the battalion managed to withdraw, even though the other flank was also being out-flanked, with the exception of the scout platoon of C Company which had become too engaged with the enemy. Lieutenant Colonel Shipton notes that "[t]his gallant action by the carriers of C Company undoubtedly contributed greatly towards the extrication of the reminder of the Battalion - no easy matter in daylight and in contact with an armoured enemy."[54]

The battalion withdrew thirty miles or so to positions north of Agedabia and was soon in action again by mid-afternoon when they were attacked by a "strong artillery concentration"[55] followed then by a heavy attack from enemy infantry and armoured fighting vehicles. German artillery barrages in the desert at that time were described as "the slamming of a million massive doors"[56] by Vernon Scannell, a deserter, who later found fame as a poet after the war. We will meet him again later. A counter attack by a tank squadron allowed the battalion to withdraw again to Antelat to the north, where they were then able to spend the night without further enemy attacks.

Over the next few days, the whole support group moved north to Sceleidima. Here the battalion was ordered to hold the line on an escarpment that ran from Sceleidima to Sidi Brahim further north. Communications were becoming patchy with the support group HQ, but an order eventually came through to continue to Msus. Communications were also becoming patchy internally with the battalion, resulting in A Company becoming temporarily separated from the battalion, catching them up when they reached their destination.[57]

When they all reached Msus, the battalion was relived to find it could refuel, despite hearing reports that the petrol dump and wells had been blown up. They seemed, however, to have greater difficulty getting water from the wells. There were issues with fuel and water throughout the retreat—something Stephenie remembers her father mentioning year later. He told Stephenie of the constant strangling thirst they had in the desert due to the heat and the lack of water. He described the relief of seeing the green fringe of an oasis on the horizon as they traversed the desert and of the frustration of finding out the oasis they thought they had found was a shimmering mirage. He told Stephenie of how his lips soon became dry and painfully cracked. The reports of the destruction of the fuel dumps highlight the confusion of the time, which would have added to the disorientating nature of the experience for the soldiers involved. They were in the middle of chaos.

The sounds and sights of the battlefield are overwhelming, and not just when first experienced as they were being experienced here by Alan. On some days in the empty desert, it must have seemed that war was all there was. On these days Alan must have often felt like closing his eyes and putting his hands over his ears.

Clear communications from higher command with accurate information can give soldiers faith that in amongst the chaos their superiors still have a grip on the situation, and by following their orders they will give themselves the best chance of survival. During the retreat from Mersa Brega, it is likely that this faith was quickly eroded. This faith would have been further eroded as news reached the men that Lieutenant-Generals Neame and O'Connor (architect of the only success in the desert so far), and, Brigadier Gambier-Parry, the 2nd Armoured Division commander, had all been captured during the withdrawal. Gunner Ron Bryant F Troop, 8 Battery, 2/3rd Light Aircraft Regiment noted afterwards that; "the retreat had, as is the nature if many retreats in history, became a rather panicky rout."[58]

Over the next few days the battalion moved again. It was during this move that Sam Spencer, in his 2011 interview with the Imperial War Museum, describes bumping in to O' Connor, who told his platoon to remain where they were, just to the east of Derna, before disappearing off to rally more troops. After waiting a few hours where they were, the news that O'Connor had been captured came to them from passing troops, and they decided to move off.[59] By dawn on 7 April, the battalion was passing through Derna. Major Bernard Cracroft's Report of Operations of the 2nd Armoured Division in Cyrenacia describes what happened in six lines in the original report:

> Units of 3 Armed Bde and 2 Sp Gp continued to withdraw to Tobruk via Derna. Throughout the day there were parties of enemy consisting of tanks, armoured cars and artillery operating in the area of Derna aerodrome; they caused considerable interference with the withdrawal and most units had to fight their way through. Several gallant actions were fought and casualties were inflicted on the enemy the fighting caused units to become mixed and disorganised but all units eventually reached Tobruk although a number of vehicles were lost and some personnel were missing.[60]

It would have been the third night running that drivers like Alan had been driving all night as well as all day. They would likely have been exhausted from lack of sleep and also exhausted from the stress of driving in very difficult conditions—both in terms of visibility, as they would have been limiting the amount of light used to avoid being sighted by the enemy, and the ground conditions.

The National Health Service (NHS) website in the UK states that "after several sleepless nights, the mental effects [of lack of sleep] become more serious. Your brain will fog, making it difficult to concentrate and make decisions.... Your risk of injury and accidents at home, work and on the road also increases."[61] It must have been an ordeal for Alan and his fellow drivers, trying desperately not to fall asleep at the wheel, knowing that if they did it would not just be themselves they would be endangering, but all their comrades in the back. Within the wider battle, in each cab of each truck, another battle would have been fought throughout the night with sleep itself.

It was a battle that could not be won. Under such conditions, you cannot help micro-sleeping— dropping off for between fractions of a second to up to thirty seconds. This must have been terrifying, constantly waking and realising that you were at the wheel on a precarious road with mine fields and precipitous drops to the sides. It would have been made more terrifying by the feeling of helplessness Alan must have experienced; no matter how hard he tried to steel himself, he would not be able to prevent himself keep sliding back into the dark abyss of dangerous sleep.

The NHS website goes on to say that "chronic sleep debt may lead to long-term mood disorders like depression and anxiety" —this would have become an issue for many soldiers as the campaign wore on. The British Army now puts its soldiers through sleep deprivation in training so soldiers understand the effects on themselves and one another. It is obviously not to the same extent as to that which Alan endured, but from my limited experience, the NHS description of a fog is a good one. It closes in on you, finally fully engulfing you in a sleep, from which you will wake in a panic as you are in an environment where if you are not alert you can be punished. The fog briefly clears as you wake with start and then slowly starts creeping back in again; whatever you try to do to waft away the fog will ultimately fail.

On operations, I was aware that a lack of sleep was adding to the background stress of the environment, that it had the potential to negatively impact decision making, and that it made it harder to grip my emotional response to events.

I was unable to find any records of how many accidents occurred on route but we do know that 3rd Armoured Brigade's Brigadier Rimington's armoured vehicle had gone off the road and fallen down a steep bank during this drive,[62] highlighting the risks involved. Units had also become intermingled and confused during the move. From 0730, the units of the Support Group of which Alan's battalion remained were slowly moving through Derna in a traffic jam. As D Company moved through the traffic jam from the foot of the escarpment to the centre of town, they would have took on rations as well as sorted themselves out back in to the correct order of march.

The 2nd Support Group War Diary describes Derna as a harbour in pleasant wooded country in contrast to the desert country so far crossed[63] (Libya has one of the lowest forested lands ratio on earth with only 0.1% of the total country covered by forest). Passing through Derna the road follows the coast for five miles before then rising up an escarpment it had previously traversed before dropping down into Derna, and then turned east across a plateau towards an aerodrome. Beyond that the road goes on to Gazala and then Tobruk. The battalion was the rear guard supported by J Battery (Bty) of the Royal Horse Artillery (RHA). By this point, the battalion consisted of the remains of A Company, the six survivors of B Company, C Company, D Company, and HQ Company.

At the same time as Alan was passing through Derna guns from the 1st Regiment RHA, who had reached Derna aerodrome at the top of the escarpment, engaged advancing German vehicles claiming to score a direct hit on one.[64] The convoy which was attempting to pass through and on to Tobruk then started to receive incoming fire. By 0800 Lieutenant Colonel Shipton describes how, as the battalion reached the top of the steep escarpment and headed to the aerodrome, the leading companies—C and HQ were "ambushed by tanks supported by anti -tank guns that had apparently cut across the desert from the west."[65]

Rifleman Albert Handscombe a wireless operator in HQ Company describes the scene as the advance units of the battalion:

> I got as far as a hill overlooking Derna and was sitting in my truck next to the driver. Suddenly I saw a German tank in the distance, there was a tremendous crash, and a shell came whistling straight through the cab. I opened the door, whipped off my headset, out the door, rolled on the ground, and ran across the road off to the far side. I got myself together and looked across the road to see if I could do anything for my pal, but unfortunately he was beyond recognition. The cab was demolished and the wireless set with it.[66]

I would imagine that Albert never forgot the sight of his beyond recognition pal, who seconds before was alive. I am sure Albert was very aware that at any point he could suffer a similar fate before this incident, but now there was no way in which he could not be aware that he was just a second or two away from death. I am also sure that Alan was also by now aware of this too. Albert's pal was mostly likely Victor Levi Newell, son of William Harry and Lottie Mabel Newell, of Cockfosters, Barnet, Hertfordshire, who was listed as the only member of The Tower Hamlet's Rifles killed in action on 10 April. He was twenty-five years old at the time.[67]

Fighting continued at the aerodrome as the Allied forces attempted to break out towards Tobruk and Rommel's Axis forces attempted to cut them off to prevent an effective occupation of Tobruk. The fighting caused what was described somewhat euphemistically as "considerable interference" by a 2nd Armoured Division report[68], but was eventually over by the end of the day. The rear-guard had bought enough time for sufficient forces to get to Tobruk. The cost had however been high, as it had been previously been at Mersa.

Lieutenant Colonel Shipton notes that the reminder of the battalion reached Tobruk about 100 miles further east about 2200 that night, eight days after the initial first contact at Mersa having withdrawn some four hundred miles across difficult terrain, with the ever-present fear of ambush from the air or ground. By this time the battalion had lost sixteen officers, some three hundred and fifty men, forty-two carriers out of forty-four, and nearly one hundred and fifty other vehicles out of two hundred. By 11 April Tobruk was finally surrounded by strong enemy forces. A group of soldiers from the battalion were left in Tobruk to help with its defence as the main body of troops moved in a mobile column, that we assume Alan was part of, further eastward another twenty miles to the aerodrome at Gambut. It continued the withdrawal on to Cairo over the next few weeks with no further contact with the enemy. On reaching Cairo they were then placed under command of Brigadier William H. E. ('Strafer') Gott as part of a temporary force. The rest of the battalion joined them from Tobruk having been evacuated by sea and then travelling by rail.

In all the descriptions of the battle and retreat from various sources I found no mention of what happened to the dead. Using the Commonwealth Graves Commission website to search for the names of those I could establish died at Mersa I found that they were all listed on the Land Forces panels of the Alamein Memorial, which forms the entrance to Alamein War Cemetery in Egypt. The website states that the Land Forces panels commemorate more than 8,500 soldiers of the Commonwealth who died in the campaigns in Egypt and Libya, and in the operations of the Eighth Army in Tunisia up to 19 February 1943, who have no known grave.[69] This memorial is for those whose bodies were not recovered. Alan would not have been able to bury any of the friends from his battalion that were lost in this his first experience of war. The bodies of his fallen comrades would mostly have been left where they fell. Relatives of their fallen comrades would later ask them what happened to the body of their son, husband, brother or father, and they would have had to tell them that they left them behind.

In Afghanistan on 15 January, 2007 a Royal Marine from 3 Commando Brigade, Lance Corporal Matthew Ford, was shot while on an operation against the Taliban in Garmsir, Southern Helmand[70]. The Royal Marines withdrew from the fort they had been assaulting, withdrawing back across a river, but in the confusion Lance Corporal Ford was left behind on the other side of the river. He had been killed instantly, but helicopters spotted the marine's body still giving off a heat signal which indicated to the rescuers that he was potentially alive. Despite uncertainty of whether he was alive or not, four Apache helicopters fired at the Taliban to keep them away from the wounded marine, while a rescue plan was worked out.

One of the Apache pilots came up with the suggestion of landing in the compound with two Royal Marines strapped to the outside of the helicopter. After touching down inside the fort the marines disembarked returning four minutes later with Lance Corporal Ford.[71] During all of Iraq and Afghanistan all the bodies of the fallen were recovered. There would have been a sense of pride that nobody was left behind—dead or alive. Soldiers risk their lives to recover comrades who have already lost theirs. This is reassuring for all and a reassurance that Alan and his comrades would not have had.

Alan's first experience of combat was nothing was nothing like combat that most British soldiers have experienced in recent conflicts. To Alan and the men of the Tower Hamlets' Rifles, they were facing an enemy that seemed superior in every way. They were in a conflict that, at that point, seemed more likely they would lose. They had had little training to prepare them for the environments in which they were operating. They suffered casualty rates vastly higher than those suffered in recent conflicts. There was no end of tour date to get to. Alan would not have known what the future was to hold in the next few months or years, yet he fought on as did the rest of his battalion (there is no mention of any desertions during this period).

Chapter Two
False Starts and Not So Quiet Times

Far be it from me to paint a rosy picture of the future. Indeed, I do not think we should be justified in using any but the most sombre tones and colours while our people, our Empire and indeed the whole English-speaking world are passing through a dark and deadly valley. But I should be failing in my duty if, on the other wise, I were not to convey the true impression, that a great nation is getting into its war stride.

—Winston Churchill, House of Commons, 22 January 1941

The battle for Greece began on 7 April 1941 and was over three weeks later, ending with the evacuation of British troops. The front established in the Balkans collapsed almost as soon as it had been established with the signing of an armistice by the Yugoslavs on 30 April after Germany and Italy began their invasion of the country on 6 April. In North Africa, there were then rumours that Rommel had been reinforced by a division of Panzers via Tripoli. Facing a desperate situation across the bulk of his area of operations, General Wavell asked London for assistance.[72] Churchill responded to the request and made the bold decision of insisting that a convoy, known as the 'Tiger convoy,' should be dispatched via the higher-risk (but significantly quicker) Mediterranean route, rather than the same route Alan had taken around Africa. The gamble paid off, and the convoy managed the successful resupply whilst also conducting a raid on Benghazi and resupplying Malta on route with limited losses.[73]

The situation elsewhere, though, continued to get worse for Wavell. Rashid Ali's Arab nationalist and pro-Nazi revolt in Mesopotamia produced another commitment for Wavell in May.

A further commitment then came after Admiral François Darlan signed an agreement with the Germans on behalf of Vichy France known as the 'Paris Protocols.' The agreement granted the Germans access to military bases in Vichy-controlled Syria. Though the protocols were never ratified, German and Italian aircraft were allowed to refuel in Syria. Disguised as Iraqi aircraft, they landed in Syria on route to Iraq to support the rebels. The Germans also requested permission to use Syrian railways to send armaments to support the rebels in Mosul. The British were forced to invade Syria in May 1941, or face the prospect of defeat in Mesopotamia.[74]

Churchill, however, who by that point was becoming famous for his micromanagement of his generals, was keen for Wavell to go on the offensive against Rommel in North Africa.[75] Signals intelligence highlighted the precarious position Rommel's forces were in, having extended their supply lines significantly, in a similar manner to that which O'Connor's victories had done to the Allied supply lines. This led to the failed Operation BREVITY in mid-May 1942, which was launched to harry Axis forces at Sollum and Tobruk, before the more significant Operation BATTLEAXE which would have the benefit of the tanks provided by Tiger.[76]

Operation BREVITY started well, achieving surprise by not using an artillery barrage in advance of H-hour (the given hour that an attack begins), and achieved the capture of Halfaya from the Italians, but this was the only real gain. It was also only a temporary gain, as it was only held for ten days. German resistance at the other objectives and then a counter attack reversed the initial tactical victories and soon resulted in a withdrawal. According to Strawson the "well enough named" two-day operation was a failure.[77]

Shales notes that the Tower Hamlets' Rifles as part of Gott's temporary force, after briefly supporting the defences against the German assault on the perimeter of Tobruk on 11 April, retreated to the Libyan-Egyptian border.[78] Here they were joined by other elements of Gott's 7th Support Group, the 22nd

Guards Brigade, and a squadron of the 7th Hussars. Shales stated that the action that followed between the 11 April and 15 May in combat with German and Italian units was "significant, and many the fire fights and small battles at the border that have been largely ignored in the build up to Operation BREVITY."[79]

The battalion war diaries note that by 3 May, the battalion vehicles were handed over, and on 4 May the battalion was moved by rail to Alexandria. By 10 May, the rest of the battalion arrive from Tobruk and the battalion took leave as Operation BREVITY begins. On 20 May, the battalion fell under the command of Brigadier Charrington as part of the 1st Armoured Brigade and then spent the rest of the month acting as a mobile reserve, receiving training to defend against an airborne assault on the Suez Canal.

In Sam Spencer's interview with the Imperial War Museum, he notes that at this point three of the four deserters who had left the battalion in Durban returned.[80] Spencer claims that they received no punishment, as all records of their desertion had been lost. One of the deserters, Charlie D—, (obscured to protect his identity) is visible in one of Alan's photographs from the desert. Seeing his name listed as one of the deserters in Durban and then appear in the photo had created a mystery solved only by Spencer's interview. Stephenie told me that her father had been mates with D—, so there is no doubt that Alan would have known about his desertion and lack of consequences of it. The deserters seemed to have been welcomed back to the battalion with little fuss. Spencer says he "wasn't too worried about them."[81]

The battle for Crete between 20 and 31 May that followed shortly after saw the Royal Navy and the Army suffer significant losses of both equipment and life (14,000 men from a force of 32,000—mostly as prisoners).[82] The fall of Crete increased the pressure on Wavell to get back on the offensive and make gains in North Africa, in particular the airfields in Eastern Cyrenaica, including Derna, where Alan had already seen combat. The Axis had now been able to open sea routes from Western Greece to

Cyrenaic. The Chief of Staffs had recognised that these routes must be "interfered with" and the airfields of Malta alone could not do that.[83] Whilst Wavell was given clear intent it is questionable whether he had the capability to achieve what the Chief of Staffs and Churchill wanted. There was a lack of preparation time for resources arriving in theatre and for refitting those depleted by previous encounters (many of the tanks that had been used in Operation COMPASS were still being refitted).

Nonetheless on 15 June, Operation BATTLEAXE was launched. Three days later, it concluded. Despite it being the first time during the war that a significant German force fought on the defensive, the operation ultimately failed as Allied forces attacked strong defensive positions that had been constructed by Rommel's forces.

On the first day, over half of the Allied tanks were lost—ninety-eight were lost in total over the three days—and only one of the three attacks launched succeeded. There were further mixed results on the second day, as Allied forces were pushed back on their western flank but still repulsed a significant German counter-attack in the centre. On the third day, a disaster was narrowly avoided. As Rommel's forces attempted to encircle the 22nd Guards Brigade, British armour managed to stall the advancing Panzers long enough for the Guards to escape. Tobruk, however, remained under siege. This failure led to changes in command.[84]

By June, Alan and his battalion had been back on the move to Beni Yussef where they received vehicles. The intense desert heat would now begin to make their lives difficult, almost as much as the enemy. They took no part in Operation BATTLEAXE. By the end of the month Lieutenant Colonel "Squeak" Purdon assumed command of the battalion from the departed Lieutenant Colonel Shipton.[85] In June, desert training began in earnest again as preparations for Operation CRUSADER, the next attempt to relieve Tobruk, began. On 19 June, Alan was promoted to Lance Corporal.[86] This was an extremely quick promotion by today's standards, but promotions happened at a much more rapid rate in the prolonged combat of the Second World War, where the high casualty rates amongst officers and NCOs combined with frequent opportunities for soldiers to prove themselves. Even so, it shows that Alan was at this point performing well and was regarded within his unit. However, this increased responsibility may have had meant that Alan had to distance himself from the friends he had made who were still at the rank of rifleman.

There are no significant entries in the battalion war diary for July 1941. August was then spent training in the desert in preparation for the next offensive. Waiting back at Infantry Base Depot to be assigned a battalion, Crimp notes in his diary that on the 18 August a large draft up to the front appeared on the detail, but his name was not on it.[87] By 20 September, the advance party from the battalion had moved through Alexandria eventually to Amirya where the main body arrived on 23 September. They moved on to Abar El Kanayis, where, on 24 September, there was a contact with the enemy. Support Group, the 7th Armoured Division then took command of the battalion. By 30 September, they were in a concentration area at Sidi Barrani and formed the "Sister Column" (a battalion minus sized mobile force, mostly consisting of infantry mounted in vehicles and artillery), which undertook patrol tasks over the next few weeks and Little Sister Observation Post (OP), through which the companies of the battalion (including Alan's D Company) rotated.[88]

Throughout October, the OP and patrols reported increased enemy activity and regular contacts. Patrol and OP reports attached to the war diaries state that enemy shelling was common and enemy aircraft that regularly passed overhead bombed battalion positions.[89] On 12 October, the war diary reports that the OP witnessed an air battle overhead.

Minefields were a constant worry and would have been at the forefront of Alan's mind as he drove often at night through the desert. He would no doubt pass the silhouettes of destroyed tanks and other less protected soft skinned vehicles more similar to those that Alan drove, both grim memorials to fallen comrades and portents about what could happen to Alan at any point. The lack of sleep combined with the stress would likely have caused Alan to hallucinate on these patrols. This would have made it more difficult for him to trust his already stressed senses. There are no records of what Alan saw in the moonlight of the desert or in the brief few seconds of bright light from a flare on dark night. He would undoubtedly have seen some visions of enemy soldiers bearing down on him or more surreal sights, maybe even more disconcerting and disorientating, but equally as imagined.

Reports do detail how often the soft skinned troop carriers that Alan drove would patrol out to a certain point and then troops would dismount and continue on foot leaving the vehicles sheltered in a *wadi* or other piece of natural cover. Alan would have either joined these foot patrols or remained with the small party left to protect the vehicles. We know he did often join the patrol as he told Stephenie about the tension of hearing a tank coming when out on patrol. He told her they would wait to see if it was one of theirs so they could ride it back to the rest of the company's position, or at least run alongside it giving themselves cover. If you did the latter Alan told Stephenie you had to be careful to not fall under the tracks as you did so. It would have been hard going on foot in the sand, the troops no doubt feeling vulnerable moving around in an area where German tanks were also patrolling and minefields had been laid by both sides. Waiting, often in the dark, would have been easier physically, but just as difficult mentally, as they would have focused in on every sound carried across the desert as they were waiting for shadows to return over whatever horizon was offering them cover, providing a brief moment of high stress before it was clear it was friendly forces. Often, patrols would not encounter the enemy, but in the day just see tracks in the sand and dust clouds on the horizon and at night see multi-coloured very lights and distant mussel flashes. Even patrols that were contacted by the enemy often did not see the source of the indirect fire; others would just see the hard-edged jarring machinery; the enemy operating it—the pilot, gunner or cavalry soldier would remain faceless.

When I was a young officer (young, but a few years older than Alan would have been) in the British Army in Basra, Iraq, I travelled around in 'snatch' Land Rovers that, despite their hard edges, were poorly armoured bullet magnets. There was a constant background fear that at any moment we could trigger an improvised explosive device (IED). Every group of men we would pass could be spotters or trigger men; every pile of rubbish we passed could be concealing the IED they would detonate.

There were small similarities with Alan's experience in the desert, but often the differentiator was scale. The heat and the dust that provided constant discomfort to Alan provided temporary discomfort to us. In the height of summer by the end of a patrol I would feel sapped by the heat, my eyes would sting with salt, and I would feel drained by the amount of sweat lost, but I would not be too far from a base that would provide me with some security to recover. By the time I was deployed to Iraq, after the initial war fighting phase, most British troops operated from bases that provided decent food, plenty of water, and a decent shower. Even in the platoon houses in Helmand Province, Afghanistan, where some troops did endure very basic conditions and much more rationed supplies, it was weeks rather than months between decent a meal and a shower. We did not have to suffer the constant dull ache of hunger that Alan did or the throbbing headaches brought on by dehydration to the same degree or for as long. The majority of troops in Iraq and Afghanistan in recent years did not degrade, physically or mentally, as much as many did in the desert back then.

Further to that, like Alan, I knew that if my vehicle was hit hot metal would rip through the paltry protection of the Land Rovers, much as it would have done to Alan's CWT, killing and maiming most of us in the vehicle. However, even though I had been to a memorial service of one of the team that was deployed before us who had died in such an incident (the second they suffered), the odds of being hit that I faced were significantly lower than that which Alan faced. The chances of surviving if anything did happen were also much greater for me. I actually feared a strike on one of the other vehicles more than my own. If my own vehicle was hit, I would not know too much about it and others would have had to respond. If one of the others was hit it was my response that could determine whether my colleagues lived or died. It would be me that would have to open the back doors of the vehicle to the shattered bones, screams, limbs, the hellish red smoke of detonated red phosphorus grenades, and the quiet of those I couldn't help. The stress was still much less acute than that which Alan must have experienced. I had also not experienced the intense combat that Alan had experienced before.

Even if Alan was not involved in a direct incident during this time, he would have been under great psychological stress as the final shaping operations (operations that establish conditions for the decisive operation) were conducted as part of the preparations for Operation CRUSADER. This would be the next exposure to significant large-scale warfare Alan would have. Richard Humble describes CRUSADER in the title of his book about the operation as the "Eighth Army's Forgotten Victory."[90] So after the "lost battle" of Mersa Brega Alan was moving on to the "forgotten victory."

Chapter Three
The Pyrrhic Victory

The battlefield is a scene of constant chaos. The winner will be the one who controls that chaos...

Napoleon Bonaparte

By 13 November 1941, the battalion handed over responsibility for its OPs and patrols and moved to the 22nd Guards Brigade concentration area for the beginning of Operation CRUSADER (named after the new Crusader Cruiser tanks that had arrived in the Tiger convoy). Following the failure of Operation BATTLEAXE, Wavell had been relieved as Commander-in-Chief Middle East and replaced by General Claude Auchinleck. The Western Desert Force of which Alan and his battalion were ultimately part was also now renamed the Eighth Army under the command of Lieutenant-General Alan Cunningham. The Eighth Army was comprised of two Corps: XXX Corps under Lieutenant-General Willoughby Norrie and XIII Corps. XXX Corps included 7th Armoured Division (commanded by the now Major-General Gott) and the independent 22nd Guards Brigade, under whose command the battalion was for the start of the operation. The Eighth Army also included the Tobruk garrison made up of Australian, British and Polish troops. In reserve, there was the South African 2nd Infantry Division.[91]

The aim of Operation CRUSADER was to relieve the siege of Tobruk and inflict a fatal blow to the German Afrika Korps by concentrating Allied armour, using the numerical advantage they now had, on ground of Allied choosing. The initial plan was to engage the Afrika Korps with the 7th Armoured Division, while the South African Division covered their left flank. Meanwhile, on their right, XIII Corps, supported by 4th Armoured Brigade, would make a clockwise flanking movement west of Sidi Omar and hold positions threatening the rear of the line of Axis defensive strongpoints, which ran east from Sidi Omar to the coast at Halfaya.

Central to the plan was the destruction of the Axis armour by the 7th Armoured Division to allow the relatively lightly armoured XIII Corps to advance north to Bardia on the coast whilst XXX Corps continued north-west to Tobruk and linked up with a break-out by 70th Division (the troops in besieged Tobruk). There was also a deception plan in an attempt to convince the Axis that the attack would not be ready until the end of the year, and when it came, it would be a sweeping, outflanking move through Jarabub, an oasis on the edge of the Great Sand Sea, far south of the actual point of attack. This proved successful to the extent that Rommel, refusing to believe the attack was anything more than a reconnaissance by force, was not in North Africa, but in Rome.[92]

According to Strawson, there were broadly four phases to CRUSADER.[93] First there was the Allied armour advance on the first day as the Allies gained an element of surprise launching their attack before dawn. By nightfall on 18 November, things looked to have progressed well; the 7th Armoured and the 7th Support Group had reached Sidi Rezegh, so they were almost in sight of Tobruk. The 22nd Armoured Brigade moved to engage the Italians at the First Battle of Bir el Gubi, and the 4th Armoured Brigade were in action east of Gabr Saleh with the German 21st Panzer Division. However, despite the appearance of progress, it was already not going to plan (operations rarely do—in my time in the army the saying "no plan survives first contact" was just as true as it was then—although some argue the plan here did not even survive before the first contact with the enemy). The plan to engage enemy armour on ground of Allied choosing and with a concentration of fire had fallen apart as Cunningham's armoured brigades became split—although it should be noted how difficult it is to keep a concentration of forces on such a vast battlefield where both sides are mobile and communications often difficult.

There followed a series of tank battles near Sidi Rezegh, a barren stony ridge, in which both sides suffered heavy casualties—the Germans suffering slightly less.

Next came Rommel's dash to the frontier. This is the border area between Egypt and Cyrenaica, marked by a long, barbed-wire fence put in place by the Italians before COMPASS—giving rise to the phrase crossing the wire, meaning to enter Cyrenaica. The bold dash nearly paid off as the threat to his rear areas almost convinced Cunningham to abandon the operation and withdraw (although his subordinates were keen to push on); however, Auchinleck moved forward to be next to Cunningham, prompting him to continue to attack.[94] The continuation of the Allied advance towards Tobruk forced Rommel to withdraw his armoured units to support his troops encircling he besieged city and protect his lines of supply between Tobruk and Bardia. After Auchinleck returned to Cairo and consulted with his seniors, he made the decision to remove Cunningham and replace him with General Ritchie. Although Ritchie served with the British Expeditionary Force (BEF) in the First World War (where he was awarded the Distinguished Service Order), and later in the Mesopotamian campaign (Military Cross), as well the evacuation of Dunkirk in the Second World War, he was one of Auchinleck's staff officers at the time and had no experience of commanding armour.

The third phase saw Sidi Rezegh again exchange hands with severe encounters between the German armour and New Zealand infantry in late November and early December. The New Zealanders took key positions through a series of attacks, which often involving hand to hand fighting, before an Axis counter-offensive re-took Sidi Rezegh at a great cost, as had the success against the South Africans the week before, and this would prevent them holding the position for long. In *The Early Battles of Eighth Army*, historian Adrian Stewart notes that New Zealand prisoners of war later reported that their captors were "practically sleepwalkers," who showed no sign of elation.[95] Rommel's troops were close to breaking point. On the other side, more New Zealand soldiers were killed or taken prisoner during

CRUSADER than in any other campaign the division fought in the Second World War, and the majority of these were at Sidi Rezegh. More New Zealanders died, were wounded, or were reported missing than in any other Eighth Army division; the New Zealanders having 879 killed and 1699 wounded—and 2042 men became prisoners of war.[96]

Lastly, despite achieving some tactical successes at Tobruk, Rommel, seeing that he could no longer relieve his Bardia and Halfaya garrisons (which did later fall) and seeing the need to preserve his remaining forces, withdrew his army to a defensive line at Gazala (west of Tobruk) and then all the way back to El Agheila. He did not do this, however, before inflicting further damage on British armour. This withdrawal finally allowed the relief of Tobruk; one of the key Allied aims. The operation was seen then as an overall victory, the first victory over the German ground forces by British-led forces in the Second World War. Alan and the Tower Hamlets' Rifles were part of it, but the victory did come at a heavy price. The failure to effectively knock out the Afrika Korps also meant it would be a short-lived victory.

The battalion had limited involvement in the first phase of the battle. For the first few days of CRUSADER, the battalion had been tasked with protecting the supply chain through a series of OPs at Field Supply Depot 62 (FSD 62).[97] They would, however, have been able to hear across the desert the fierce fighting on 20 November when the 22nd Armoured Brigade fought a second engagement with the Ariete Division and the 7th Armoured repulsed an infantry counter-attack at Sidi Rezegh. The 4th Armoured fought a second engagement with the 21st Panzer, and on 21 November one hundred guns were there to bombard positions on the Tobruk perimeter with 40,000 rounds to support the breakout of the 70th Division from Tobruk. This was warfare on an extraordinary scale. In *The Portrait of an Artist as a Young Man*, James Joyce describes the round of applause in a Dublin as like the sound of "dwarf artillery."[98] This must have been the sound of forty thousand giants clapping. Hearing high explosive ordnance detonating always had the same effect on me as standing in front of a rough sea in a storm or hearing rolling thunder seconds after seeing lighting; it makes me feel insignificant and powerless in comparison.

They would have possibly heard the fighting as the 70th Division advanced some three and a half miles on the main supply road, costing the Black Watch an estimated 200 men and their commanding officer as they failed to link up with the 7th Armoured advancing from Sidi Rezegh. The following day, Sidi Rezegh witnessed intense fighting when Rommel attacked with his 21st Panzer and captured the airfield. The desperate fighting here saw Brigadier Jock Campbell commanding the 7th Support Group, awarded the Victoria Cross for his heroic leadership, moving across the battlefield in an open staff car "regardless of shells or bullets,"[99] banging on the sides of tanks to attract attention and lead them against the enemy tanks, leaping out to serve his guns and encourage anyone he thought needed encouragement.

During the second phase of the battle, however, Alan and his battalion would see action. On 23 November, as Rommel looked to move his forces to the frontier, the battalion (less B Company who were left protecting the six-mile square FSD 62) received orders to move forward. However, on 24th November, the battalion received new orders to move immediately back to protect FSD 62, which was then being threatened by a column of enemy tanks. D Company was given the task of protecting the left flank.[100] This column is likely to have been part of Rommel's attempt on 24 November to relieve the Axis supply base at Bardia and pose a large enough threat to the British rear echelon to force the abandonment of the wider operation—which we know did give Cunningham serious doubts.

The Afrika Korps and Ariete division headed for Sidi Omar, causing chaos and scattering the mainly rear echelon support units in their path, splitting XXX Corps and almost cutting off XIII Corps. The battalion was engaged in protecting these rear echelons. On 25 November, the battalion received new orders to protect the lines of communications threatened by another column of enemy tanks moving south down the Libyan Sheferzen. The battalion formed part of the advanced guard. From 25 November to 30 November the battalion provided strong point of Libyan Sheferzen for the 4th Indian Division's initially failed attack on Libyan Omar.

During this period, the third phase of the battle began (which saw the Tobruk garrison finally linking up with the New Zealanders and the intense fighting at Sidi Rezegh). It was not until 6 December, however, that the battalion War Diary notes the first significant contact of the operation involving the Tower Hamlets' Rifles. Following the withdrawal of the 2nd NZ Division, Ritchie had reorganised his rear echelons and sent the 4th Indian Infantry Division's 5th and 11th Brigades as well as the 22nd Guards Brigade up to the front line.

By 4 December, the 11th Indian Brigade was heavily engaged in action against a strongpoint near Bir el Gubi. Italian forces holding this hilltop position successfully fought off repeated attacks by the British armour and Indian infantry. On 5 December, the 11th Indian Brigade continued its attritional attack against point 174. As dusk approached, the Axis armoured division intervened to relieve the Italians and cause mayhem in the 11th Indian Brigade. The Brigade was broken and had to be withdrawn to refit and arrangements made to bring the 22nd Guards Brigade, to which Alan's battalion was then attached, to their place. The Tower Hamlets Battalion War Diary notes that the 11th Brigade withdrew through the battalion defensive position on 5 December. By 6 December, the battalion was in contact from a large enemy column. Throughout the afternoon, the battalion was shelled and, at one point, heavily bombed by 11 Stukas resulting in one fatality. The battalion pushed out listening posts and all through the night there was lots of enemy activity noted.

On 7 December, A Company came under attack and a very large enemy column appeared to the north. There was very heavy shelling, and the battalion could see a tank battle to the south of Gubi. By 1200, the artillery troop of 18-pounders with D Company was engaged by ten enemy tanks. Two of the guns were put out of action, the troop sergeant and one OR ("other ranks" —a term used in the war diary to refer to soldiers who were not officers or senior non-commissioned officers). ORs were never referred to by name in the diary even when they were killed in action. According to the Commonwealth War Graves Commission, there were six members of the Royal Artillery killed in North Africa on that day, and only two of these six came from the same regiment, with one being a sergeant and one a gunner. It is likely therefore that the diary is referring to Sergeant John Stapleton, son of Charles and Jessie Stapleton; husband of Harriet Anne Stapleton, of Tarporley, Cheshire, and, Stanley Spurr, son of Edgar M. Spurr and Mary Spurr, of Congleton, Cheshire; husband of Rose Spurr, of Newchapel, Staffordshire.[101] It is also likely Alan would have witnessed their deaths. He would have felt the ground shake as the shells from the German tanks smashed into the guns and likely seen the impact those shells can make on British equipment and British bodies.

As the dust came down he would have heard the rising screams of pain. He would have witnessed first-hand what some would replay for years in flashbacks and nightmares as they suffered silently from aftershocks from the impacts of those German shells.

Following this four M13 tanks (Italian) advanced to within 1800 metres of C Company. The Allied plan had been for Allied armour (tanks and mechanized infantry) to destroy Axis armour, but as we have seen often, it was Allied infantry that faced Axis armour. This would have been a terrifying experience. The men facing the tanks would not have been comforted by the fact that the Allied Forces had an overall numerical advantage in terms of tank numbers. By 1800, that day the battalion was out of contact. The diary notes that the battalion had seven ORs wounded during the contacts throughout 6 and 7 December and one shell shocked, as a result of the intense shelling received throughout the day. This is the only mention of shell shock in the diary for the period, but demonstrates the intensity of battle the soldiers of the battalion were being exposed to. Also during this period, the battalion liaison officer went missing with two ambulances. Stewart notes that the Afrika Korps was now down to 40 tanks after suffering heavy losses in the tank battles that the battalion witnessed.[102]

Rommel was now told that supply could not improve until the end of the month when the airborne supply from Sicily would begin.[103] This saw the battle moving into its final phase. Realising that success was now unlikely at Bir el Gubi he decided to narrow his front and shorten his lines of communication by abandoning the Tobruk front and withdrawing to the positions at Gazala, 10 miles to his rear, which he had occupied by 8 December.[104] The remnants of the Afrika Korps were placed behind the southern flank, ready to counterattack. Rommel left the Italians to hold out as long as possible in the Sollum, Halfaya, and Bardia area. They continued to fight for another month and a half. This allowed 70th Division in Tobruk to now finally be relieved. They captured the German-held strong points without any resistance, however they met resistance from the remaining Italians, suffering heavy losses as they took Point 157. In a final action on the part of the Division, the Polish attacked Italian elements covering the Axis retreat. The Tobruk defenders were finally relieved after a nineteen-day battle.

The battalion moved into a reserve position between 9-11 December with 22nd Guards Brigade and come under 7th Armoured Division, who in the hope of getting better co-ordination between his infantry and armour, Ritchie transferred to XIII Corps. On 12 December, the battalion with a squadron of tanks from the Kings Dragoon Guards were ordered to advance to contact—which they did—and then took up defensive positions. The Eighth Army launched its attack on the Gazala line on 13 December with only limited gains at the cost of significant losses. On 14 December, the battalion moved from the Guards Brigade to the 4th Armoured Brigade, who were to make a wide sweep around the enemy. The battalion moved with the B Echelon and found the going very difficult in the soft sand and winter rain. It would have again been exceptionally difficult driving conditions for Alan to navigate.

On 15 December, the offensive was renewed all along the line but without significant success. The same day also saw an Axis counter attack against Point 204, which Rommel considered a key position. The Buffs holding this point lost almost 1,000 men killed or captured[105]. Fortunately for the rest of the 5th Indian Brigade it was by then too late in the day for the attacking force to collect itself and advance further. By 15 December, the Afrika Korps were down to eight working tanks. Rommel now became concerned about the flanking move to the south that Alan was part of. He ordered an evacuation of the Gazala line on the night of 15 December.

By the afternoon of 15 December, the 4th Armoured, having looped round to the south, was at Bir Halegh el Eleba, some 30 miles northwest of Alem Hamza and ideally placed both to strike at the rear of the Afrika Korps and advance north to cut the Panzer Group's main lines of communication along the coast. However, early on 16 December, refuelling difficulties meant that only a small detachment was sent north (which did cause confusion among enemy rear echelons, but wasn't decisive) while the rest of the brigade headed south to meet its petrol supplies. In the afternoon, the 15th Panzer moving west were able to pass by the rear of the 4th Armoured and block any return move to the north. Rommel began a further retirement on the night 16 to 17 December. Over the following ten days, Rommel's forces withdrew to a line between Ajedabia and El Haseia, maintaining his lines of communication and avoiding being cut off and surrounded as the Italians had been the previous year in O'Connor's offensive.

On 17 December, D Company was attached to the 7th Support Group and came under heavy dive bomb attack from the wailing Stukas.[106] The following day, two trucks from the company came under friendly fire from two hurricanes. Even now, friendly fire incidents are always upsetting for all involved and somehow seem worse than deaths caused by the enemy—

somehow more pointless, as if deaths caused by the enemy are an accepted part of war but mistakes in amongst the chaos that result in friendly fire are less acceptable.

In *Where Men Win Glory: The Odyssey of Pat Tillman*, US author Jon Krakauer tells the story of Tilman, a professional American football player who left his sports career and enlisted in the US Army in the aftermath of the September 11 attacks. He was later killed by friendly fire in Afghanistan, and Krakauer claims that; "according to the most comprehensive survey of casualties (both fatal and nonfatal), 21 percent of the casualties in World War II were attributable to friendly fire, 39 percent of the casualties in Vietnam, and 52 percent of the casualties in the first Gulf War. Thus far in the ongoing conflicts in Iraq and Afghanistan, casualty rates are 41 percent and 13 percent, respectively."[107]

The company received congratulations from the brigade commander Brigadier Campbell for the night patrols they conducted to Fort Mechili, suggesting the challenging nature of the patrols and the professionalism of Alan's unit.[108] By the 19 December, the battalion again change command coming under the 22nd Armoured Brigade. As Rommel's lines of supply shortened, he was able to rebuild his tank force while at the same time the Eighth Army lines of supply (especially fuel) became more and more stretched as they continued the pursuit. Thus strengthened, the Germans once again turned on the pursuers. On 27 December, the Axis forces were able in a three-day tank battle at El Haseia to inflict heavy damage on the 22nd Armoured Brigade, to which the battalion was now attached. The attack was aimed at the brigade flank so the battalion was involved despite its position within the brigade. On 28 December, the war diary notes that they were ordered to move to the Brigade HQ and again came under heavy shelling as they did. D Company with A Company brought up the rear and found themselves almost cut off. The going was rough, and vehicles got hit by shell fire when they became stuck. A Company had to fight through to try to avoid being captured; however, the OC, one other officer, and twenty-five ORs became cut off and the diary noted they were missing ever since. The battalion was in further contacts on 29 December, and on 30 December the brigade HQ was again under threat as it moved north. At the end of December's entries in the war diary, there is a section entitled "General Comments." In it, the author states that in the last three weeks of December, the rations were worse in variety and water shortages were more acute with no more than half a gallon a day.[109]

The counter attacks ultimately allowed the Axis forces to fall back to a tactically more desirable defensive line at El Agheila which they reached on 6 January, without in Stewart's words, "further molestation."[110] The battalion war diary does, however, describe a number of contacts during that withdrawal. The battalion was formed up in "Jock Columns" which, similar to the earlier "Sister Columns," were small highly mobile mixed groups of motorised infantry and field guns, named now after the VC winner from Sidi Rezegh. From late on in Operation CRUSADER, they became popular formations. D Company was in the Squeak Column named after its commanding officer Lieutenant Colonel "Squeak" Purdon, the Commanding Officer of the battalion. On 1 January, the column was in close combat with the enemy consisting of some 20 tanks and 50 Mechanized Enemy Transport (MET). On 2 January, they were taking incoming mortar and machine gun fire when trying to occupy OPs. On 3 January, while moving south to engage the enemy with 25-pounders, they received more accurate shelling than on previous days but took no casualties. The night of 3-4 January, D Company sent out a night recce of one officer and fifteen ORs to search area occupied by enemy in the day, but they found nothing of interest. On 5 January, the column moved and successfully engaged the enemy. Contacts with the enemy included a mounted anti-tank gun approaching a protective detachment from D Company and fired, 25-pounders and small arms fire were returned and it made off.[111]

On 6 January, the column moved to a day reserve position and a sandstorm hit. D Company sent out three patrols under the cover of the sandstorm to recce enemy positions. Two returned without incident. The third patrol that was sent out on the night of 6-7 January and was composed of one officer and ten ORs from the company in two 15 CWTs trucks. Its' task was to recce some potential enemy positions reported in Belandah. The war diary reports that at Kilo 26 on the Agedabia-Belandah track, the second truck was hit by a mine and the driver was killed. The crew, with as much kit as possible, transferred to the leading 15 CWT and the patrol returned. The driver was quickly buried at the scene. Throughout the patrol no enemy was sighted. The enemy were now at El Agheila, where they were before the original battle for Mersa Brega and Operation CRUSADER was over.

Alan told Stephenie that on one patrol his unit was selected, but then at the last minute a second unit was tasked with the patrol and he stood down. That unit that then went out in place of Alan's unit suffered casualties. He spoke to Stephenie of his guilt all those years later that he was not sent out and that he survived when others did not. He felt that it was his fault they died, as if he had gone on the patrol they would not have been there, even though the decision was not his. It was quite possibly this patrol he referred to when speaking with Stephenie, although we cannot be sure. Like so many who survived guilt was one of the most common emotions Alan felt about his time in the desert. For him, though, it was not just the guilt of having fate intervene and change a patrol task, throwing others in harm's way. It would become guilt over all the fighting that Alan missed after he had deserted and guilt over all the others he believed ended up dying in his place on every patrol he would miss after he deserted. This must have been a massive burden to bear for all those years.

The Commonwealth Graves Commission website has one fatality listed for the period of 6-7 January 1942 within the battalion and it is a Sydney Albert Kennedy aged 22, son of William Edward and Mary Ann Kennedy, of Fulham, London. He has an entry on the Alamein memorial.[112] Sydney would have been one of the last of the 2,900 British deaths in the operation.

According to Ken Ford in *Operation Crusader 1941: Rommel in Retreat*, there were a further 7,300 British wounded and 7,500 British missing, whilst the overall Eighth Army losses were fifteen percent of troops involved,[113] revealing the intensity and true scale of the fighting in this little-known operation. These figures dwarf those from the conflicts I was involved in.

Strawson quotes Robert Crisp from his book *Brazen Chariots*, which gives an insight to what is was like fighting in Operation CRUSADER at the level of the individual soldier:

> From that moment on I can truthfully say none of us had more than the vaguest idea where we were from day to day and hour to hour, or what was happening either to our own force or the enemy's. The campaign swung violently from one end of the desert to the other...We chased mirages and were chased by mirages...We went without sleep, without food, without washing or change of clothes, without conversation beyond the clipped talk of wireless procedure and orders...the long day of movement and vigil and encounter, death and the fear of death, until darkness put a limit to vision and purpose on both sides.[114]

During the operation, the battalion never remained under the same command for a significant amount of time it was switched from one brigade or division to another at twenty-four hours' notice or less at times. This does not help in trying to follow the battalion's progress and its role in some of the bigger operations such as CRUSADER. All the history books consulted make no mention of the battalion at all; it is only the original dusty and largely unread war diaries in the National Archives that seem to record the battalion's presence. It would also not have helped the men of the battalion's confidence in their leaders or their appreciation of how the operation was progressing. Always being the attached battalion can lead you to believe that you are always going to get the worst tasks and you are unlikely to have the same level of trust with command and the other units, as those who are long established members of the formation.

Operation CRUSADER is presented in most texts as an Allied victory, as the siege of Tobruk was relieved and the Axis forces were pushed west all the way to El Agheila, although most texts note it was not the complete victory that Churchill, Auchinleck, and his generals wanted.[115] Rommel while suffering significant losses had got the bulk of his fighting troops off the battlefield. A fact that, Stewart notes, Churchill at least appreciated.[116] Alan and his fellow soldiers would not have seen the operation as self-contained period of time and experience. Time in the area of operations is one continuum. History puts artificial lines in the sands of time. They would not have sat back, at the point we now declare was the end of the operation, celebrating a victory—for a start, they were still in contact with the enemy. Secondly, would have seen the operation in the context of what happened to them next which certainly did not feel like a victory, but much more a defeat.

Chapter Four
The Gazala Gallop

Between January and June 1942 the desert war, so like an occasionally interrupted game of battledore and shuttlecock, was to reach a previously unknown pitch of speed and violence. For the second time Rommel had the battledore firmly in his hand. 8th Army was the shuttlecock.

The Battle for North Africa, John Strawson

And war is not but what you have learnt it to be, and
what you have experienced, and what is said concerning it
is not a story based on suppositions.

When you stir it up, you will stir it up as an accursed,
thing, and it will become greedy when you excite its greed
and it will rage fiercely.

Then it will grind you as the grinding of the upper millstone
against the lower, and it will conceive immediately after
one birth and it will produce twins.

The Mu'allaqat, Zuhair

While CRUSADER was still in progress in December 1942, one of the key actions of the Second World War took place: the Japanese attacked the US fleet at Pearl Harbour. This attack, coupled with the Japanese attacks on British-held Malaya, saw the US and Britain becoming allies against the Japanese in the Far East. A few days later, the US joined the Allies and also declared war on Germany and Italy. Whilst in the long term the US entry to the war was good news for the Allies, in the short

63

term the attacks in the Far East were bad news for the Allies in North Africa. Reinforcements for the Middle East were now sent to the Far East and, worse than that, some of the resources Auchinleck currently had in theatre were also donated to the Far East, including, but not limited to, six RAF bomber squadrons and 110 tanks from the 7th Armoured Brigade.[117]

At the same time as Auchinleck's resources were decreasing, Rommel's were increasing. The Axis assault on the island of Malta increased in intensity. Hitler instructed Field Marshall Albert Kesselring, the commander of all naval and air forces in the Mediterranean, to; "ensure safe lines of communication with North Africa," going on to highlight that "the suppression of Malta was particularly important in this connection."[118] In the last week of December 1941, over 200 aircraft attacked the island. In January and February 1942, the attacks increased again. Malta held out under seemingly endless air attack with a level of stoicism that saw King George VI award the George Cross "to bear witness to a heroism and devotion that will long be famous in history."[119] It is the only time in history that such an award has been made to a community as a whole. While Malta held out, it could not sustain its offensive capability. The RAF bases on the island had been key in disrupting Axis supplies. While Malta was under pressure the Axis could resupply Rommel. On 5 January, a significant convoy broke through to Tripoli with, amongst other supplies, fifty-four Mark III tanks with their crews.

At the end of CRUSADER Auchinleck, however, was not planning to defend his gains, but had begun planning a new offensive: Operation ACROBAT. This would drive the Axis forces further west, through Libya, taking Tripoli and had the potential of removing them from the continent altogether. This was a key aim of Allied strategy according to the memorandum that came out of the grand strategy conference in Washington that now included the US combined staffs for the first time.

Even after Churchill, usually more bullish than his commanders, questioned whether the offensive could still occur after the 5 January convoy resupplied Rommel, Auchinleck was dismissive of the state of Rommel's forces and keen to proceed. Stewart suggests that Churchill's questioning may have, even at the subconscious level, actually hardened Auchinleck's intent to proceed abandoning his more prudent assessments of Rommel's strength before the reinforcements and before Churchill's enquiry.[120] Stewart suggests that Auchinleck had become so unhappy with the Prime Minister's interference that he was rejecting any suggestion on principle.

The 18th-century Scottish philosopher David Hume said "reason is and ought to be a slave to the passions,"[121] and modern psychology has done much to support his claim.[122] At best this is a form of sentimentalism, a belief that distinctions between morality and immorality are discovered by emotional responses to experience. At worst, though, I think this means that key decisions are often made not on the evidence in front of the decision-maker, but due to an emotional bias that can emanate as much from psychological flaws as positive emotions such as empathy. Resultantly, so often in the history of war, and humankind more generally, decisions that profoundly affect the lives of men and women, are made not by reasoned thought, but due to one individual's emotional reaction to another individual—maybe this is sometimes for the best; here though, if this was at play, it was not for the best.

Before ACROBAT could be launched, Auchinleck faced a more tactical decision as to whether to sacrifice ground to be able regroup around Msus and Benghazi and provide a stronger front line, or, to maintain contact with the enemy further forward in Agheila risking the widely dispersed British light forces in that area, being driven back by reconnaissance in force. Auchinleck chose to walk the tightrope of maintaining contact. By 7 January, the Squeak Column had moved on to try and regain contact with the enemy, who it was reported had withdrawn from Agedabia. Although the 22nd Armoured had withdrawn to Tobruk to re-equip after the casualties, it sustained in the final phases of CRUSADER, the battalion remained at the front with the 200th Guards Brigade (the renamed 22nd Guards Brigade), who were spilt, one half forming Jock Columns in the area around Mersa Brega and the other operating without artillery around Agedabia. This was as part of the higher formation of the 1st Armoured Division commanded by General Messervy, which also included the newly arrived, inexperienced 1st Support Group (also split into columns) protecting the Guards left flank in the area and the 2nd Armoured Brigade conducting training between Antelat and Saunnu. The 7th Armoured Division was the next formation back, but they were re-fitting all the way to the rear in Tobruk.

Strawson summarises that the "intelligence was inadequate, supplies uncertain, training inadequate and adaptability non-existent."[123] Add to all this the fact that the Axis air situation was more favourable than it had been for months and what followed seems inevitable.

On 8 January, the Squeak Column dispersed to allow armoured car patrols to search for the enemy and regain contact. The D Company Scout party was one of the key patrol elements and found contact. The war diary also notes that on the same day that one of the scout platoons met with "Arabs" from a Bedouin village and questioned them about German movements.

It is not noted what the Bedouins made of the foreigners with their strange and terrifying machines of combat creating carnage in their lands. Oral poetry is the most popular art form among Bedouins, capturing the history, wisdom, and values of the various tribes. Those of us outside of oral cultures are dependent on the generosity of those who dedicate the significant time necessary to immerse themselves within it, and write the stories and poems down for us. There have been several such individuals in history who have done this for the Bedouin. Probably the most well-known was Hammad 'the Transmitter,' a man of supposed prodigious memory, who in the eighth century memorized the poetry he encountered in his travels among the Bedouins. From his memorized collection, seven odes by individual poets were written down in an anthology called *The Mu'allaqat*, (most frequently translated as the *"Suspended Odes)*.[124] While poetry remains very important across the Arab world, as far as I am aware there are no poems written down that tell of the North African Bedouins meetings with the Europeans.

It is unlikely Alan was on this patrol. He told Stephenie that he saw the Bedouin on the horizon a number of times, but when they moved to where they thought they had seen them they had always disappeared back into the desert. This left them unsure whether they had just seen a mirage or that the Bedouin knew ways to move and hide that the foreigners in their land did not. The harassing continued on 9 January, with D Company providing the majority of forward party engaging the enemy.

On 10 January, the 200th Guards Brigade took over the Haban area from the Squeak Column. A sandstorm limited movement for the rest of the day. Alan told Stephenie how they hid under their canopies and just waited until the sandstorms passed. He said the sand got in everything; you ate it, drank it, and dressed in it. It was the sand you find in your shoe weeks after the day you spent on the beach, but also in every single item of clothing and every bit of kit you owned. I remember in Iraq the helicopters supporting us needed to be grounded for a number of days due to sand that had got in to their engines turning to glass in the heat. Like much of the equipment and vehicles Alan would have used, the helicopters supporting us had not necessarily been designed to operate in such hot and sandy conditions. It was not just the soldiers that would overheat and struggle to function in the desert. The battalion then spent the next two days in reserve before moving twenty-nine miles southwest on 13 January. They received reports that the enemy were now digging in to the south.

On 14 January, they were dive-bombed by Stukas in the morning, resulting in one attached gunner (a soldier from the accompanying artillery troops—this was mostly likely Joseph Birchall son of William and Alice Birchall; husband of Mary Elizabeth Birchall, of Cheadle, Staffordshire) killed in action and one rifleman from the battalion injured. There was damage done to one of the artillery guns and battalion vehicles also. They were dive bombed again in the evening, but this time with no physical casualties; there is no mention of the mental toll this constant harassment from the terrifying Stukas was creating. The battalion was starting to feel the consequences of the strategic battle in the Mediterranean and the increasing Axis air power.

Alan talked about one occasion when his officer came running up the parked-up column, shouting at the troops to get moving. As the air would have filled with wailing from the Jericho Trumpets, he yelled at Alan (who was the front vehicle) to put his foot down and get them the "F" out of there. Alan urgently jabbed his foot flat to the floor, but frustratingly the truck only lumbered forward. As the truck slowly started to gather momentum, Alan looked in his side mirror and saw the Stukas dive bombing the end of the column.

Later, after the war, when Stephenie and her sister were children, Alan had a Dormobile caravan that he used to drive the whole family all the way to Italy for holidays. Alan told them that just like his wartime truck, when you put your foot down in the Dormobile it still just went at the one speed. He told Stephenie that he would tell them that; "You couldn't get it to move fast even if you wanted to," and he would tell them that that was how the lorries were like when he was driving in them in the desert. I had not heard of a Dormobile before, so I looked it up. When looking at the specifications, I stumbled upon the reason why Alan thought it was like the lorries he had driven in the desert. It was because the engine and chassis of the Dormobile was also made by the Bedford Company that made the CWT Alan drove in the desert, and they were based on the same engine and chassis of that same truck.

We will never know for sure whether this was a conscious decision by Alan—with his background and interest in engineering, it is likely that he knew. His family, however, had no idea, and often wondered why they didn't fly, or at least why he seemed so happy to drive for such long periods in such a difficult vehicle. The long drives to Italy, with his family in the back in peacetime must have provoked many memories for Alan of his war.

Maybe on one level, this was a cathartic experience for him, or at very least it may have provided a familiarity that was of comfort. Maybe every hill start he did when crossing the Italian Alps gave him another chance to pull away quicker, to get his lumbering vehicle clear of the dive bombing Stukas, saving the rear vehicles from their bombs and machine guns. Maybe sometimes when he looked in his side mirrors, unbeknownst to his family in the Dormobile with him, he sometime saw those terrifying planes again. With each small discovery, I wondered what Alan would have made of the someone he did not know poring over the details of his life, trying to piece together bits of his story that he would have thought no-one would ever know. Stephenie believed he would have been very surprised that anyone was interested in him.

There may well be future generations who pore over the digital records of the conflicts I was involved in. My generation has left less paper to gather dust in national archives or family attics. There are blurred and grainy head camera clips that in no way convey the violence of the kinetic activity involved or the impact on the individuals they are attached to. There are also the talking heads in documentaries, speaking after the event seemingly for entertainment purposes rather than posterity. So far though, there has been very little on what it was like day to day for the majority of troops involved, and even less on what it was like for the larger number of civilians who had to live in the impacted communities. The latter group, who endured more than anyone, are rarely heard from in the present despite the strong oral traditions in the region. They could be completely silent in the future if their voices and experiences not captured in the coming years and conflict rumbles on despite the exit of Western troops.

The war diary for those days also noted that the going in the soft sand was extreme. Alan said they were continuously putting down planks, blankets, tarpaulins, and anything else they could to get them out when they were stuck. He said how tiring it was as they never seemed to get very far, even though the distances they covered during the retreat from Mersa Brega, Operation CRUSADER and were about to cover now in the face of this Axis assault were vast. At least now they were spared the added exhaustion of the energy sapping desert heat, which they would have to endure again in the coming months. The fact that the battalion repeatedly found itself back in the same locations, time and time again as they advanced and withdrew across the desert, would have no doubt added to the feeling of a lack of progress. There was also the impact of just being in the desert for a prolonged period of time. Crimp wrote in his diary after being in the desert for just under three months:

> Just lately I have been feeling a bit browned off. there's a sort of psychological compliant some chaps get after long exposure on the Blue [the desert area of operationscalled 'desert weariness', though I can hardly claim to have reached that yet. But for months now we have been cut off from nearly every aspect of civilised life, and everyday has been cast in the same monotonous mould. The desert, omnipresent, so saturates consciousness that it makes the mind as sterile as itself. It's only now you realise how much you normally live through the senses. Here there's nothing here for them...Then over and above the physical factors, there's the total lack of change or relaxation; nothing even certain to ever look forward to, that after such a term of vacuum living, would make it tolerable... For weeks more, probably months, we shall have to go on bearing an unbroken succession of empty, ugly, insipid days...Then of course there are the flies....[125]

The contrast of the sterility and stillness of the desert that Crimp describes, with the screaming and thudding violence of the detonating high explosives that both sides were hurling at each, or had placed lying in wait under the quiet sand, must have made it all the more jarring for Alan and the others.

On the afternoon of 15 January, one soldier from D Company was wounded as well as two other soldiers in the column.[126] On 17 January, the Brigadier commanding the 7th Support and 1st Support Groups had his recce party dive bombed. The main Squeak Column was then heavily strafed by Messerschmitts, and three Savoia bombers flew over column and dropped approximately 500 bombs to the south and east. Vehicles were damaged, but there were no casualties. The column was at this point pushing out numerous reconnaissance patrols ready for handover to the 1st Support Group. More air attacks followed the next day, but no casualties were taken. No doubt by Alan and his fellow riflemen would fear the clear blue sky and pray for bad weather that might limit the chance that at any moment a fast-moving black spec could emerge that would at first hum, but then scream as it grew in size and began to deliver injury and death from above.

On the night of 18-19 January the Squeak Column handed over to a column from the 1st Support Group and the next day met up with the rest of the battalion and the rest of the 2nd RHA and the 102nd (NH) RHA. The three moved off on a two-day journey towards Giofardun to meet up with the 2nd Armoured Brigade (who remained part of the 1st Armoured Division), who they then fell under the command of. Their orders were then to rest and refit when they arrived on 21 January. Auchinleck's official dispatch on 21 January, however, noted how at dawn "the improbable has occurred and without warning the Axis forces began to advance."[127]

Spearheaded by the 15th and 21st Panzer, the initial Axis advance was both along the Via Balbia and through open desert in the area of Wadi Faregh. After encountering resistance on the first day, the Axis troops broke through on the second day. German commander Von Mellenthin described what followed— "the pursuit attained a speed of fifteen miles an hour and the British fled madly over the desert in one of the most extraordinary routs of the war."[128] By 1100, Agedabia had been captured. By 1530 Antelat was taken, which resulted, according to Stewart, in the "cutting off 2 Armoured Brigade and the remaining advanced infantry units which were still south-east of Antelat."[129]

The battalion arrived to meet the 2nd Armoured Brigade at the pre-determined meeting point on 22 January, but the war diary notes that the 2nd Armoured Brigade moved off as they arrived without sharing the code-words and call signs necessary to pass orders securely over the radio. The diary notes that this made communications with them impossible.[130] Orders were left for the battalion that they should remain in current location and refit. The diary also notes somewhat sardonically that since the Squeak Column had been relieved on 18-19 January, the enemy had made rapid advances and reached Agedabia. At this point in Auchinleck's headquarters in Cairo, they still believed that this was an enemy reconnaissance in force and not a major offensive.[131]

On 22 January, the battalion received orders to move with the 2nd RHA and the 102nd (NH) RHA to meet any threat coming from Agedabia towards Antelat.[132] However, as they had been moving around 120 miles a day for the last few days, without replenishments, they were out of petrol and immobile until a resupply arrived. The could not move as ordered and it was impossible to let the 2nd Armoured Brigade know that, due to lack of communications with them. The battalion decided to spilt back in to three columns. D Company were again in the Squeak Column with one battery each from accompanying artillery regiments. B Company were in the "Len Column," and C Company in the "Pumfrey Column" (named after Major Pumfrey). In the late afternoon, the resupply arrived so replenished and stayed the night where they were.

On 23 January, Rommel hoped to destroy the cut off forces; however, the Germans left an escape route when German armour failed to replace the mobile infantry group leaving to pursue the trapped forces.[133] Covered by artillery fire, the remains of the 1st Armoured Division fought its way to safety. The three columns comprised of soldiers from the battalion set off west, while the 200[134] Guards Brigade withdrew north and east and the 1st Support Group was also on the withdrawal. The 2nd Armoured Brigade had now been diverted from their original destination, so by now, due to the communications issues, the battalion had no idea where their higher command was. It is noted in the war diary that the three columns were "completely without information,"[134] which is as strong and emotionally charged language for a war diary that you could get. The battalion adjutant had to physically drive to XIII Corps HQ. He returned with orders and the columns moved forward on these, again getting dive-bombed, resulting in an unnamed soldier from D Company being wounded.

On 24 January, Axis air engaged withdrawing Allied forces once more. At this point, XX Corps were finally ordered to prepare a defensive line running south from Gazala to protect Tobruk and give the withdrawing troops a firm base to fall back on, as higher command accepted the fact that this was developing into a major offensive as Rommel exploited his success.[135]

The Squeak Column remained in an observation post throughout the day; unaware of the pursuit they would be involved in the following day. On 25 January, Rommel struck north for Msus. The three columns of the battalion were placed under command of the 1st Support Group and received reports of three enemy columns of tanks on a wide front north east from Antelat towards Msus.[136] The 200th Guards Brigade withdrew through Squeak Column heading for Msus. Soon after, the column was engaged by a column of twelve German tanks and received orders to withdraw to Msus themselves. They had to leapfrog, sub-units taking it in turns, one unit firing while the other moved past them and took up a new firing position so they could then put down fire while the other unit then moved and so on, withdrawing in contact. As the route previously given to them was now blocked by enemy forces, they received orders to withdraw eastwards along a narrow lane. The lane cut between two of the many salt lakes scattered south of Msus, one lake lying north and one south of this lane, for ten miles. The column then became involved in what is described by the official regimental history, *The Rifle Brigade in the Second World War 1939-1945* by Major R.H.W.S Hastings (retd), as a "lively little action."[137]

The situation was now chaotic, with many Allied units being cut off behind the rapidly advancing Axis forces. The official history notes that not only were there vehicles of both sides appearing at speed from the south and southwest, but many British vehicles were being driven by Germans. The Squeak Column took the narrow lane between the impassable salt lakes, but before reaching the end of the lane the observation post of the leading platoon of the column spotted a column of six German tanks, armoured personnel carriers, guns, and some 400 MET moving north towards Msus. The rear of this column was blocked the end of the lane.

They were trapped.[138]

The Squeak Column was then faced with two options. The first option was that the column could retrace its steps westward back to end of lane and try to find a way through the enemy in more open ground. The second option was to engage the more heavily armed column in front of them, which had yet to spot them, and fight their way out. The war diary states in a brilliantly understated way: "it was decided to take the latter course."[139] The column made the bold decision to charge straight at the enemy. The column's 25-pounders fired over their sights at a range of 1000 metres at several of the MET who made their way north as quickly as possible. They knocked out a gun tractor and 105-mm gun with Mortar Platoon D Company taking the crew prisoner. Another patrol was engaged, and twenty-eight further prisoners taken. Their bravery and decisiveness paid off.

The Squeak Column then made haste to push out east from between the two lakes to engage the remaining column from the south. By this point, the column was under heavy shelling from at least two 88-pounders that had been brought back along the enemy column. The Squeak Column then moved eastwards and halted waiting for its other observation post it had sent out to return, which had been cut off by enemy tanks and had been forced to move through the salt marshes and wait for the enemy to pass. No casualties were sustained however it was noted that a high number of soft skinned vehicles had suffered and the column was now low in fuel.[140]

The column continued north, having one further engagement with the enemy before the light faded. They moved into close leaguer formation and continued on driving through the darkness. During the night, the Squeak Column could hear the sound of the enemy moving close by and see numerous very lights and flares. At several intervals, the column halted and tried to get communications with other columns. Just after 2020, they halted as another column passed 800 metres to the front of them—a patrol was sent out to see if it was friend or foe, but could not catch up with it. There are many accounts from other units describing similar encounters as darkness fell, encounters where columns moved past each other, often in very close proximity, unsure of whether they were on the same side or if the guns and tanks passing by so closely were those of the enemy. This confusion was accentuated by the fact that throughout the previous advances across the desert, both sides had commandeered vehicles from the other side as they withdrew. There are many accounts from the retreating Allied forces of instances when they were aware that it was enemy troops passing right by in greater number, and all they could do to avoid capture or destruction was remain silent, stick a bayonet in the side of any prisoners as a pointed warning against shouting out to their comrades, and hope they would not be discovered.[141]

As the fast-moving column moved off two halted trucks were spotted up ahead. Two 15 CWT trucks from D Company were sent out to investigate, but the trucks were found to be derelicts blown up in a minefield. For the second time in a month, a D Company patrol then suffered a fatal mine strike; as one of the trucks hit a mine and burst into flames. The war diary notes that two other ranks were wounded—one of whom died of wounds the following day.[142] This is likely to be 23-year-old Lance Corporal Alfred Fredericks, son of Herbert and Mary

Fredericks, husband of Jane Fredericks.[143] It is very likely that Alan knew all those involved. At times like these, as well as feeling the loss of your comrades, it is impossible to not also reflect on the fragility of your own mortality.

The column then decided to stay in place and navigate the minefield in the morning after an eventful day. Thus, the column continued north where they met up with the 11th Hussars who passed them orders from the 1st Armoured Division, which instructed them to continue to the division rally point at El Charruba where they remained in reserve and took up defensive position. On 28 January, the 1st Armoured Division decided to move south to harass enemy rear forces as they advanced the columns re-organised and were attached to tank columns. D Company travelled with the HQ 2nd Armoured Brigade and was responsible for its protection. The force joined up with the 200th Guards Brigade in contacting the enemy. By evening, the 2nd Armoured Brigade received orders to return to Charruba. Squeak Column reformed and moved back independently. On 29 January, they found themselves now back under command of the 1st Support Group and in defensive positions. They sent out a harassing party and standing patrol consisting of members of D Company, but saw nothing of the enemy. This continued the next day.

The day following that, 31 January, the battalion was in defensive positions east of Wadi el Hamma. The Tower Hamlets Rifles were on the right, the 2nd Kings Royal Rifles Corps on left, and the 200th Guards Brigade stood to the south. The Pumfrey column, consisting of C Company and attached artillery, was sent forward from the battalion from these positions and came in contact with 150 MET and guns from south and southeast, as the column withdrew northwards Major Pumfrey and his HQ ran into some German armoured carriers as they crossed a ridge, who engaged at a range of 100 metres, causing casualties. The war diary notes that Major Pumfrey and his HQ were missing and assumed captured.[144] The rest of the column managed to escape via a path cleared by 25-pounders engaging over open sights at 1,500 metres. The rest of the column re-joined the battalion.

The going was noted as again being extremely bad and dusty as the battalion continued its withdrawal passing through the area of Derna, where the battalion was previously engaged in the retreat from Mersa, stopping briefly in defensive position on 2 February where they sent out patrols.[145] The following day, they conducted an overnight move as a battalion and attachments. By 4 February, they had taken up defensive positions south of Trigh El Abd with the 200th Guards Brigade. North of the track the Poles, Free French, and Indian Division continued the line north to Gazala. By 5 February, the 1st Support Group had moved into the line and taken over from the 200th Guards Brigade, and a minefield was laid in front of these positions. On 6 February, the 1st Support Group ordered the battalion north of the track into all round defence. They then formed the left flank of defensive line with the Kings' Royal Rifles to the north.

So, by 6 February, the Eighth Army including Alan Juniper and the rest of D Company and the Tower Hamlets Rifles' were back on the Gazala-Bir Hacheim line that only two months previously the Germans had fallen back to during CRUSADER. The latter phase of this withdrawal was a more orderly affair as Rommel's forces began to suffer their own supply issues and fuel became scarce. It was now 312 days since the battalion first contacted the enemy at Mersa Brega and 402 days since they had arrived in North Africa. The attrition and confused nature of the fighting, the difficult physical conditions, and the way hard fought victories were quickly turned into defeat and panicked withdrawals was now having an effect on the morale of the British soldiers. Stewart notes that the troops had the "haunting fear that victory was a mirage that would always disappear," just as the Bedouin that Alan saw on the horizon had done, "when it seemed within Eighth Army's grasp; that successes would always be but temporary ones; the Eighth Army was doomed to fight up and down the Western Desert for all time."[146] The pattern of advance and then retreat was given various names by the troops; "The Annual Swan up the Desert" or "The Gazala Gallop."[147] And it was Gazala where the next significant action would occur.

Chapter Five
Death by Drowning

"For in tremendous extremities human souls are like drowning men; well enough they know they are in peril; well enough they know the causes of that peril;—nevertheless, the sea is the sea, and these drowning men do drown."

Pierre or the Ambiguities, Herman Melville

From 6 February to the beginning of Rommel's next offensive at the end of May, there was a lull in fighting. The front line had been stabilised, from Gazala on the coast 30 miles west of Tobruk, to an old Ottoman era fortress at Bir Hacheim, 50 miles to the south. The Gazala Line was a series of defensive "boxes" with a brigade manning each one, laid out across the desert behind minefields and wire, watched by regular patrols and OPs in gaps between the boxes. The line was not evenly manned, with a greater number of troops covering the coast road, leaving the south with less protection in terms of troops. There was a deep minefield, however, and from an Axis perspective, attacking to the south would place a greater stress on its supply chain. Behind the Gazala Line there were more defensive boxes at Commonwealth Keep, Acroma, Knightsbridge, and El Adem, all sited to block tracks and junctions. A box at Retma was also finished just before the Axis offensive, but work on further boxes at the Point 171 and Bir el Gubi did not begin until 25 May, so they were unfinished at the time the Axis crossed their line of departure.[148]

The battalion remained in the line until 12 February in defensive positions "in readiness to launch counter offensive measures if required."[149] They dug in and camouflaged their vehicles. Attached artillery units were sent out on harassing patrols. On 11 February, unwanted vehicles that had been sent to the rear were brought back up to the line in prep for evacuation the next morning and, on 12 February, they moved out of the line and came under the 200th Guards Brigade. The attached gunners who had been with the battalion for nearly two months left the battalion command. As ever change was the only constant for the battalion. Through the rest of February and March the battalion would now be in reserve. Individual companies however would rotate through tasks that included guarding fuel dumps, conducting patrols out through the gaps in the minefield and OPs.

There were few notable incidents during this period. On 22 February, a party lead by the Battalion Technical Officer and fourteen drivers set of to find vehicles abandoned in the withdrawal. They took with them six days rations and petrol. We don't know if Alan was part of this patrol or not. Separated from the rest of the battalion and the rest of the Allied troops, they would have been a vulnerable target and would have been very much aware of this. The risky nature of the patrol indicates the importance of retrieving the supplies and the pressure on the Allied supply chain. Although there was a lull in the ground offensive, the threat of attack from the air remained. On 22 February, as the patrol left, the rest of the battalion was strafed by three Messerschmitts, which resulted in three wounded ORs. On 25 February, in preparation for D Company taking over the OP from C Company, a party of officers went up to the forward observation post. The post was attacked by ME 109s and twenty-six year old Lieutenant Harold Adler from D Company, son of James and Ellen Augusta Adler, of St. John's Wood, London, was killed as he was firing at one of the planes with a light machine gun.[150] The vehicles in the OP were all hit, but as they were dug in no serious damage was done. The air attacks continued into the next month, when on 6 March, the war diary notes that the battalion was strafed by air, resulting in one OR wounded.[151] Then on 12 March, a C Company officer Second Lieutenant Hugh Preston, son of (Ivor) Kerrison Preston and Agnes Evelyn

Preston, of Merstham, Surrey, was seriously wounded by air attack and would die a few days later in 62 General Hospital on 18 March, most likely before his parents even knew he had been injured.[152] Periods described at the strategic level as "lulls" can often not feel as such at the tactical level to the individual soldier.

Meanwhile at the strategic level, Churchill renewed his communications with Auchinleck, repeating the pattern he had set with his previous commanders, pressing him to attack to push Axis forces out of Cyrenaica and relieve the pressure on Malta, which Churchill felt was essential to the war effort:

> ...having particular regard to Malta, the loss of which would be a disaster of the first magnitude to the British Empire, and probably fatal in the long run to the defence of the Nile delta.[153]

Auchinleck was now determined, however, to buy time to re-organise, train, and supply his army. In particular Auchinleck wanted to better co-ordinate the relationship between armour, infantry and artillery. He wanted to ensure the Allies would also fight as more of a co-ordinated division rather than in piecemeal independent brigades, or sub-brigade formations, unable to support one another as had been the case thus far. This would allow him to bring about the concentration of fire power he needed to defeat the Panzer divisions. Strawson notes that Auchinleck's intent was sound, but it never progressed past the theoretical.[154] In reality, infantry divisions were split up into the series of box formations, which were designed to resist attack from any direction and were supported by guns and surrounded by mines and barbed wire to achieve this. Both Strawson and Stewart note that the various box formations spread across the Gazala line again spread Allied forces so thinly that they could often not support one another as had previously been the problem, especially as the use of box formations reduced the manoeuvrability of the army (even in motor battalions, trucks were sent away from the boxes so to not present easy targets for the enemy when stationary).[155] [156]

In March and early April, there is note in the war diary of only sub-unit training occurring during this period.[157] Training and the cycle of patrol, OP, and guarding tasks was disrupted by enemy movements more than once during late March and April. Although we now know that the German offensive was not launched until the end of May, the troops on the ground did not have the luxury of knowing this in advance and remained in a state of hyper alertness and high stress as they expected an attack at any moment. On 6 April, enemy were sighted moving east in force. The battalion was put at two hours' notice to move. By 1200, the Guards Brigade was placed at immediate notice to move. A general enemy advance was reported. By 7 April, the gaps in minefields closed and forward OPs were withdrawn. By 8 April, the battalion was back at two hours' notice to move again, and from there it was again down-graded. However, by 10 April at 0030, the battalion received instructions that enemy was likely to advance in force again. In the end, the war diary notes they had a very quiet day.[158]

There are many psychological experiments that demonstrate the negative effects of prolonged expectation of stressful events. The threat of violence can create a stress in comparison to the actual experience of violence, a principle widely understood by terrorist groups.

After moving up in to the line to provide relief for the Scots Guards, the battalion joined a 1st Armoured Division Exercise that began on 22 April. The war diary notes that they were given the task of protecting Transporter Company.[159] However, because fifteen of the sixty-two transporters got stuck, the battalion ended up moving separately from them and took virtually no part in the exercise due to the lack of co-ordination. The exercise finished on the afternoon of 26 April, with the battalion no doubt feeling no further integrated into a more co-ordinated divisional unit.

By 27 April, they finally moved to a rest area by the sea. Each company was given a 300-yard beach frontage. The diary notes that some tents were made available, providing an unaccustomed degree of comfort for the men of the battalion, now very much used to sleeping out under the stars. On 28 April, however, a signal arrived informing the battalion that due to the operational situation all units of the Guard brigade, which they were currently under, must remain at two thirds effectiveness and on three hours' notice to move. Twenty-five members of D Company were dispatched to the Guards HQ the following day, while on 30 April, the battalion managed to send 230 soldiers— mostly from B Company—off on leave. The rest of the battalion —minus B Company—remained in the rest area for the first week of May on three hours' notice to move.

The only entries in the battalion diary from 1 May to 8 May detail the visits of three VIPs. The Colonel in Chief of the Regiment, the Duke of Gloucester, visited on 1 May. The Army Commander visited on 6 May (which was presumably General Ritchie the then Commander of the Eighth Army), and the King of Greece, George II, visited on 8 May. The procession of VIP visits suggests that finally the battalion was in a safe area free from air attacks. They would have been able to relax for the first real rest since the beginning of Operation CRUSADER back in November, the rest only being interrupted by having to present themselves to the undoubtedly well-meaning visitors who would have unaware of the extra work their visit created in the small window of downtime the troops had.

The then-Prime Minister Tony Blair was guest of honour at my pass out parade from the Royal Military Academy Sandhurst, the 141st Sovereign's Parade, in April 2003. He took the time to stop and speak to almost every cadet. No doubt the thought that many on parade would very soon be heading out to the conflict that had begun in Iraq only weeks before, very much on his mind. This, however, meant that we were on parade for a significantly longer than expected. Standing on parade in full military blues with either a sword or a rifle is a painful experience as time wears on. He asked me what unit I was joining. I replied; "Intelligence, sir."

He told me I would be busy.

There is then a significant entry to Alan's war record on 9 May. According to his record, he went absent without leave (AWOL).[160] The day before Alan went AWOL, the battalion war diary reports that while the battalion were enjoying their first real bit of leave since combat started for them, one OR drowned while bathing. No further details are given. The Commonwealth War Graves website notes there was one death from the battalion around this date, that of a Rifleman, twenty-two-year-old John Fogarty—it is not noted how he was killed or any other details about him.[161] When I shared this with Stephenie, asking her if Alan ever mentioned a drowning, she told me that he didn't. She then, however, went on to tell me that as long as she remembered, Alan had been afraid of the water: "Dad has always been petrified of the water. Would never go in above his knees so I wonder if that is why?"[162]

We will never know whether Alan's fear of the water was related to the drowning of John Fogarty. We will never know if John was his friend or whether Alan was right there by his side when he drowned, searching frantically in the water for him as the waves rolled in. We will never know if this was the reason he then went AWOL. Alan never spoke about this incident to his family. All we do know is that he went absent without leave. No reason is noted in his war record. The entry just reads: "absent 9.5.42 to 11.5.42."[163]

Finding out from Stephenie that Alan had a fear of water felt like we were tantalisingly close to uncovering something significant about Alan's time in the desert, but this time it was Alan, rather than the Bedouin, who remained just out of reach on the horizon.

Alan's punishment was eight days CB (assumed to be "confined to barracks") and the forfeit of two days' pay. It does not state if he returned or was apprehended. We can assume from the lenient punishment that he returned under his own steam. In both the UK and US militaries, you are classified as a deserter after thirty days regardless of assessed intent. In US military law, the difference between going AWOL and deserting within those initial thirty days partly surrounds intent. If you desert, you have no intent to return. Whilst not considered within UK military law, the assessed intent would very likely be considered by those at the frontline deciding on punishment.

Alan at this point did not appear to have been trying to leave the battalion for good even after all he had been through. Despite whatever he was struggling to deal with at the time, he came back, continued to soldier, and was accepted back by a frontline unit that would want to know it could trust him to carry on.

In amongst all the organised killing of war, a death from drowning while relaxing in the first place they felt safe in months is likely to have had a profound effect on the men. The incongruity of it all must have been bewildering. That time of year, the low sun would have reflected off the water while the men bathed, finally cleaning themselves of the sand that they had carried with them back and forth across the desert. As the water washed away the dirt, they maybe even began to feel like the people they had been before they had been exposed to the war. The gentle sounds of the waves breaking on the shore would have contrasted with the thunder of metal breaking on metal or bone they were more used to over the preceding months.

From the sun, the sea, and the sand, they had to go back to death again.

In my time of service, when I heard of soldiers being killed in car accidents on leave after their they had returned from the dangers of Iraq or Afghanistan it somehow seemed worse—their deaths seemed more fruitless than if they had died in combat. To the men of the battalion, it must have seemed like there was nowhere in this land they were in where they were safe. Every victory was followed by defeat, and the moment they felt they could relax they were cruelly reminded that death was always close by in this unforgiving land.

Chapter Six
Into the Cauldron

At the end of May, the German Afrika Korps and their Italian allies, struck against the Gazala line in Cyrenacia. Within a month, Tobruk, which had been regarded as impregnable, had fallen, and the Eighth Army had been harried back across the Western Desert. The incidence of absenteeism, particularly in the rear areas, reached a disquieting level. General Claude Auchinleck, Commander - in - Chief Middle East, requested that the death penalty should be restored for desertion in the face of the enemy and cowardice.

The Thin Yellow Line, William Moore

During early May, the British received new equipment—including M3 Grant tanks equipped with a 75-mm gun and better armour, and large numbers of 6-pounder anti-tank guns—that provided some optimism. This was in spite of the pressure that Malta was under. The air attacks directed by Kesselring on Malta that had reduced its offensive capacity were judged to have been so effective that by 10 May, he announced the island's neutralisation to be complete and released two bomber squadrons to the Russian Front.[164] Malta was soon to receive Spitfire re-enforcements and would within months be a strong offensive asset again, but at this point it could do little to stop Axis re-supply making it through in numbers vastly superior to Allied re-supply.

The Axis commanders knew that the entry of the US into the war would eventually give the Eighth Army access to an increase in material, so they sought to forestall an Allied offensive before these supplies could be brought to bear. They were also tempted by the successes that Rommel was attempting to sell as he strained to be let off the leash and push on into Egypt. The Italians tried to restrain Rommel by advocating the capture of Malta, which would postpone another offensive in Africa until the autumn, but they agreed to an attack on Tobruk for late May. An advance would stop at the Egyptian frontier, another 150 miles east and the Luftwaffe would redeploy for Operation HERKULES.

The Axis plan to attack the Gazala Line (Operation VENICE) involved armour flanking to the south of the defensive box at Bir Hacheim. On the left flank, the Italians would neutralise the Bir Hacheim box, and on the right flank, the 21st Panzer Division and the 15th Panzer Division would advance north, behind the Allied defences, attacking from the rear. On the far right of the offensive, a 90th Light Afrika Division Battle Group was to advance to El Adem just south of Tobruk to cut the line of supply and attack supply dumps. Italian motorized troops would then open a gap in the minefield north of Bir Hacheim to create a supply route to the German armour.

Rommel, having defeated the British armour, planned to then capture El Adem, Ed Duda, Sidi Rezegh and the Knightsbridge defensive box. His ultimate goal, however, was Tobruk. By late May the Axis forces comprised 560 tanks and around 90,000 men.[165]

In a letter to Richie, Auchinleck stated his belief that there were two courses of action open to the enemy. The first was a flanking movement around the south of the line with a diversion to the north. The second was an attack on the centre of the line driving straight through to Tobruk, with a diversion to the south. He believed the second course of action was more likely and advised Ritchie to place his armour accordingly. Ritchie, although he believed the attack would come from the south, passed on Auchinleck's assessment to his sub-commanders, leading some to further question him whether he disagreed with the orders.[166] His disagreement was obvious from his placement of armour further south of Auchinleck's suggestion.

Auchinleck, nonetheless, awaited the attack confident that it would be repelled. On the Gazala Line, in the series of box formations were the 1st South African Division nearest the coast, the 50th (Northumbrian) Infantry Division to the south, and the 1st Free French Brigade furthest south at Bir Hacheim. The 1st and 7th Armoured Divisions waited behind the main line as a mobile counter-attack force, the 2nd South African Division, formed a garrison at Tobruk and the 5th Indian Infantry Division (which had arrived in April to relieve the 4th Division) was in reserve. The British had around 110,000 men and around 720 tanks.[167]

On 14 May, the battalion received a warning order from the Guards Brigade to move to re-join the 1st Armoured Division in an area north east of El Gubi as part of a mobile counter attack force.[168] On 15 May, the advance party moved off, followed by the rest of the battalion, including Alan, who was by then back with his company. By 18 May, the battalion had dug defensive positions and transport had left to pick up B Company from leave. On the same day, Colonel Purdon moved to Divisional HQ to take part in a divisional war game. On 19 May, the leave party returned and the battalion prepared for the start of a divisional exercise. Reinforcements from six separate regiments were also received.

On 21 May, the company commanders went with Colonel Purdon to recce the Field Maintenance Centre (FMC), where they suspected their next tasking would be. FMCs were developed for CRUSADER and even included POW cages. They were so huge and dug in that you would have been able to drive through one and not even realise it was a supply base instead of open desert. The following day, the exercise began. The diary notes that the code-word for the battalion to move off did not come and the decision was made to move off anyway. Half an hour later the code-word arrived to start the exercise followed by the code-word to finish. Again at the battalion level, the experience of a higher formation exercise appears to have been a confusing one.

By 24 May, the battalion had taken up a permanent defensive position in the FMC. On 26 May, they received an operational order as JoForce. Strawson broke the battle of Gazala in to three phases. The first from 26 May to 29 May saw the Axis forces attempt to overcome the British defences from the rear as planned.[169] This began at 1400 on 26 May, the Italian X and XXI Corps, after a heavy artillery concentration, launched a frontal attack on the central Gazala positions. A few elements of the Afrika and XX Mobile Corps were attached to these assault groups, and during the day, the bulk of the Afrika Korps moved to give the impression that this was the focus of the Axis assault.

The battalion diary, however, makes no mention on 26 May of the initial assault happening at the line to their west; instead it notes that on 27 May the German offensive had begun. When darkness fell on 26 May, the armoured formations turned south. This movement was observed by a number of Allied units and reported, but they were dismissed as a diversion as had been predicted in Auchinleck's assessment. In the early hours of 27 May, Rommel had led the elements of the Afrika Korps, the Italian XX Motorised Corps, and the German 90th Light Afrika Division—in a flanking move around the southern end of the Allied line, using the British minefields to protect the Axis flank and rear.

By the time the reconnaissance aircraft confirmed this, it was too late. Allied forces had been outflanked. The Ariete division of the XX Motorized Corps was held up for about one hour by the 3rd Indian Motor Brigade of the 7th Armoured Division. They dug in approximately four miles south east of Bir Hacheim, then overcame the defenders, killing or wounding 440 men and taking about 1,000 prisoners, along with most of its equipment. The 21st Panzer Division advanced south of the position and did not take part in the action.

Further to the east, the 15th Panzer Division had engaged the 4th Armoured Brigade of the 7th Armoured Division, which had been ordered south to support the 3rd Indian and the 7th Motorised Brigades. In a mutually-costly engagement, the

Germans were surprised by the range and power of the 75-mm guns on the new M3 Grant tanks. The 4th Armoured Brigade then withdrew and spent the night of 27 May near the Belhamed supply base east of El Adem. By late morning 27 May, the Axis armoured units had advanced more than 25 miles north, but by midday they were stopped by the 1st Armoured Division, resulting in more intense fighting resulting in heavy losses on both sides. At 1200, the battalion first sighted enemy tanks; the diary notes that they were seen moving along the track between Bir Gubi and El Adem. C Company—with a section of anti-tank guns from B Company—went out to engage. They destroyed nine enemy motorised transport vehicles and took two German prisoners.

On the far right of the Axis advance, the 90th Light Afrika Division engaged the Jock Columns of the 7th Motorised Brigade at Retma and forced it to withdraw eastwards on Bir el Gubi before continuing on as planned to reach the El Adem area by mid-morning, capturing a number of supply bases and the advanced HQ of the 7th Armoured Division, dispersing it and capturing the commander, General Messervy, who pretended to be a batman and escaped. This left the division without effective command for the next two days. The same day, at 2000, the battalion was put under command of the 7th Motor Brigade. Unaware of this change of command, it was forced into a withdrawal. The war diary notes that by the following morning, 28 May, there was no sign of the brigade and that there was "uncertainty all day as to whose command we were under until 1930 when we were placed under command of 29th Indian Infantry Brigade together with Kings' Dragoon Guards, all to come under 7th Armoured Brigade."[170] Meanwhile, the 4th Armoured Brigade was sent to El Adem, and the 90th Light was driven back to the south-west.

The second-in-command of D Company went at first light on 29 May to liaise with the 29th Brigade, but before he returned, the previous order was cancelled and the battalion was again placed under direct command of XXX Corps, still with the role of defending 83 FMC. The battalion then received orders provide an escort for a convoy of ammunition and supplies for the Free French at Bir Hakiem. The escort was to be D Company with one platoon of anti-tank guns from B Company. Owing to incomplete orders, the convoy was postponed twenty-four hours. On 30 May, five enemy tanks were spotted. Patrols from B and C Companies were prepared to move out to engage them when further reports of twenty-seven and of twenty-five tanks in the area were received. These reports turned out to contain inaccurate grid references and the tanks were not in fact in the battalion's area.

A further inaccurate report later claimed that eight enemy tanks were moving through the battalion's area that afternoon. No doubt, these inaccurate reports would have further eroded the confidence the soldiers in Alan's company would have had in the tactical intelligence they were receiving. At 1915, the D Company convoy departed for the Bir Hakiem Box. This was held by the 1st Free French Brigade, commanded by General Marie-Pierre Koenig. They had been attacked by the Ariete Division on 27 May in what became known as the start of the Battle of Bir Hacheim. The Ariete had ultimately made little progress against the French guns and mines.

The wider tank battle continued for three days. Lacking possession of Bir Hacheim, Rommel was exposed, so he drew the Afrika Korps into a defensive position, using the extensive Allied minefields to protect his western flank. This marked the end of the first phase of the battle. The second phase saw Rommel resupply and re-concentrate his forces. On 29 May, supply vehicles supported by the Italian divisions, worked through the minefield north of Bir Hacheim and reached the Afrika Korps with much needed supplies and helped repel British armour counter attacks. Auchinleck was now pushing Ritchie to watch out for a pincer attack from the north and plan for an attack around the Axis southern flank.[171] This prevented him taking resources out of the battle and caused disagreements between the Eighth Army's senior commanders. However, despite this, the Allies managed to concentrate armour from 2nd, 4th, and 272nd Armoured Brigades to attack the exposed main body of the Axis forces. This, though, resulted in heavy Allied casualties from the Axis anti-tank guns. The following day, British armour attacked again with the same result. The same day, Rommel pulled the Afrika Korps back westward against the edge of the minefields, creating a defensive position at 'The Cauldron.' A link was formed with elements of the Italian X Corps, which were clearing two routes through the minefields from the west. Rommel then surprised the Allies by going on the offensive, overrunning the Sidi Muftah Box between 31 May and 1 June, destroying the British 150th Infantry Brigade with, according to Rommel, the Axis forces taking around 3,000 Allied prisoners.[172]

On May 31, the battalion received an order to draw six-pounders to Ed Duda.[173] Ritchie was now concerned by Tobruk so brought reinforcements up to the El Adem box and created new defensive boxes opposite the gaps in the minefield. It is likely that this was the reason for the orders. Further orders were then received to send out a company to deal with stragglers from the fighting to the east and south east of Bir Hacheim. D Company also received a warning order to be prepared to move to Bir Hacheim to replace the Free French on 31 May. This was subsequently cancelled.

The following day, the battalion HQ was strafed from the air injuring three ORs, one of whom would subsequently die. The Commonwealth Graves Commission notes that a John William Tillott, aged 31 years old, son of Jessie M. Tillott of Ealing, died on 3 June 1942. He is buried at Halfaya Sollum War Cemetery, approximately 12 kilometres from the Libyan border, adjacent to Halfaya Pass, the scene of heavy fighting in 1941 and 1942. All the graves in the cemetery were brought in from the surrounding area. The cemetery now contains 2,046 Commonwealth burials of the Second World War, of which 238 are unidentified.[174]

Orders finally arrived to move to Hachiem to form part of GREYFORCE with the 1st Free French and 9KRRC under command of Lieutenant Colonel C E Grenville-Grey. Later that day, the advanced party moved to Hachiem, which was being heavily bombed by Junkers 88 bombers, but the main body remained.[175]

On 2 June, the main body of the battalion moved south to Hacheim to intercept column of fifteen enemy tanks moving towards Hachiem. As they moved south, they heard that it was now fifty enemy tanks thought to be moving along the west side of the minefield to their position. These were likely to be Italian tanks as on the night of 1-2 June, the 90th Light and Trieste divisions were sent south to renew the attack on Bir Hacheim. The battalion was about to dispatch B Company, but instead it was instructed to hold Hachiem as a separate column was approaching—leading to shelling and a return of contact. The war diary notes that visibility was very poor due to dust from a sandstorm, which according to the history "caused most of the battalions" rather antiquated trucks and carriers to "boil like so many kettles."[176] Once again, Alan and the others would have been battling the conditions as much as the Axis forces. The battalion's machine gun platoons and anti-tank guns got off some rounds into the sandstorm to unknown effect.

Despite the Battle of Hacheim continuing on for another ten days, on 3 June the battalion received orders in the night to move east of the Knightsbridge Box, where they would be drawn into the main battle. They re-joined the 201st Guards Brigade and spent most of the rest of the night mining the area north east of Knightsbridge. By 4 June, they were given orders to establish themselves at Taman under command of the 2nd Armoured Brigade.

Ritchie was planning to launch the all-out counter-attack on the Cauldron he had previously hesitated from doing.[177] It would be called Operation ABERDEEN. The battalion arrived at Taman after, according to the war diary; "a very laborious journey at 1700 to find astonishing congestion including part of 1 Rifles Battalion."[178] During the night, they were put under command of the 4th Armoured Brigade, and by the morning of 5 June, the congestion cleared and battalion spent the day digging in while the counter attack launched.

The counter-attack was met by accurate fire from tank and anti-tank guns positioned in the Cauldron and stalled.[179] By early afternoon on 5 June, Rommel split his forces, as he decided to attack east with the Ariete and the 21st Panzer divisions, while he sent elements of the 15th Panzer Division northwards against the Knightsbridge box. The eastward thrust towards Bir el Hatmat dispersed the tactical HQs of the two British divisions, as well as the HQs of other smaller units, at which point command and control broke down.

The 22nd Armoured Brigade, having lost sixty of its 156 tanks, was forced from the battlefield by renewed attacks from the 15th Panzer. Of the Allied attackers, three Indian infantry battalions, a reconnaissance regiment, and four artillery regiments were left behind. Unsupported by armour, they were overrun by the enemy. During the night, the 4th Armoured Brigade was ordered to move to meet the enemy thrust eastwards from Harmat, threatening El Adem. The 5th Royal Tank Regiment were left to support the battalion. The Battalion received orders placing them under the 1st Armed Division's direct command and informing them to stay in position as long as possible. In that position on 6 June, the battalion was dive bombed by Stukas, resulting in three ORs being wounded. One of them died later of his wounds. The Commonwealth Graves Commission suggests this was Lance Corporal Albert Edward Drew, the 21-year-old son of Thomas and Ann Drew, of Poplar, London. He is buried at Knightsbridge War Cemetery.[180]

Rommel continued to hold the initiative over the following days, maintaining his strength in the Cauldron while the number of operational British tanks diminished.[181] A number of probes were sent to test the various opposing strong points, and from 6 -8 June, further attacks were launched on Bir Hacheim, which were repulsed by the French. On 7 June, A Company accompanied the 339th Battery to a position in order that they could provide counter battery fire against the enemy who were shelling the Knightsbridge box. On 8 June, the war diary notes that "[a]s result of some confusion over the aim, the battalion moved a few miles east to Point 187 and returned immediately to Tamar."[182] They were back in position by midday. When they got back they came under command of the 22nd Armoured Brigade.

Reinforced with a further combat group, the Axis attacked Bir Hacheim again on 9 June. Alan's company was ordered to be part of a column, to be known as "Arduous," standing by to operate west of the minefield.[183] However, Axis forces overran the defences at Bir Hacheim on the following day, and the column was cancelled. Ritchie ordered the remaining troops to evacuate as best they could, under the cover of darkness. Under fire through the night, many of the French found gaps in the line through which to withdraw. The survivors then made their way some five miles to the west, to rendezvous with transport from the 7th Motor Brigade.[184] About 2700 troops (including 200 wounded) of the original garrison of 3600 escaped.

In his essay, *The Legend of the Legion*, the British poet, writer, and explorer Robert Twigger notes that it was Susan Travers, the only woman ever to be officially recognised as a full member of the French Foreign Legion, who drove the two commanding officers out of the box to escape capture during this evacuation.[185] Travers was the bilingual daughter of a British Navy officer who grew up in France. She was thirty-two when she unofficially joined, first a nurse and then an ambulance driver. She became the mistress of several Legion officers, ending up with General Koenig. Travers, the only woman allowed in the defensive box perimeter, demonstrated real courage under fire on numerous occasions. The senior legionnaires let her drive not because it was her job, but because she was apparently the coolest behind the wheel. In the end car suffered only eleven bullet holes and ruined shock absorbers. About 500 French troops, many of whom were wounded, were captured when the 90th Light Division occupied the position on 11 June.

On 11 June, Rommel pushed the 15th Panzer Division and 90th Light Afrika Division toward El Adem. By 12 June, the day the battle was to reach its climax, he had forced the 201st Guards Brigade to withdraw from the Knightsbridge Box to the Tobruk perimeter.[186] The battalion at this point was placed under the command of the 2nd South African Division and after being visited by Corps and Divisional commanders. At 1800, the diary notes that they "received cypher message instructing us to unless seriously engaged to move into the perimeter of Tobruk."[187] They left A Company and moved at about 1945. The battalion war diary goes on to note that the "South Africans were most helpful over a difficult journey through the minefields, providing an abundance of Liaison Officers and guides." Nevertheless, the column became very split up, and there were some casualties to vehicles due to the very dark night, and no doubt also due to drivers like Alan battling with sleep deprivation. Apart from stragglers, they all reached allotted area by 0200.

The 29th Indian Infantry Brigade repulsed an attack on the El Adem box on 12 June, but the 2nd and 4th Armoured Brigades on their left were pushed back almost four miles by the 15th Panzer Division and obliged to leave their damaged tanks on the battlefield. The commanding officer of the 4th Armoured Brigade, Messervy, had left his brigade in search of General Norrie to question his orders and attempt to impose a different course of action; however, he encountered enemy forces on route. This left his brigades without direction, creating an opportunity for Rommel to thrust the 21st Panzer forward from the Cauldron, striking the rear of the 4th Armoured.[188] As the 21st Panzer Division advanced from the west in to the battle, they then engaged the 22nd Armoured Brigade sent to assist the 4th Armoured. Combining tanks with anti-tank guns while on the offensive, and acting rapidly on intelligence obtained from Allied radio intercepts, Axis forces inflicted big losses on Allied tanks; British tank strength had been reduced from 300 tanks to approximately 70 tanks.

At 1800, the battalion moved out to support a night attack against enemy located north of El Adem, but by the end of 13 June, the Knightsbridge box was virtually surrounded. It was abandoned by the Guards Brigade later that night after the 21st Panzer Division attacked in the middle of a sandstorm and overran part of the 2nd Battalion Scots Guards in the box at the west end of Rigel ridge, after resolute defensive by the guards. South African gunners covering the box kept firing until their guns were destroyed, allowing the withdrawal of other Allied formations.[189] The South African battery commander had decided to stay and maintain fire against the German tanks, in order to delay them for as long as possible.

The remaining guns were commanded individually and fired over open sights. The Germans attacked from the rear, cutting off all escape, and the gunners kept firing until the guns had been destroyed. Approximately half the gun detachments were killed or wounded. The entire Natal Field Artillery Regiment was captured. The 2nd and the 22nd Armoured Brigades were ordered to move to support the defenders, but this just resulted in more losses to the German anti-tank guns and left the way clear for a thrust by the 15th Panzer to the east of Knightsbridge. The Germans captured over 3000 Allied prisoners. The Afrika Korps had established a superior number of tanks and held the dominatin ground, posing a serious threat to cutting off the XIII Corps units on the Gazala line. Due to these wounding defeats, 13 June became known as "Black Saturday" to the Eighth Army.[190]

Auchinleck, on 13 June, issued firm orders that Ritchie should hold the Gazala line. The battalion however were on the move, off to join the 7th Motor Brigade. It was another arduous journey described in the battalion diary as a "very slow journey due to sandstorms."[191] Visibility was poor, and it would have been another stressful and tiring journey for Alan and the other drivers. For much of the night, Alan would have been driving blind, hoping he could react in time when the convoy lights on the back of the truck in front appeared out of the eerily yellow darkness of the sandstorm. At points, he would have likely questioned whether there still was a truck in front, disoriented by the lack of visibility. I am sure he more than once panicked that he had lost the rest of the convoy and had potentially veered off towards enemy lines or into a minefield. The battalion, in-between the sandstorms, did manage to bring down a Messer-schmitt on the way, which had been strafing the column.

On 14 June, Auchinleck authorised Ritchie to fall back and to hold a line running south-east from Acroma (west of Tobruk) through El Adem to Bir el Gubi.[192] R.H.W.S Hastings describes the journey the 1st Battalion Rifles made on 14 June as they moved down an escarpment towards the coast road to support Tobruk after providing cover to forces withdrawing from the line in front of the German advance:

> The vehicles bumped, crashed, stopped, restarted, stuck on boulders, got ditched, drove in the dark and without lights into the truck in front and found their way to the bottom [of the escarpment].... Drivers slept and some-times failed to wake when others in front of them went on. It was like a nightmare dream, for everyone knew that behind them the German tanks were approaching.[193]

That night plans were made for a retreat. The Germans were driving hard towards Tobruk. The defenders in the El Adem and two neighbouring boxes held firm (which action later saw Lieutenant Colonel Henry Foote of the 7th Royal Tanks being awarded a Victoria Cross), and the 1st South African Division was able to withdraw along the coast road (Via Balbia) practically intact. The road could not accommodate two divisions and after the South Africans escaped it quickly became a "bottle neck." To make things worse, the 32nd Army Tank Brigade, which was supposed to keep the road open, misunderstood its orders and fell back to Tobruk early on 15 June. The remaining two brigades of the 50th (Northumbrian) Division could not retreat eastwards because of the presence of the Axis armour, so they attacked southwest, broke through the lines of the Italian divisions opposite them and headed into the desert to make the long march south before they turned east to retreat.

By the evening of 15 June, numerous Allied strong points and defensive boxes had suffered significant attacks and become overrun. The battalion received orders to withdraw to the wire in three tactical bounds. At 1200, the battalion moved to Bir Ed Dleua, where it would remain on 16 June. On 17 June, the battalion war diary notes that an attack involving a platoon from B Company resulted in 2nd Lieutenant Peter Dalbiac and 3 ORs killed.[194] The Commonwealth Graves Commission records their deaths as 16 June. It tells us that the 21-year-old Peter Dalbiac was the son of Major Richard Dalbiac (Royal Engineers) and Kathleen Dalbiac of Knockholt, Kent. It also tells us that the three other ranks referred to were 30-year-old James Reggie Porter, son of Alfred and Elizabeth Porter, of Woodford Green, Essex; husband of Edna Porter, of Woodford Green; 21-year-old John William Smith, son of Albert V. T. and Alice Smith, of Laindon, Essex; and 22-year-old Charles Joseph Strobl, son of Joseph Strobl, and of Edith Elizabeth Strobl, of Rotherhithe, London. All are buried together in Halfaya Sollum War Cemetery.[195]

Ritchie ordered the Eighth Army to withdraw to the defensive positions at Mersa Matruh, some 100 miles east of the frontier. Tobruk was again left to hold out, but this time without the number of forces that would guarantee its survival. Despite confirming Ritchie's intent not to reinforce Tobruk, before he was then no longer being able to due to his retreat, Auchinleck reassured Churchill that it would be reinforced.[196] Hastings, in his history, quotes a letter home from an unnamed rifleman that said, "After Hachiem was evacuated we started withdrawing and for some reason never clear to me seemed unable to stop."[197] The history notes that the Allied forces were unable to hold Matruh and the fortress there, specially constructed in peace time at the cost of considerable effort, and was abandoned just before it was used for the purpose it was built.[198] The effectiveness of the fortress depended on the existence of an armoured force to its south, and such a force was no longer in existence. Hasting follows this by recounting a story that the Axis forces crossed the minefield to the south of the town by driving a herd of camels in front of them.

On 19 June, the battalion engaged an enemy column of fourteen tanks and sixty-six MET, who would have had a combined firepower much greater than their own. The battalion was obliged to withdraw. It observed the enemy moving to Bir el Gubi, on the line that only a few days previously the Allies had held, and then coming out of Gubi again in the evening prompting a second contact. It might have been during these contacts and this withdrawal that Hastings notes the following:

> When the battalion was sharply attacked by tanks... a herd of camels looked after by Beduin Arabs became involved in the battle and had the same ideas about withdrawing as the carrier platoon, which was nearest the enemy. The carriers, having by then completed some two thousand miles had the worst of the race. There are few more unpleasant situations than to be withdrawing with an enemy close behind you across an endless desert in an ancient and rickety truck.[199]

The next day the battalion pushed north during morning. It had received information that Tobruck was in danger and all columns were instructed to move north as far as possible. Auchinleck had urged a major counter attack on 20 June, but those orders only reached Ritchie at 2120 that same evening. Ritchie had already given orders to bring as much pressure on the enemy as possible which the battalion orders were part of. The battalion reached escarpment overlooking Sid Rezegh and engaged targets there on the axis road. Stewart notes however that the only unit in a position to do so, 7th Motor Brigade, which was still operating in "Jock Columns," its efforts, as might have been expected, had "virtually no effect."[200]

During that night, they moved back in preparation for joining the 3rd Indian Brigade. Tobruk, which had held out for nine months at tremendous cost to human lives, fell during the early morning of the following day. A white flag was raised over what had been the symbol of Allied resistance the year before. Not everyone in the garrison, however, surrendered at that moment. The Gurkhas did not surrender until that evening, the Cameroon Highlanders until the following day, and some did not surrender at all, such as a Major Sainthill from the Coldstream Guards who led 200 of his own men and almost 200 South Africans in a successful escape to Allied lines, claiming that the Coldstreams did not know how to surrender having never practiced such a manoeuvre.[201]

The speed of the fall of Tobruk was a shock to all. Even though the defences at Tobruk had not been well maintained due to the emphasis on building strength at the Gazala position for Operation BUCKSHOT, Allied leaders expected it to be able to hold out for at least two months with the supplies and the forces they had. The exact circumstances of the fall, even after a later court of enquiry, remain confused. What is clear, though, is that its fall saw 35,000 Allied troops surrender. The entry for the battalion war diary for that day makes no mention of Tobruk falling, although all those in the battalion would have been aware of this demoralising news, if not on that day, very shortly afterwards.

On 22 June the battalion moved, passing through Beida Gap, taking up position six miles east of the wire. The Battle of Gazala had been lost. Unsurprisingly it was a confusing time. There were bewildering changes of command. Orders and counter orders were frequent and complicated. All the accounts of the battle speak of confusion and disagreement between the senior commanders. I highlight some of this confusion not to take a side in the various debates as to which senior commanders were to blame and which are to be admired, but to highlight how it must have seemed for those lower down the command chain. If at these senior levels there was uncertainty over the aims, and confusion as to what was actually happening at any given point of the battle, then at Alan's level, that of the average soldier on the ground at the front, they would not have had any idea as to what was happening in the wider battle and little confidence in senior command.

Confidence in leadership is crucial on the battle field. A lack of clarity and consistency undermines confidence. Orders come down from senior commanders; if they are not trusted then orders that place troops at greater risk are not followed by many of those troops. In interviews with the Imperial War Museum in-between 2002-2007, Douglas Waller from B Company described the situation from this level:

> We were under about forty different commands in two years...You really did not know what the hell was going on. It was just a question of we want you there. [You] didn't really know where you were. It was completely confusing.[202]

All the while in their own corner of the battlefield, they could not even tell whether the British vehicles approaching them in the confusion were manned by Allied or enemy forces. Every day fires, appeared on the horizon as dumps of supplies were burnt. Sandstorms reduced visibility to almost zero as they moved across vast areas where it was often impossible to tell where the minefields began and ended. When the sandstorms cleared again, more vehicles would appear out of a mirage as if from nowhere, and out of the clear skies enemy aircraft would scream down and release their ordinance. All the while, the men on the ground had to cope with these conditions whilst also dealing with the disorientating effects of the heat, lack of sleep, and lack of water. In *All Hell Let Loose: The World at War 1939-45*, historian Max Hastings highlights the issue:

> Eighth Army's fighting men had little confidence in their higher commanders. The colonial contingents, especially, believed that their lives were being risked, and some-times sacrificed, in pursuit of ill-conceived plans and purposes. There was bitter resentment about the huge 'tail' of the army, indulging a privileged lifestyle in Egypt while fighting soldiers endured constant privation 'up the desert'. A British gunner wrote sourly: came to realise that, for every man sweating it out in the muck and dust

of the Western Desert, there were twenty bludging and skiving in the wine bars and restaurants, night-clubs and brothels and sporting clubs and racetracks of Cairo.[203]

Hastings goes on to say that, although conditions in North Africa were not as bad as the horrific conditions on the Eastern Front (which I am certain would have provided little comfort for Alan and his fellow soldiers in the Eighth Army) those fighting in the desert "suffered from desert sores, jaundice, dysentery" and that; "both sides learned to curse *khamsins*, sandstorms that reduced vision to a few metres and drove yellow grit into every crevice of vehicles, equipment and human bodies."[204] The conditions on the Eastern Front were no doubt horrendous, but their severity does nothing to soften the experience of being in the unforgiving sand and heat of North Africa at that time.

Hitler rewarded Rommel for his victory at Gazala and the taking of Tobruk with a promotion to the rank of Field-Marshal, the youngest German officer ever to achieve the rank. Rommel allegedly remarked that he would have preferred that Hitler had instead given him another Panzer division. Churchill wrote of the loss:

> This was one of the heaviest blows I can recall during the war. Not only were its military effects grievous, but it had affected the reputation of the British armies.[205]

A few days later, on 25 June, Ritchie was dismissed by Auchinleck, who assumed command of the Eighth Army himself. The Eighth Army had lost 50,000 men to death, wounds, or capture. They also lost thousands of tons of supplies, nearly 800,000 rounds of artillery ammunition, nearly 13 million rounds of small-arms ammunition and a huge number of tanks and other vehicles.

The end of Gazala, however, gave no respite to the battalion. Operation AIDA, the Axis advance upon Egypt continued, while the Eighth Army fell back to El Alamein. On 23 June, the battalion moved north to cover Sheferzen Gap.[206] D Company was involved in a contact with MET in the afternoon in the Libyan

Sheferzen area. In the evening, a general withdrawal to Matruh line started, and the battalion moved back to Hamra, arriving at 0330. It was decided not to hold Mersa Matruh; instead, X and XIII Corps would fight (a delaying action).

Auchinleck sent a message to his commanders on 25 June, informing them that he no longer intended "to fight a decisive action at Matruh," but instead wanted to engage the enemy across the area between Matruh and the El Alamein gap.[207] He was now focused on keeping the Eight Army intact rather than holding ground. On 24 June, the battalion moved east again— they spent all day being chased by a German column, which the battalion engaged at intervals throughout the day. Due to a heavy German presence in the area they continued to move south throughout the night until they were far enough south to turn eastwards which they did in the early hours of 25 June.

The Afrika Korps, who had now been on the move since 26 May, and whose logistics chain was now being stretched, were, however, delayed at Mersa Matruh in a battle that continued on to the early morning of 29 June. Commanders on both sides recognised after the battle that a resolute and properly concentrated counter attack by the Allies at Matruh could have resulted in a significant victory for the Allies.[208] As it was, Auchinleck had instructed his commanders that remaining intact was the greater priority, so what could have been a victory for the Allies became another victory for the Axis and another demoralising retreat for the Allies.

The Afrika Korps were soon on the move again and cut off the X Corps retreat along the coast road. The corps had to break out at night to the south, colliding with Axis forces several times and losing more than 6000 prisoners, forty tanks, and a large quantity of supplies. The Eighth Army continued to retire another ninety-nine miles to El Alamein.

By 27 June, the battalion received orders to move to protect eighty-six FMC in the rear.[209] They drove all day to arrive just in time to discover that the FMC was moving a further ten miles southeast. They leaguered for the night and moved on in the morning to reach 86 FMC, where they were also told to guard ninety-one FMC. These orders were cancelled immediately and they became a column once more. A Company were ordered to put a roadblock just east of Fuka as the rest of the column moved south of the road arriving at 0500.

The next day, the battalion engaged MET in the day—the roadblock eventually having to withdraw in the afternoon. During evening, the whole column moved east and C Company set up new roadblock. On 30 June, the road block party destroyed fourteen MET-captured prisoners of war and an Italian tank. The column moved on the left flank of the 1st Armed Division in a dust storm arriving in leaguer position at 0200 with no further contacts.

On 1 July, the battalion took up a defensive position and engaged MET. The following few days saw the company taking up a number of defensive positions and at some point, D Company was dispatched to on guarding tasks in the B Echelon away from the frontline. The first few days of July are known by some as the First Battle of El Alamein. What is recognised by most as the Battle of Alamein would not begin until 23 October. Stewart settles on the title "First El Alamein." Whatever title was given between 1 July and 3 July, Rommel's advance was finally checked. In *The Daily Express of London,* the Second World War correspondent Alan Moorehead, claimed the advance was finally halted:

> Not because Rommel made a mistake, or because Auch-inleck achieved an eleventh hour miracle, but because the German army was exhausted... The German soldiers were wearied to the point where they had no more reserves either of body or will-power.[210]

Stewart, whilst recognising the stresses on the Axis force (in particular the supply chain), gives more credit to the Eighth Army and General Norrie, commander of XXX Corps, in particular.[211] While Auchinleck was still issuing orders emphasizing the importance of protecting his forces and reminding commanders of provisional plans for a withdrawal to

Cairo, Norrie decided that XXX Corps would stand and fight. He ignored Auchinleck's orders and dug in, creating a series of fortifications that Rommel's increasingly stretched and exhausted forces would throw themselves against, while they were picked off from above by the Desert Air Force.

The intense fighting resulted in Rommel eventually conceding that he could go no further, and on 3 July he halted his advance just a day after in Parliament a disgruntled minority of MPs put forward a motion of no confidence in Winston Churchill's leadership that they would lose 475 votes to 25. The motion proposed:

> That this House, while paying tribute to the heroism and endurance of the Armed Forces of the Crown in circumstances of exceptional difficulty, has no confidence in the central direction of the war.[212]

The battalion would not take part in the fighting over these days. The war diary has no significant entries for the first week of July in terms of the wider conflict, although many commentators see this week in July as the turning point of the whole war, the nadir from which the Allies begin clawing their way back. There is just one entry for 5 July, which notes an uneventful patrol by A Company, and a field return of officers and ORs is attached.[213] This first week in July was, however, also a key week in Alan Juniper's life and possibly the nadir of his time in the desert, maybe his life. Alan would not have been listed on that return, if ORs were listed, as Alan's service record notes that on 5 July 1942 he deserted, leaving his fellow soldiers behind to face the stalled, but by no means defeated Axis army.[214]

As Alan never discussed this day and the war diary mentions no desertions, we can only speculate as to what was going through Alan's mind and how he actually deserted. He may have just gotten up and walked away on his own in a daze, heading east through the rear echelons. He may have deserted with others in a more calculated decision, having weighed up his chances of survival, his ability to continue to soldier, and the punishment he might receive if caught. All we do know is that

Alan Juniper would now play no further part in the Battle for North Africa. He will now, after 551 days in North Africa, and aged twenty-three years old, be known for the rest of his life a deserter.

Chapter Seven
A Few Square Metres

Such a sufferer from war shock is not a weakling, he is not a coward. He is a battle casualty.

Psychology for the Fighting Man

Four days the earth was rent and torn
By bursting steel,
The houses fell about us;
Three nights we dared not sleep,
Sweating, and listening for the imminent crash
Which meant our death.

The Bombardment, Richard Aldington

All the time we are out here the days at the front sink into us like stones the moment they are over, because they are too much for us to think about right away. If we even tried, they would kill us.

All Quiet on the Western Front, Erich Remarque

Alan took cover from the exploding shells landing all around him. In the poem *Anthem for Doomed Youth* Wilfred Owen describes "The shrill, demented choirs of wailing shells" and elsewhere in *Mental Cases* the "Batter of guns and shatter of flying muscles, Carnage incomparable." Alan took cover from the chaos in a bunker with a small number of his fellow soldiers as the shells continued to pound their position. As they huddled there in the bunker, covering their ears from the unnatural noise, a shell landed with great violence in the doorway.

Unlike the other shells exploding with ground shaking force all around the position, the shell did not explode. The shell just sat there. The hard, smooth metal was almost within touching distance to Alan, a live, fused, shell of high explosive ordnance that could have detonated at any second. It blocked the only entry or exit, not that leaving the bunker to go outside into the murderous hail of Axis artillery was an option to those not driven mad by the trauma, like the new recruit in *All Quiet on the Western Front* by First World War veteran Erich Remarque. The recruit cracks under a barrage and, despite the attempts by his comrades to stop him, runs from the bunker outside to his death.[215] If it had of detonated, it would have almost certainly killed all those in the bunker instantly. Anyone who was not ripped to pieces by shrapnel from the shell would have died of blast injuries, as the shock wave emanating from the shell would have caused physical trauma to internal organs—in particular the lungs. The effects of blast injuries are particularly acute in confined spaces. The bunker would have become a tomb.

We don't know for how long Alan and his comrades would have sat there staring death in the face, struggling to breathe in the suffocating atmosphere, whilst the barrage continued to shake the foundations of the bunker, but for young twenty-three-year-old Alan Juniper, every second must have seemed like an hour. Every violent shaking of the earth by other shells landing and detonating would have caused those in the bunker to fear the detonation of the shell in front of them. He eventually told Stephenie that it felt like an eternity sitting waiting for either the shell to explode or the barrage to stop and help to arrive in the form of a bomb disposal team—not knowing which would come first.

There is no way to establish who else was in that bunker with Alan, but Stephenie believes, from comments Alan made to her, that he was with an officer and a few other ranks like himself. Stephenie thinks that they tried to barricade themselves in to a corner with whatever they could get their hands on, which was unlikely to be much, something Alan would do towards the end of his life with furniture in the corner of his room when the dementia took him back to that bunker. The size and construction of the bunker, suggested by the few bits of information we have, is bigger and more permanent than a temporary shell scrape that would have been dug every time the battalion leaguered. It would have to have been in a location where the battalion (or another force, friendly or enemy, if they inherited it) was for a period of time.

After Alan and the others barricaded themselves in, they apparently then sat quietly and prayed to themselves. Alan told Stephenie that he was paralysed with fear. Maybe even though they had one another, each one of them felt more alone at that point than any other time in their lives. They were alone like the condemned men spending their last night together in the cellar in *The Wall* the short story by Jean Paul Sartre. Like the fictional men in the story waiting to be executed in the morning, struggling to comprehend the closeness of their own deaths, they may have been afraid to even look at one another in fear of seeing one another as "grey and sweating...alike and worse than mirrors of each other."[216]

Unlike the cold stone slabs of Sartre's cellar, we think from what Alan told Stephenie that Alan's bunker was a sand bag construction, built to shelter troops from artillery. It was dug into the sand, which provided the walls and some of the protection for the roof also. It would have been more like Remarque's fictional bunker, in which his narrator, while taking cover during an intense barrage, claimed that; "we cannot even look at one another for fear of seeing the unimaginable."[217]

Up until that point, Alan would have feared the clear skies that Axis aircraft launch their deadly attacks from, what enemy formation was lurking in the approaching dust clouds and what was buried in the sand ready to detonate on contact. A bunker, such as the one that Alan found himself in, should have been a haven from all these dangers, but instead what was built to protect would become part of the weapon that would kill him. The incongruity of it was similar to the death of John Fogarty on the beach. For Alan and his comrades, there was no corner of the desert they were safe, nothing they could do to protect themselves from the harsh environment to which they had been seemingly indefinitely condemned.

The barrage did eventually end, and all those in the bunker, Alan included, managed to walk away from the incident, unlike many of their colleagues who could no longer walk after similar bombardments. We do not know exactly when and where this occurred. It could have been at some point during either the Battle of Mersa Brega, Operation CRUSADER, the withdrawal to the Gazala line, or the Battle of Gazala. We do know, though, that it was an incident that would profoundly affect him for the rest of his life. It is not mentioned in the battalion war diary, and as you can now appreciate, his battalion moved back and forth across the desert, visiting many of the same places again and again.

Stephenie believes it likely happened somewhere outside of Tobruk from some of the comments Alan made, but she is not certain about this, and does not know in which direction the battalion was heading at the time; as we have seen, Alan and his battalion were involved in fighting around Tobruk numerous times during the campaign. From the battalion war diary, it seems unlikely that the incident occurred in the days immediately prior to Alan deserting; he would have been nowhere near Tobruk, and there are no contacts with the enemy mentioned in the days leading up to and including 5 July, the day he deserted. It is possible that he continued to soldier on after this incident, deserting days, weeks, or months afterwards.

There were no desertions on D-Day. Despite the horror of the beaches, there was nowhere to go. Desertions happened only in the weeks later as the Allies moved off the beaches into the French countryside. There is a massive spike in court martials in the months after D-Day, which no doubt includes a high number of desertions due to the psychological damage done to those on the beaches and close combat of the initial advances from hedge to hedge, house to house, as well as the opportunities provided in the towns and cities of liberated Europe.[218] I suspect the incident in the bunker occurred in sometime in mid-June in the days following 14 June when the battalion was moved up to support Tobruk during the Battle of Gazala, due to the proximity in time to when Alan deserted, the location of the battalion, and level of fighting that was occurring at the time.

Alan did not discuss the incident in much detail to his family. As far as we know, none of those within the bunker received a physical injury, but this does not mean that they walked away from the incident unscathed. From how Alan lived the rest of his life—his fear of confined spaces, the anxiety he suffered, the flashbacks he endured when suffering from dementia, and the conversations he had with Combat Stress and his family—we can see that while he was able to physically walk away, damage was done to him in that bunker for which he did not receive treatment.

During the research for the book, I was struck by the number of veterans who had both PTSD and dementia. Interested in understanding if there was a causal link to the correlation, I contacted the Alzheimer's Society, the UK's leading dementia support and research charity. It seemed intuitive that when an individual started to suffer from the debilitating effects of dementia, their ability to control or even repress the impact of traumatic memories would decrease.

Dr. Louise Walker, Research Communications Officer at the Alzheimer's Society, responded, stating that the society was "not aware of any research into this [a reduced ability to control PTSD due to onset of dementia], although it is a very fascinating subject." Dr. Walker did, however, go on to say that there has been some research into a link between PTSD and dementia, in terms of PTSD increasing the likely of dementia:

> ...[S]ome studies have found an association, however the underlying mechanisms don't appear to be known. It may be that PTSD does cause a physical effect on the brain, with some studies finding that people with PTSD have a smaller hippocampus—the brain's memory centre. There could also be a role for a hormonal or immune response triggered by the event or the subsequent stress that play a part in development of dementia. However, as not everyone with PTSD goes on to develop dementia and not

everyone with dementia has experienced PTSD, it seems likely that there are other factors that feed into this risk.[219]

The link is by no means proven, but it may be that future studies can establish with more certainty such a relationship between PTSD and dementia. In that case, far from walking away unscathed, the unexploded shell in the bunker eventually killed Alan. If this is true for Alan, then it would have also been the case for many, many more soldiers and for many civilians who also witnessed the trauma of the war. The already varying estimates given at the start of this book might need to be revised upwards again from their already almost uncomprehendingly vastness. It would mean that there are still soldiers dying today due to injuries they received all those years ago.

In the years following the Second World War, historians, when writing about the desert, remember the decisions of Rommel or Montgomery, the movements of the grand formations at the battles at Alamein, the fall of Tobruk, comparisons of the technical capabilities and numbers of tanks and guns, and, the grand left hooks where brigades and divisions manoeuvred. Individual soldiers remember the face of a mate they saw die next to them in the cab of truck, the feel of the mess tin in their hand, the sight of a patrol they were meant to be on returning with a truck missing, how they felt the first time a shell exploded nearby and how it made the leg of their trousers pull tight on their leg, the pattern of prominent stones on the few square metres of ground that they had to dig into or sprint across under fire.

In the years to come, historians will debate the reasons why the conflicts I took part in were started and the merits of the strategic plans on the ground by which they were fought, but my memories of Iraq and Afghanistan will be more personal and specific. For Alan, it was the few square metres encased by the bunker, the claustrophobic fear he felt staring at the unexploded shell and then the few metres encased by the walls of the detention centre that would stay with him. These square metres would be where he would keep returning to years later when a door shut violently, reminding him of the detonation of a shell or the corner of a table in a waiting room reminded him of the corner of a joist in the bunker he stared at for what seemed like hours as those shells kept falling again and again. Alan walked away from the bunker, but it kept dragging him back, and when the dementia made it hard for his mind to resist it dragged him back more and more.

Chapter Eight
The Impact

Come to me, all you who are weary and burdened, and I will give you rest.

Matthew 11: 28, The Bible

After a traumatic experience, the human system of self-preservation seems to go onto permanent alert, as if the danger might return at any moment.

Trauma and Recovery, Judith Lewis Herman

Alan Juniper became one of the approximately 100,000 British deserters in the Second World War. Most of these 100,000 were frontline troops like Alan, and in *The Deserters: A Hidden History of World War II*, journalist Charles Glass claims that "for the most part they left the lines because they'd had nervous breakdowns... Too much shelling, close friends killed, not getting any sleep—the daily stresses were too much." Glass notes that "[f]ew deserters were cowards," adding that the people who "showed the greatest sympathy to deserters were other frontline soldiers. They had, at one time or another, felt the temptation."[220] In *The American Soldier: Combat and Its Aftermath*, a work that surveyed over half a million US infantrymen who fought in the Second World War and became the essential source of data on soldiers for scholars working in military, organizational, and social psychology, Samuel Stouffer and his associates noted that:

> Enlisted men with combat experience adopted a permissive attitude to fear in combat... the majority of men regarded men who crack up mentally in combat as genuine casualties rather than cowards and...the majority of

troops showed little tendency to deny having experienced emotional reactions to combat but rather appear to have been willing to admit readily that they experienced fear and anxiety.[221]

In *Enduring Battle: American Soldiers in Three Wars, 1776-1945*, Associate Professor of History at George Mason University and Visiting Professor at the U.S. Army War College, Christopher H Hamner, when discussing US GI's in The Second World War, notes that "exposed to the acute rigors of the twentieth century combat, soldiers increasingly came to believe that everyone had a limit on the amount of stress that could be endured." Hamner also explains some of the research into this subject:

> The common World War II adage "Every man has his limit" had an empirical basis: studies conducted among American GIs during the Second World War found that, in general, troops could tolerate a fixed number of days of battle. More than 200 or 250 days in combat, it seemed, and few soldiers could bear the terror and stress of battle. The incidence of psychoneurotic breakdown—"combat fatigue," in the parlance of that war—increased sharply. Past a certain point, chronic and repeated over-activation of the body's alert systems simply ground down then psyche until all but the most exceptional could no longer function.[222]

This adage was repeated by Prof. Neil Greenberg in 2016 at the appeal hearing of Sergeant . Al Blackman, referred to as "Marine A" in court, the British Royal Marine convicted on a charge of killing a mortally wounded Taliban insurgent prisoner in Afghanistan in 2006, when he told the hearing that everybody had their "breaking point."[223] He went on to say, "[t]here is no such thing as a Rambo type, an Arnold Schwarzenegger soldier, who can face all sorts of stresses and appear to be invulnerable...That sort of person only exists in the cinema."

The verdict in the appeal, after evidence from Greenburg and two other psychiatrists, who all gave a diagnosis that

Blackman was suffering from an abnormality of mental functioning at the time of the killing caused by an adjustment disorder of moderate severity, substituted a verdict of manslaughter by reason of diminished responsibility. In the same way, every individual has different physical breaking points everyone has different mental breaking points.

Alan's behaviour after the war and his diagnosis by Combat Stress strongly suggests that he reached his limit and was psychologically damaged by his experiences during the war. We cannot know for sure his state of mind when he deserted; however, there is a significant chance that Alan was, at that point, an undiagnosed psychiatric casualty, either due to the incident in the bunker, the built-up stress over a prolonged period of time (including multiple near death experiences and deaths of comrades), or a combination of both. At the point Alan deserted, unless a commanding officer made a personal intervention (very unlikely with other ranks), there was no triage system or subsequent support for those suffering from "battle fatigue."[224] It was only months later, as Montgomery took command of the Eighth Army, that forward physiological support stations were brought in. This was obviously too late for Alan, who then had to wait over sixty years later to finally get such support.

Most Western militaries today recognise psychiatric casualties and, what was known as 'battle' or 'combat fatigue' in Alan's time is now most commonly diagnosed as Post Traumatic Stress Disorder (PTSD). In 2013, the American Psychiatric Association revised the PTSD diagnostic criteria in the fifth edition of its Diagnostic and Statistical Manual of Mental Disorders (DSM-5; 1) which is seen as the definitive textbook for all mental disorders. PTSD is included in a new category: Trauma and Stressor-Related Disorders.[225] All the conditions included in this classification require exposure to a traumatic or stressful event as a diagnostic criterion. For PTSD, the criteria required for diagnosis are summarized below:

Criterion A (one required): The person was exposed to: death, threatened death, actual or threatened serious injury, or actual or threatened sexual violence, in the following way(s): Direct exposure, Witnessing the trauma, Learning that a relative or close friend was exposed to a trauma, Indirect exposure to aversive details of the trauma, usually in the course of professional duties (e.g., first responders, medics)

Criterion B (one required): The traumatic event is persistently re-experienced, in the following way(s): Intrusive thoughts, Nightmares, Flashbacks, Emotional distress after exposure to traumatic reminders, Physical reactivity after exposure to traumatic reminders

Criterion C (one required): Avoidance of trauma-related stimuli after the trauma, in the following way(s): Trauma-related thoughts or feelings, Trauma-related reminders. Criterion D (two required): Negative thoughts or feelings that began or worsened after the trauma, in the following way(s): Inability to recall key features of the trauma, Overly negative thoughts and assumptions about oneself or the world, Exaggerated blame of self or others for causing the trauma, Negative affect, Decreased interest in activities, Feeling isolated, Difficulty experiencing positive affect

Criterion E (two required): Trauma-related arousal and reactivity that began or worsened after the trauma, in the following way(s): Irritability or aggression, Risky or destructive behaviour, Hypervigilance, Heightened startle reaction, Difficulty concentrating, Difficulty sleeping

Criterion F (required): Symptoms last for more than 1 month.

Criterion G (required): Symptoms create distress or functional impairment (e.g., social, occupational).

Criterion H (required): Symptoms are not due to medica-
tion, substance use, or other illness.[226]

The Combat Stress psychologist determined, when examining
Alan all those years later, that he met these criteria.

In *Aftershock: The Untold Story of Surviving Peace*, British
journalist Matthew Green quotes the US/Dutch psychiatrist and
trauma specialist Dr. Besell Van de Kolk, who states unequivocal-
ly when talking about soldiers with PTSD that "we now know
that their behaviours are not the result of moral failings or signs
of lack of willpower or bad character—they are caused by actual
changes in the brain."[227] Green documents the history of PTSD
and our treatment of it both on the battlefield and after those
impacted have made it home. Green notes that by the beginning
of the Second World War the military seemed to have forgotten
the lessons learnt on the Western Front. There were only a
handful of regular Army officers with varying degrees of
psychiatric training, when war was declared. The British
Expeditionary Force that deployed to France in 1939 made no
plans to adopt any of the forward psychiatry support that was
developed at the end of the First World War to support shell
shock victims.[228]

When Tobruk was first surrounded by the Germans in May
1941 after their initial advance from Mersa Brega, Australian
medics set up a war neurosis clinic, similar to those in operation
at the end of the First World War, in a bunker in which casualties
would still have been able to hear both incoming and outgoing
shelling. Whilst the location of the clinic was more out of
necessity, in this instance in the First World War psychiatrist
had found they had better success rates in returning soldiers to
the front line if they were treated within earshot of the battle.[229]

The forces that had retreated past Tobruk on their way from
Mersa, which included Alan and the majority of the Tower
Hamlets Rifles, had no such provision. There was a psychiatric
consultant to the Middle East, a doctor "Jimmy" James, who had
no administrative powers, but could advise senior command.
James had served as a young doctor at the Battles of Loos, the

Somme, and Passchendaele in the First World War. When he arrived in Egypt in September 1940, he saw more similarities than differences. In *A War of Nerves: Soldiers and Psychiatrists in the Twentieth Century*, author Ben Shephard notes there was nowhere, in all the vast area served by the Middle East Force, where a soldier could be "treated on modern lines for psychiatric breakdown;" indeed, army doctors "appeared to have no conception of breakdown in war and its treatment, though many of them had served in the 1914-18 war." Visiting the troops at the front in July 1941, James found "more frequently than before evidence of battle nerves...yet as a rule, men would object to leaving their units and going into hospital."[230]

James, despite his lack of administrative power, managed to gradually acquire the means to treat troops sent back to Cairo. His methods were simple: "fluid, food, sleep, and stool." This was because "men who broke down in battle came down to their distant psychiatric centres dehydrated, remarkably constipated and often sleepless." [231]James noted that the incidence of breakdown was much higher with support troops, those who had to drive great distances, who were frequently dive-bombed by the enemy, yet did not have the pride and exhilaration of the fighting troops—those like Alan. Although Alan was not a support troop as he was serving in a frontline infantry regiment, he drove great distances and was regularly dive bombed. Yet serving in a frontline regiment through the confused defeats he fought, there would have been little pride to offset the stress of this. A year later, after the withdrawal to Alamein, James reported that the men "had got tired of fighting," had become "apprehensive of the German power and leadership" and were "fed up" with the desert. For some, if not the majority of these men, there was no one incident that created the psychological damage they were suffering from. It was the accumulation of highly stressful situations over time.[232]

It was not until 1942 that the War Office established its first Directorate of Army Psychiatry. Treatments, however, continued to vary according to the individual psychiatrist involved.

Winston Churchill voiced a widely held view when he warned in a memorandum that letting psychiatrists loose amongst the soldiers might cause more issues than it might solve. Churchill wrote that psychiatrists "are capable of doing an immense of harm with what may very easily degenerate into charlatanry."[233] In a *War of Nerves*, Shephard notes that "even three years into the war, parts of the British Army refused to accept that psychiatric casualties were inevitable." It can be argued there remain parts of the British Army that refuse to accept this fact today. The 2014 paper entitled *Stigma as a Barrier to Seeking Health Care Among Military Personnel with Mental Health Problems* by Marie-Louise Sharp et al at the Kings Centre for Military Health Research, King's College London, opens with a statement about this issue:

Approximately 60% of military personnel who experience mental health problems do not seek help, yet many of them could benefit from professional treatment. Across military studies, one of the most frequently reported barriers to help-seeking for mental health problems is concerns about stigma.[234]

By the time Operation TORCH was launched in November 1942 (after Alan had deserted), the invasion of Algeria and Morocco aimed at finally pushing Axis forces out of North Africa, through a pincer movement with the now victorious Eighth Army after Montgomery's victories at Alamein, "made no provision at all for psychiatry." When Dr. John Wishart made it to the frontline in January 1943, he noted that he was initially very unwelcome and was told he was the "most unwanted man in North Africa." The Corps commander:

> [W]as afraid that, since he had a psychiatrist, discipline... would be ruined. A man who was under arrest for some breach of discipline, it was thought, had only see a psychiatrist, tell a tale of his mother being frightened before he was born or some other such plausible tale, and he would be let off any punishment.[235]

Ultimately, commanders cared more about the wider discipline of their forces than they did about any individual soldier such as

Alan. Senior commanders, no matter how much they genuinely do care for the men under their command, cannot help but see them as means to an end, when faced with mission critical decisions in a conflict as grave as the Second World War when the consequences of defeat are so immense.

One quote in *Aftershock* used by Green from his meeting with Surgeon Captain John Sharpley, a current defence consultant advisor in psychiatry, highlights that even today in the military where the role of the psychiatrist is more established than in 1942, there is a belief that recognising the mental effects of war on soldiers could hamper the ability of the military to achieve its overall mission. Sharpley tells Green, "Stigma is bad for the individual but good for the group."[236] The suggestion here is that, for the military, stigmatising any condition that impacts the overall capability of a unit over the welfare of any individual solider is still preferable. Military psychiatry's goal (if not always the individual psychiatrists' goal) is to provide the military with the most effective fighting force, not support any particular individual soldier. However, often these goals can align when psychiatrists did get access to the frontline. After Alan's desertion rest centres allowed some soldiers to overcome and return to duty, curing soldier and giving the military back men who could still fight.

If the Eighth Army at the time of Alan's desertion had the processes and resources in place it later developed to deal with psychiatric casualties, things may have been very different for Alan. He may have been given the support he required to be able to return to the line without deserting, or he may have been diagnosed with a psychological injury that ended his war with a medical discharge. However, as Nafsika Thalassis, who completed her PhD thesis; *Treating and Preventing Trauma: British Military Psychiatry during the Second World War* at the University of Salford,[237] told me via email the following:

> The perspective you might want to take is one that moves away from 'good' psychiatric casualties and 'bad' deserters. Different people had different ways of coping with

the extremely difficult circumstances they were in. Military psychiatry isn't about benefiting the individual soldier but about benefiting the army, its functioning principle is to help those that can fight longer to do so and to get rid of those who can't or won't.[238]

My instinctive reaction has been to distinguish between the two. On hearing of a soldier who has been diagnosed with PTSD, my immediate reaction is sympathetic. This is not a universal reaction, and there is still some stigma attached to PTSD in both today's military and wider society, something Green covers well in *Aftershock* and I witnessed during my service. In paragraph 35 of the appeal verdict in the case of Sergeant Blackman (Marine A) in 2017, Dr. Philip Joseph, a twenty-nine year consultant forensic psychiatrist, one of the three psychiatrists consulted by the defence, concluded that in the original trial "the appellant [Sergeant Blackman] would not want to rely on a psychiatric defence because of the stigma that was perceived to attach to it" and later in paragraph 65 noted that "additional factors [as to why a full psychiatric assessment was not included in the original trial] were the stigma, perception of weakness and the likely end of his career."[239]

In his book *Justice*, the American philosopher Michael J. Sandel also uses the debate around what qualifies someone for a Purple Heart to highlight this stigma in the US military. Advocates for US veterans with PTSD have proposed that they, too, qualify for the Purple Heart (the medal awarded to soldiers who are wounded or killed in battle by enemy action). In 2009, after a Pentagon advisory group had looked at the issue, the Pentagon announced that the medal would be reserved for just those with physical injuries, saying psychological injuries were not intentionally caused by the enemy and were hard to diagnose objectively. I would question both parts of this argument. Firstly, we have seen that even though the wounds maybe invisible, there are clear medically established criteria for diagnosis. Secondly, militaries have for thousands of years understood the benefit of attacking the enemy's mind. From

Genghis Khan's soldiers catapulting decapitated heads over besieged city walls and using arrows specially notched to whistle as they flew through the air, creating a terrifying noise, to the Stukas' Jericho trumpets to US forces in Vietnam playing tapes of distorted human sounds during the night to make the Vietnamese soldiers think that the dead were back for revenge, armies have long used tactics designed solely to break their enemies' minds. In modern militaries, these activities are usually led by specific psychological warfare departments.

Regardless of this, a veteran's group called the Military Order of the Purple Heart opposed awarding the medal for PTSD as it would "debase" the honour. Sandel quotes a former US Marine officer Tyler E. Boudreau:

The same culture that demands tough-mindedness also encourages scepticism towards the suggestion that the violence of war can hurt the healthiest of minds... Sadly, as long as our military culture bears at least a quiet contempt for the psychological wounds of war, it is unlikely those veterans will ever see a Purple Heart.[240]

Boudreau believes that, ultimately, there is a deep-seated attitude in the military that psychological injuries are a sign of weakness that should not be rewarded within the honour code of the military. Overall, though, I would suggest that a significant proportion of civilian society in the West today would have a mostly sympathetic reaction, but I think this reaction is dependent on a diagnosis—an official confirmation of psychological injury.

Steven Hyman MD, Director of the Stanley Centre for Psychiatric Research and a core member at the Broad Institute of MIT and Harvard, however, questions, the notion that mental disorders are discreet and discontinuous (with good health and with each other) categories as laid out by the DSM.[241] Depression, for example, has nine criteria, and you need five of the nine to be diagnosed as officially suffering from depression. For those with the requested amount, any two individuals with the same diagnosis may only have a couple of criteria that are the same.

This also means that someone with four very severe criteria can fall outside the category, yet someone with five mild criteria is diagnosed. According to Hyman, when work on the DSM first began in the 1970s, those working on it wanted to be able to create a system of diagnosis that would clearly state whether an individual had a mental disorder or did not, in the same way you either had smallpox or you didn't. Hyman believes these created categorical thresholds that are rigid and arbitrary. He suggests a better way to see disorders is to think of a spectrum. If Hymen is correct, there are important consequences when considering PTSD and its diagnosis in the military.

For those in the military who accept the validity of psychological injury, this strict categorisation can potentially promote a way of looking at soldiers as being able to cope right up until an arbitrary point where they become classified as having been broken psychologically. This can especially be the case when PTSD is thought of as being linked to one specific trauma rather than the slow build-up of witnessing trauma on a daily basis. An approach to understanding PTSD as on a continuous spectrum could promote a way of viewing the disorder that allows the military to better care for individual soldiers' psychological well-being. In some cases, it could prevent the upper limits ever being reached as was the case with the successful treatments that James administered. Having this line in the sand created by the discontinuous category approach can also leave the system open to abuse, by keeping that line out of reach, when pressure from senior commanders is intense as it was in Alan's time. In an email to me, Hymen explains this:

I think you have a very interesting story to tell, which exemplifies the human cognitive heuristic which leads us to categorize each other based on a few salient traits. Psychiatric diagnosis is a special case of reducing complexity to categories, and of course whether one is 'in' or 'out' of one of these arbitrary categories can have enormous implications in some systems of treatment and systems of justice, military or civilian

In theory, making criteria for PTSD today could have the secondary consequence of being considered mad as opposed to bad when being charged. In fact, the acceptance of psychiatric diagnoses is far from uniform in the US military given the invisibility of the underlying neural, cognitive, and emotional mechanisms from the outside. Thus many decision-makers in various hierarchies can always doubt the veracity of a person's symptoms or even the truth of the entire diagnostic category.[242]

If you accept Hymen's approach, it removes the need to answer conclusively whether Alan had PTSD as diagnosed by the DSM at the point of his desertion, and it encourages us to consider more closely the complex the impact of war on mental states of other individuals accused of wrongdoing not officially diagnosed, but exposed to high stress environments, maybe even Bergdahl and Sergeant Blackman.

When considering Alan's story, I think it is important to look not just at the incident that Stephenie now believes was the main cause of his PTSD, but consider everything that led up to that point. We have already at least seen that there was potentially one other key traumatic incident at the beach the day before he briefly went AWOL and many traumatic incidents when the battalion was in combat. We have also heard of the obvious physical stressors of the heat, lack of water, flies, lack of sleep, and the physical exhaustions of combat over a prolonged period due the lack of rotation that would have made everyone else on the frontline more susceptible to psychological damage.

If we accept the idea of mental disorders as existing on a spectrum rather just dividing those past their limit and those who are "healthy," we can phrase it differently and say that these stressors moved numerous soldiers fighting at the time along the spectrum, at differing rates due to their own psyches. However, there were many other factors at play in the desert at that time in particular outside of the stressors the soldiers were feeling, that we should also consider when making any comment on deserters. To consider these factors we need to think about the duties we think we owe to ourselves and our communities, the values we give our relations and commitments to others, whether we think the means can justify the ends or we think that some acts are just right or wrong and principles matter more than consequences, and what rights we think an individual should have.

A Devil's Advocate was formerly an official role within the Catholic Church. It was one who argued against the canonization of a candidate put forward for sainthood. It was their job to take a sceptical view of the candidate by looking for holes in the evidence and question any miracles and their character. The Devil's Advocate opposed the God's Advocate, whose task was to make the argument in favour of sainthood. It is also the title of a Morris West novel about a priest and a fictional Second World War deserter in post occupation Italy.[243] Father Blaise Meredith is the cynical English priest with a terminal illness sent to rural Italy from Rome to play Devil's Advocate for the canonisation of the deserter. The deserter had become a figure in the local community, helping them survive whilst undergoing a conversion to the Catholic faith. Father Meredith has to decide whether the deserter Giacomo Nerone is a saint or sinner before his own time runs out.

On setting out to tell Alan's story my intention was not to attempt to portray him or any other deserter as a saint. My aim was more to play Devil's Advocate to my own prejudices and my initial reaction to hearing that someone was a deserter. To do that I needed to better understand the factors that can push someone closer to desertion, and even question if there are some contexts where I feel that desertion is a morally permissible act. What is it about these contexts that that could make me, an ex-soldier who never considered deserting, feel this way?

During the Second World War, there were certainly those that deserted for more questionable reasons, including greed. Glass gives the example of one deserter who deserted to join one of the sizeable criminal networks, run by gangs of deserters that sprouted up in post-liberation Naples, Rome, and Paris.[244]

Another motivation identified by Glass is that of disgust. The "disgusted" soldier is one we have already met: John Vernon Bain who became a famous poet after the war in the UK under the pen name Vernon Scannell.[245] Scannell deserted three different times: once during training while in the UK; once after he witnessed one of his fellow soldiers taking a watch from an unknown dead Allied soldier in North Africa in the aftermath of a firefight; and once after VE Day, when he was in England recovering from serious leg wounds. He was convicted but discharged after a brief stint in a psychiatric ward. We have seen that three of Alan's battalion deserted before they even arrived in North Africa. Desertions before leaving the UK occurred in significant numbers across the wider army. Motivations for desertion here were again diverse, ranging from fear, ethical beliefs against killing, the valuing of other commitments such as new born babies, sick relatives or new loves, to name but only a few.

All of these individuals would have the same one word on their records: deserter. But my reaction to their actions is different, and I would argue that both the context of their desertion and motivation makes the act different in terms of ethics. Alan was a psychological casualty, but think now of Alan II, who deserts after going through similar to that which Alan went through but is not a psychological casualty as we would diagnose according to the DSM- what should we think of his actions? To understand how these differences come about using Alan's story as an example, we need to look again at the state of the Eighth Army at the time, the wider context of the war, the specific contexts that Alan was facing and ask the question, why do soldiers fight at all?

Chapter Nine
Why Fight?

Morale still seems reasonably high and, while the desertion rate has risen, it is still limited to those who can walk.

Woody Allen

Every day and every hour, every shell and every dead man wear down that thin handhold, and the years grind it down rapidly. I can see how it is already giving way around me.

All Quiet on the Western Front, Erich Remarque

When Alan deserted, almost to the week, morale in the Eighth Army was at its lowest and desertion was a serious problem. In *All Hell Let Loose: The World at War 1939-1945*, Max Hastings quotes one of Auchinleck's soldiers:

> The order came to us, "Last round, last man." This was chilling. It was curious to see that this legendary phrase of heroic finality could still be used. Presumably it was intended to instil a steely resolve... But being interpreted, it meant that there was no hope for Tobruk and that we were being left to our fate -the very reverse of morale building... We were a downcast, defeated lot.[246]

Hastings follows this quote by stating that "Britain's fortunes in the Middle East, and the global prestige of its army, had reached their lowest ebb."[247] Auchinleck repeatedly asked the War Office to bring back the death penalty during early 1942 for desertion in the face of the enemy and cowardice. The alarming numbers deserting convinced the War Office to re-open the issue. In *A War of Nerves*, Shepard highlights that there were a couple of key issues in doing this—firstly, bringing it in would suggest they were losing the war, and secondly, it was unlikely that the public back home would approve.[248] The public's attitude had changed after the First World War—when men suffering from what was then termed "shell shock" were executed for desertion. The public had by then come to recognise that there were non-physical injuries caused by war that needed treatment rather than the harshest military justice possible in the form of a firing squad.

Auchinleck did not see any issue with his request, believing, very questionably, that his men at least would approve of the measure. Auchinleck was from a different generation to his soldiers—generals always are. The decision was made to not reinstate the death penalty, and Auchinleck was sacked not long after. The tide of the conflict in North Africa, and indeed the war, began to turn and support began to reach the small percentage of troops who were used with limited rotation at the front line who were suffering from battle fatigue. The support introduced was based on some of the work done in the First World War. Desertions decreased and would only increase again at the end of the war in the intense fighting in the countryside of Northern France and the hills of Italy. This, however, came too late for Alan. It was not until late 1942 that this happened.

Journalist and writer Neal Ascherson, who himself served in the Malay conflict, reviewing Glass' book in the British newspaper *The Guardian* makes further claims about desertion:

> Desertion in war is not a mystery. It can have contributory motives—'family problems' at home, hatred of some officer or moral reluctance to kill are among them. But the central motive is the obvious one: to get away from people who are trying to blow your head off or stick a bayonet through you. Common sense, in other words. So the enigma is not why soldiers desert. It is why most of them don't, even in battle and even in the face of imminent defeat. They do not run away, but stand and fight.[249]

As the Eighth Army finally stopped retreating at El Alamein, it was as an important question as it had ever been for a British

Army: why do soldiers continue to fight when facing the very real risk of death or serious injury at any time, let alone in a desperate situation such as the Eight Army found itself in?

In *Enduring Battle: American Soldiers in Three Wars, 1776-1945*, Christopher H Hamner looks to answer this question and identifies the key factors that keep men fighting when 'a soldier's instinct for self-preservation in direct opposition to the army's insistence that he does his duty.'[250] Many soldiers, academics, and writers looking at this question over the years have focused on group cohesion theory as a major part of the answer.[251] The theory describes how the close bond between soldiers in small units keeps them motivated to do their duty. The fear of letting a comrade down or even contributing to their injury or death by failing to do your duty motivates them. Interviews from soldiers who fought in the American Civil War through to the Second World War and more modern wars have been provided as evidence to support this. Stouffer's already-cited study concluded that in the Second World War, neither ideology nor patriotism was the major motivating factor for soldiers in combat.[252]

That is not to say that the just or unjust nature of the war has no impact; rather, that is has less of an impact that other motivational factors. During the Vietnam War, the large protests regarding the perceived unjust nature of the war had a direct negative impact on the motivation of the US Armed Forces and individuals signing up or responding to their conscription. Many did not need to be swayed by public opinion and reached their own conclusions on the unjust nature of the war.

During my time in Iraq, I witnessed soldiers citing the questions being raised back in the UK over the just nature of the war when considering whether an operation should go ahead that could place troops at risk. To Stouffer, though, the main motivations were unity and the bonds soldiers formed with one another.[253] They valued the bond between themselves (often more than their own lives) rather than the bonds with people from the same nation (known or not) or an ideology—certainly when they were there in the heat of the battle. Hamner notes that "the pressures and confusions of ground combat are so intense that ideology is simply disconnected from behaviour when the bullets and shrapnel are flying."[254] Hamner concedes that ideology is a powerful motivator in leading soldiers to join the army, but this power is diminished in the heat of battle. Ideology may be a luxury for those away from the frontline or on operations such as the one I experienced in Iraq in late 2005 to early 2006 when there was more time for reflection than there were periods of intense combat.

Hamner cites the ground-breaking *Men Against Fire,* by US Army combat historian S L A Marshall,[255] in which he concludes that the thing which "enables the infantry soldier to keep going is the presence or presumed presence of a comrade."[256]

Most recently, the US Army's own 2003 study *Why They Fight: Combat Motivations in the Iraq War* concluded that such emotional bonds remained a "critical factor in combat motivation."[257] Hamner notes that the group cohesion theory of why soldiers fight can be traced back past when Shakespeare has his Henry V encourage his men on the morning of the Battle of Agincourt "we happy few, we band of brothers."[258] Ultimately, soldiers fight on for their comrades, due to the special bond that forms between them. The British Army currently uses the slogan on its recruitment adverts, "[t]his is belonging." To desert is to break this almost sacred bond. This is what, in his interview with Koenig, Thurman refers to when he accuses Bergdahl of betrayal,[259] and I think this idea of betrayal informed my initial reaction to desertion. For both Thurman and me, without waiting to know the context of the act, we instinctively conclude that the act of walking away from your comrades is an inherently bad as it is breaking an almost sacred bond that is inherently good.

In his article *The Associative Account of Killing in War*, the Australian philosopher Seth Lazar makes the key assumption that "our associative duties [the duties we have to those we share a close association with] are genuine moral reasons."[260] Lazar claims the following:

> Most of us share a number of morally important relation-ships with those closest to us—our families, friends and other loved ones. Combatants enjoy similar significant relationships with their comrades-in-arms. When aggres-sors attack, they threaten those with whom we share these relationships—our associates... We have duties to protect our associates grounded in the value of these spe-cial relationships.[261]

Lazar starts the article noting that warfare can involve justified intentional killing, yet at the same time we believe humans enjoy fundamental moral protections against being deliberately killed— commonly expressed in the language of human rights.

The challenge is to render these two commitments mutually consistent. Lazar lays out two ways of doing this. The first, which Lazar claims is the approach the vast majority of contemporary philosophers in the ethics of war affirm despite disagreements in how it is applied, is that in a justified war those who we intentionally kill are liable to be killed as they have lost or forfeited the protection of their rights. For example, Walzer would argue that combatants on both sides lose their right from attack,[262] while non-combatants on both sides retain them, whilst McMahan would argue that combatants and some non-combatants on the unjustified side lose their rights against attack, but those on the justified side do not.[263] In the article, he investigates how the duties soldiers have in war to their comrades, whether they are on fighting a just war or not, can provide moral reasons to fight and indeed kill.

The other approach is accepting that war involves violating rights, but weightier reasons can override these violations. The article goes on to explore to what extent associative duties can override the rights of others. In the case of desertion, the question becomes to what extent do your duties to your own right not to be killed outweigh your associative duties, and to a certain extent your duty to loved ones who may rely on you?

Lazar understands duties in this context as "a kind of moral reason, distinguished by being non-voluntary, having a particular weight,"[264] so they include the scenario where you are conscripted. You inherit the associative duties to your comrades by being there of your own choice or not (interestingly this would to me suggest the greater the association the greater the duty—so deserting before even setting sail as some of Alan's battalion did absolved them of the same level of associative duty). Therefore, Alan did have a duty to his comrades and to the community to which he belonged, but what was the point when that duty to his comrades and those back home was outweighed by his duty to himself and/or his loved ones? I would say that the scales were certainly tipped by the point when he reached the level of psychological injury he did, in the same way they would have been if Alan had had his legs removed in a bombardment.

If Alan had not been suffering from psychological injuries, would there be a point where the scales were tipped by other factors, especially when others with an equal duty, to certainly the wider community, were not fulfilling their duty in anywhere near the same way due to the lack of rotation of frontline troops? For a version of Alan who was not injured—who we have called Alan II—was there a point where his desertion was justified? To answer this question, we need to explore what value we should place on associate duties (the assumption of many who accept group cohesion theory is a great value), what value we should place on our duty to our wider community and measure that against the duty we have to our love ones to survive, and the rights we have as individuals, particularly the right to life.

Hamner questions some of the assumptions of previous thinkers when looking at the bonds created between soldiers. He points out that the way that the battlefield has been transformed over time due to new technologies, has changed the way that this bond can motivate soldiers to fight and is valued by them. In the eighteenth and nineteenth century wars, Hamner claims that as infantry soldiers fought in a line, the presence of fellow soldiers, shoulder to shoulder provided an example to follow and physical reassurance. There was also a powerful discouragement to not perform their duties, as their actions were under constant observation by others nearby.

Hamner then compares the motivations that made men fight on these linear, low-technology battlefields to the dispersed industrialised higher technology of the mid twentieth century that Alan would have experienced. Although the modern infantry soldier is still reliant on his comrades to provide covering fire, provide eyes and ears for other individuals seeking cover, and still works together more closely with comrades on crewed weapons, the lack of the feel of the elbow from the tightly packed columns and lines of the past is missing. Hamner then goes further and questions the importance given to group cohesion theory. Though consistent with soldiers' own anecdotal accounts and intuitively appealing Hamner believes there is a large body of historical evidence that questions the validity of the theory, identifying three issues in particular.

Firstly, Hamner cites a number of sources, including *Hitler's Army* by Israeli historian Omer Bartov and the writing of combat journalist Ernie Pyle, who was embedded with the US 1st Division in the Second World War, that highlight that the group cohesion theory is difficult to sustain in heavy combat as the group itself is destroyed through losses to the group. Bartov looking at the German Army on the Eastern Front noted that group cohesion theory was difficult to sustain because of primary groups' "unfortunate tendency to disintegrate when they are needed most."[265] Pyle noted the high turnover of replacements within the small units of the 1st Division due to casualties that meant that over time small units eventually retained no original members.[266]

Replacements during some battles in the Second World War would join their units at night time, and they would only see their comrades for the first time when engaged in combat at first light. This issue is often dealt with by the military by developing loyalty to the regiment, company, or platoon, establishing a continuity of loyalty with those serving at any point in time with all others who have served in that unit, including recently lost comrades. You may not have the chance to form a bond with new recruits, but you fight on due to the bond you still have with lost comrades and comrades who embodied the regiments ethos and won it the battle honours you are still proud of hundreds of years later.

Secondly, Hamner cites a body of theories developed in psychology and sociology. He highlights research that shows that tight cohesion within small units can actually work against the goals of a wider organisation. The tightness of the group emboldens each individual to resist authority. The controversial Stanford Prison Experiment run by US psychologist Philip Zimbardo is the most well-known example of this.[267] In this experiment, volunteers were randomly designated as either guards or prisoners in a mock detention centre. Zimbardo found that the prisoners were compliant at the beginning of the experiment, but as they got to know one another and form a group, they began to challenge authority together. Despite questions around the accuracy of Zimbardo's accounts of the experiment, and his role as an observer rather than instigator, there are real world examples that Hamner uses to highlight this phenomena, including incidences of fragging (soldiers deliberately killing their officers) where he cites military sociologist Charles Moskos, who estimates that 80% of fraggings in Vietnam were the results of group action[268] (see Fabre for an interesting consideration of the ethics of Internecine War Killings).[269]

Thirdly, Hamner questions the basic principle of group cohesion theory—that the bond makes soldiers more willing to fight. He cites Roger Little's work on buddy pairs during the Korean War, in which he records interviews with infantry soldiers who revealed that if they were wounded, they would expect their buddy to stay with them rather than continue with the mission.[270] A strong bond between comrades does not equal a strong loyalty to the mission or the wider organisation. Group cohesion could just as likely cause soldiers to stop fighting to protect their comrades than to carry on. It is an argument often used against allowing women in to frontline combat roles—that male colleagues would desert the mission to focus on protecting female comrades who were injured or in danger—the assumption being that male soldiers would feel a stronger drive to do this than with their male comrades.

None of this denies the existence of associative duties—much of Hamner's understanding is based on the assumption of such duties. He is highlighting that they may be overstated in contributing to soldier's motivation to fight. Hamner moves on to try to explain what keeps soldiers fighting if group cohesion is overstated. Weaknesses in group cohesion theory have led some social scientists to look at the distinction between social cohesion and task cohesion.[271] The distinction between how well members of a group identifies with each other, versus how well the group identifies with a collective goal. The former does not guarantee the latter and vice versa. Hamner believes that it is task cohesion in fighting units that is the critical factor encouraging soldiers to face fire. He goes on to highlight a tension within task cohesion. For the military, the groups' task is the mission; for the individual, the task is often to simply stay alive.[272] The key is aligning the two and convincing soldiers that by following orders, they give themselves and their comrades the best chance of surviving combat. And the key is to convince as many soldiers as possible this is the case so a critical mass is reached that allows the chance of success of the mission to seem realistic.

This begins in training and also involves an attempt to give soldiers a sense of controllability (the belief that individuals could improve their odds of survival by behaving in certain ways).[273] By the Second World War, training given to Allied troops implied a correlation between ability and survival. Be good at the skills you are trained to do and follow instructions and you will survive.[274]

As the war went on, training changed from drills by rote to become increasingly realistic. Battlefield inoculation training—

where the sight, sounds, and pressures of the battlefield were created—was developed to prepare soldiers mentally and to give them confidence in the training when they later experienced those same conditions in combat. It presented the battlespace as filled with decisions that had markedly different influences on the chances of survival. It was designed to create a belief that committed participation in battle was not necessarily a death sentence. Getting specific decisions right could help increase the soldier's odds of survival.

The British Army also focussed on basic intelligence and aptitude tests to screen recruits as there was a belief that "dullards" and "neurotics" were more likely to be vulnerable to the effects of battle fatigue.[275] Psychologists helped design command tasks (group activities involving leaderless exercises, usually involving an obstacle crossing using a variety of planks and barrels) for officer selection, versions of which I went through when attending the Regular Commissions Board in the 2000s. The British army still operates on the maxim "train hard, fight easy." This encourages a level of training that creates a belief that you will cope with anything the battlefield can throw at you through the knowledge that you have done worse and survived.

From my experience, travelling around in the back of vehicles in Iraq, when there was a constant threat from unseen IEDs, felt more stressful than when I was deployed in Afghanistan, where there was a greater threat of being engaged directly in a firefight with the enemy. I believed that, in the latter situation, by deploying my skills, I would have much more control over my fate. In Iraq, I felt I had no control over the situation, because I was often passive in the back of a vehicle with no chance to deploy skills that would allow me greater agency. This was a belief that was not based on any statistical analysis of the actual risks. To attempt to counter the seemingly random nature of the IED threat, much of the pre-deployment training before Iraq focussed on skills that could help you avoid routes where they might be deployed and how to safely identify potential IEDs. The message was clear—we are teaching you skills that, if executed to a high standard, will keep you alive. We have seen from Alan's training record and descriptions of training by other members of the battalion in the Imperial War Museum archives, that those in Alan's battalion did not receive realistic or sustained training. Max Hastings quotes a Lieutenant Michael Kerr who served with the Eighth Army:

> In 1941 and early 1942 the morale of the British Army… was very low… the standard of infantry training was really quite terrible. Soldiers were unable to understand what they were meant to be doing and what everything was about.[276]

In 2009, to increase the sense of controllability in their soldiers, the US Army began to roll out a programme called Comprehensive Soldier Fitness to teach resilience to all of the US Army's 1.1 million soldiers. This program was based in part on ancient Greek philosophy and the latest insights in psychology including in the area of Cognitive Behavioural Therapy (CBT). The programme trains soldiers to evaluate what they can control and what they cannot, and then focus their energy on changing what they can control. In their own words, they are training their soldiers to "take control of their emotions before they take control of you."[277]

The military wants soldiers who can control their emotions and see that the logical option to increase their chances of surviving is to stay and fight with their comrades. Each soldier faces a version of the prisoner's dilemma. The prisoner's dilemma is the thought experiment where two prisoners are put in a position where, whatever the other does, each is better off confessing than remaining silent. But the outcome obtained when both confess is worse for each than the outcome they would have obtained had both remained silent, showing the conflict involved when a group whose members pursue rational self-interest may all end up worse off than a group whose members act contrary to rational self-interest. In a combat unit, all those involved are bonded together in a mutually beneficial relationship that is held together by the trust that everyman will do his duty (underpinned by the notion that this will give all the best chance of survival through the successful completion of the mission). Hamner notes that "many veterans and scholars acknowledge simply remaining alive as a powerful component of the bonds linking the members of a combat unit."[278]

Hamner cites Moskos who dismissed the band of brothers phenomena as a "semi-mystical bond of comradeship" arguing instead that the more pragmatic needs—particularly the instinct of self-preservation—had underlain these bonds rather than allegiance to some idealised band of brothers.[279] If this view is to be accepted, while we still need to acknowledge the associative duties soldiers have, the value of the association is lessened as it is potentially based more on selfish motivations than because it is the right thing to do, and to me this therefore reduces the duty one has.

From my experience of military training, those highly thought of by their peers were first and foremost competent, before any other moral characteristic was spoken of. Hamner notes in his chapter on leadership that surveys of soldiers asking them to rate qualities they most wanted to see form their officers - competence was often the highest ranked response.[280] This was underpinned by the belief that if their officers were competent that gave them the best chance of survival.

By the Second World War, acts of individual bravery that might grant immortal glory were less celebrated than competence that might increase the chance of a longer mortality. In *The Mighty Dead: Why Homer Matters,* English author Adam Nicolson questions the assumption that, for even some of those in the past associated most strongly with beliefs in immortal glory, it was valued so highly. Nicolson identifies the great central statement of both *The Iliad* and *The Odyssey* as that made by a dead Achilles to Odysseus when he meets him in the Underworld. Achilles, whose epic deeds on the battlefield have reserved for him a special position in Hades, tells Odysseus, "[i]f I had a chance of living on earth again I would rather do that as a slave of another, some landless man with scarcely enough to live on, than lord it here over all the dead that have ever died."[281] Homer at least seems to suggest that, in Nicolson's words, "the reality of the human heart, is the only one worth having." Homer shows us Achilles, the ultimate warrior, who earlier in the poems chose death and glory over a long life, in death seemingly regretting his choice.

This reading of Homer shows that, although the idea of obtaining glory through death on the battlefield was alive in such times, Homer at least was already questioning its worth to mortal man. Traditional military values that would have been familiar to Homer, like strength, bravery and self-sacrifice, are still highly valued. Armies and their regiments still endeavour to sets of values that would have been similar to soldiers of the past and of Homeric myth. However, according to Hamner, the ranking of importance has subtly shifted, from at least out perceived idea of their importance in the past.

Wider beliefs in society have shifted too and this has changed the relationship individuals have with both their wider web of associations, and even who is seen as part of that web. In Homer, the authority of the gods' and man's position in the cosmos was a frequently recurring theme. There are many myths detailing the fate of those who challenge the natural order of the world. In *Homo Deus*, the Israeli Historian Yuval Noah Harari, notes this:

> A catholic soldier fighting at the Battle of White Mountain [an early battle in the Thirty Years' War fought in 1620, in which an army of Bohemians and mercenaries were defeated the combined armies of the Holy Roman Emperor and the German Catholic League] could say to himself; 'true I am suffering. But the pope and the emperor say we are fighting for a good cause, so my suffering is meaningful.[282]

Harari claims that "for thousands of years, when people looked at war, they saw gods, emperors, generals and great heroes. But over the last two centuries the kings and generals have been pushed to the side, and the limelight shifted on to the common soldier."[283] Harari contrasts the soldier from the Thirty Years War with Otto Dix, the German First World War soldier and then artist, who was profoundly affected by the sights of the war, and later described a recurring nightmare in which he crawled through destroyed houses. He represented his traumatic experiences in his art and was later designated a degenerate artist by the Nazis. Harari claims Dix used an opposite kind of logic to his Catholic counterpart. He saw personal experience as the source of all meaning, hence his kind of thinking said, "I am suffering—and this is bad—hence the whole war is bad. And if the Kaiser and the clergy nevertheless support the war, they must be mistaken."[284]

In the poem *The Charge of The Light Brigade* by Alfred Lord Tennyson that describes a suicidal British cavalry charge after a failure in communication at the Battle of Balaclava in the Crimean War, he claims:

> Theirs is not to reason why,
> Theirs but to do and die:
> Into the valley of Death
>   Rode the six hundred.[285]

By the time of the Second World War, lessons from the carnage of the Great War and wider changes in society, meant frontline troops felt more empowered to reason why. By the time Alan was fighting in the desert, it is likely that he would have seen his wider duty not to a religious leader, nor distant monarch, but to his community; in other words, to other people like himself, particularly those he knew. He would have understood these duties as being in tension with his own rights, and he would have recognised that his own inner life, which was as important to him as anyone else's was to them.

Troops today, while still being prepared to make personal sacrifice, endure hardship and recognise that there will often be a higher mission and intelligence to which they are not privy, expect at the very least competency from higher command, the right resources to achieve their mission, the right legal framework to operate in and the right welfare support. They will question if any of these are not in place. The verdict in Sergeant Blackman's appeal trial noted the gap in his pre-deployment training (due to his father's death), the lack of access to Trauma Risk Management (TRiM) trained individuals to support Blackman and his multiple in the field after suffering lost comrades, the difficult physical conditions (including the heat and lack of sleep), the feeling of insecurity and regularity of attacks, and, crucially, the perception of a lack of leadership by senior commanders, as important factors to consider when looking at the circumstances under which the appellant was operating.[286]

In 2000, the Military Covenant, which sets out the relationship between the nation, the armed forces and the government, was introduced as an informal rather than legal agreement.[287] It recognised the moral obligation to members of the armed forces and their families and it established how they should be treated. Members of the armed forces and their families are now much more aware of their own rights than in any time previously. Recent inquires, such as the 2016 Chilcot Inquiry, into the Iraq war that have examined the lack of body armour for troops during the 2003 invasion and the legal justifications of the conflict are evidence of this.[288]

The covenant did not exist in Alan's time, and if it did, the profound nature of the threat the country faced would have most likely given the government the moral justification to suspend it until the threat was defeated. For individuals like Alan, though subjected to what they were subjected to, were, from their point of view, entitled to feel that they were being let down? Harari believes that for is humans in the modern era "[m]odernity is a surprisingly simple deal. The entire contract can be summarised in a single phrase: "Humans agree to give up meaning in exchange for power [over their own lives]."[289] Many within today's Western societies from which militaries come, believe less in the divine power of their leaders and believe more in their own ability to have control over their own lives.

Alan was not particularly religious. Stephenie told me that although he did not believe in God, he did believe that one's family remain watching over you after that have passed away, believing that his brother was still with him after he died.

Whatever their beliefs, Alan and thousands of others surrendered power over their own lives in a very one-sided deal with the government and military hierarchy, with no legitimate means of objecting when they felt those on the other side of the deal were not holding their end up. Due to the existential nature of the threat faced, the government and military hierarchy adopted a very consequentialist approach (often contrasted with the deontological or duty based approach, that prioritises the positive or negative ethical value of the consequences of an action are more than the means used to achieve it). Military operations such as the Allied strategic bombing campaign over Germany and the dropping of the H-Bomb in Japan were recognised by some Allies at the time as being unethical acts, only justified as the lesser evil, and judged acceptable due to the aimed-for consequence of ending the war as swiftly as possible with the defeat of the evils of German fascism and Japanese militarism.[290] Later generations have judged the actions more harshly, focussing their arguments on principles rather than results.

It is interesting to note that it was the German and Russian armies who executed the highest numbers of their own soldiers for desertion and other derelictions of duty. Estimates for the number of Russians shot go as high as 160,000 (but are very disputed), while more accurate figures for the German Army record that approximately 15,000 soldiers were shot after sentencing, while a further 15,000-35,000 were executed without trial, with the final year of the war seeing a massive spike in executions.[291] There are several potential explanations for this. These include the fact that both suffered very high numbers of deserters, due to the tough conditions on the Eastern Front and the fact that these two armies were also two of the largest and suffered the greatest number of casualties. If British numbers continued to increase and Auchinleck remained in place, would British deserters have eventually been shot?

However, I would suggest that there are two other key factors here that meant these two armies increasingly adopted more extreme means to justify their ends that are common to other times and states throughout history. Firstly, it was due to the desperate nature with which they found themselves in—when executions peaked the threat of existential defeat for both the German and Russian armies was at its greatest. Secondly, both armies were working for political masters who believed in utopian (or maybe more accurately dystopian) futures for their countries. The ends they were justifying were not just the survival of the current political state as it was, but the destiny of the superior race and the universal freedom of humanity respectively. The perceived magnitude of the greater good of these ends meant that they allowed increasingly unethical acts, which could still be justified by a form of consequentialist thinking.

This consequentialist approach was frequently taken in less known and smaller military engagements. Soldiers like Alan were seen as a means to end by senior commanders, especially when the war for the Allies was at its nadir, as it was when Alan deserted. Soldiers were sent on operations where the chance of them being killed or captured was higher than them surviving. In the year that Alan deserted, numerous commando raids were launched from the UK, with the expectation that few of the men would return. The 1942 raid against the dry docks at Saint Nazaire, named Operation CHARIOT, despite successfully disabling the dock, saw only 228 men return to England out of the 622 men who took part (169 men were killed and another 215 became prisoners of war).[292] Deontologist philosophers like eighteenth-century German philosopher Immanuel Kant would say that Alan and all those other soldiers treated as a means, even voluntarily, were done a wrong by being treated as such, and even by treating themselves as a means to end were committing an unethical act.[293]

Extreme situations like the Second World War test the assumptions and claims of various approaches to ethics. I do not necessarily ascribe more weight to one approach than another. The point is to highlight that, when giving duty primacy in an ethical approach, competing duties must be weighed, and also that there are competing ethical frameworks with which to examine an act such as desertion that can give different readings of the same act.

Within militaries, such ethical questions are rarely discussed. Behaviour by an individual that is seen to prioritise the individual's rights over that of the group is punished. During my training, it was drilled into me that the opposite of being a good soldier was someone who was 'Jack.' This is taken from the phrase 'I'm alright, Jack,' which, according to the Collins English Dictionary, is a well-known English expression indicating smug and complacent selfishness.[294] 'Jack' was used to describe any behaviour deemed as selfish, especially any behaviour where an individual would cut corners to make his or her life easier at the expense of the group. The group would seek out this behaviour and punish it. Without using the same phrase, Hamner highlights this as crucial.[295] You maximise your chances of survival if the rest of the group are looking out for you, have your back and care about your fate. Competence alone will not guarantee this, even on the modern battlefield.

The only way for a trust to develop within the group, a trust that every group member is looking out for the next, is for each group member to display selfless behaviour and seek out the opposite behaviour in others. Any displays of 'Jack' behaviour threaten this trust. Desertion could be seen as the epitome of this behaviour. Desertions threaten the critical mass of the mission, reducing the chances of successes and the chances of survival for those who remain. Every desertion that occurs slightly changes the balance of the prisoner's dilemma every remaining soldier faces. Even with the scale of Second World War—where each individual soldier would feel insignificant when compared to the vast Armies moving across the desert, jungles and countryside—at the group level individual losses could be seen to threaten the bonds of trust of armies. This explains why Auchinleck pressed for the most serious of punishments. Denied the death penalty the military was more limited in what threats to its personnel that previous militaries had been. Hamner notes:

> Because the armies direct control over soldier's behaviour waned dramatically on the empty battlefield, the power of disgrace aimed at soldiers who refused to go in grew even more important in the twentieth century.[296]

It was, and still is, in the military's best interests to ensure any failure to do your duty be seen as a shameful act. Alex Bowlby, a soldier in Alan's battalion in Italy who we will meet later, sympathised with those who deserted, suggesting that his own courage was simply "fear of disgrace."[297] I was very aware that how I behaved on operations would define how others saw me, both my peers and my family and friends back home. I cared that they thought that I had not failed to do my duty, even if I did not make it home.

In *Death and the Afterlife*, American philosopher Samuel Scheffler examines how many in the West, who despite not believing in any life after death, seem to care very much about the memory of them living on past their death.[298] Many who believe in no God and accept they will be no heaven for them to watch on from still care that others will remember them. Scheffler suggest that this extends to the hope that there are not just people who knew them preserving their memory, but a much longer continuity of recognisable society, made up of people who would have never personally known them. It is in part why groups use the threat of 'disappearance' in conflicts. The 'disappeared' in any conflict often seem to have a degree of tragedy greater than those whose fates are known, no matter how tragic the known story is.

We are narrative creatures, and we care deeply what the end of our story is even if we are not going to be around to hear it. There are a complex set of connected beliefs that stem from this that cause diverse behaviours. These include soldiers risking their lives to recover fallen comrades they know are already deceased. It also explains why soldiers throughout centuries of conflict have attempted to provide identification in the case of their death, from US civil war soldiers writing their names on to their inside of their collars to Argentinean conscripts scribbling their names on their hands in pen to the development of and the importance placed on dog tags. For many years, soldiers have written letters to be sent on becoming 'Killed in Action' and requests to comrades to give their loved ones messages that will arrive post mortem. Even when death seems inevitable, remaining in the military system can seemingly help the survival of the story of what happened to the soldier (not just preservation of reputation), giving closure to loved ones and allowing them to live on in memory and ensuring that story is one that reflects well.

It could be argued that the military takes ownership of how your story will be told, of how you will be remembered. This can be a powerful hold over a narrative creature. Step out of the system and you will be forgotten, stay and do your duty and we will remember you. The concept of memory and living on through remembrance is a complicated and exceptionally important one in the military.

It is undoubtedly easier in times of peace to preach of values that place the individual in extreme risk in war. On the limited operations in which I served, it was undoubtedly a combination of faith in the skills and drills I had been taught, faith in the orders I was given, and professionalism of my colleagues, a fear of being 'Jack,' and concerns to how others would remember me if something happened, that kept me going.

I, though, never had to face the levels of risks that Alan did for such a prolonged period. I never experienced the feeling that I was fighting a war where the units I was with could be completely overrun and the larger British Force routed (I know others in some of the most isolated outposts of Helmand Province did experience something close to this). I do not know what that exposure would do to me. When I served, I did believe in a bond between myself and the other soldiers in the units I served with and with the wider coalition I served in. I am aware, however, that there is a growing body of research in modern psychology that suggests that the role of our conscious in decision making is to provide post-hoc explanations of our actions that fit in to an ongoing narrative of who we think we are.[299]

Reading the work of Hamner and others has led me to question how much of my behaviour was motivated by both my desire to stay alive and the military's desire to keep me on mission. Determining individuals' motivations is a near-impossible task, and I would suggest that there are rarely actions determined by one single motivating factor. If soldiers are coming up with a post-hoc explanation of their actions to explain why they fight and undertake selfless heroic acts, the explanation that they were doing it for their comrade next to them would be one that would fit well with what the military units I experienced claim they stand for. Was my initial reaction to desertion based in a belief in a fictional sacred bond?

We shall return now to the example of the Irish deserters in the Second World War. At first look, it seems that my reaction is determined by the motivation of the Irish soldiers more than anything else, followed by the end result, which was countless examples of their bravery and their contribution to the defeat of fascism. They intentionally exposed themselves to great danger to fight the tyranny that was Nazism (although there are other interpretations, such as that they were leaving to pursue adventure and glory, and, before the reality of the horror of the conflict becomes apparent, this is more attractive course of action than staying at home where there is no promise of either).

Even though, at the start of this project, I believed that desertion in itself was a bad act, the good motivation seems to outweigh the badness of committing the act, and the ends—defeating a great evil—justify the means of committing that bad act with good motivation. If pushed, I would claim that this judgement was made on an objective weighing up of the facts.

The criticism of many in Ireland towards the deserters was that it was their duty to stay and protect Ireland from potential German invasion (and also British, if certain circumstances prevailed). As a former British soldier, whilst I should be able to easily see the importance of this from an Irish perspective, I place much greater value on the deserters' positive contribution to fighting alongside the British and other Allies against the Axis forces than their negative contribution to Ireland's defence. I also chose to focus my judgement less on the national priorities than at the strategic level, focussing on the greater good for Europe and the world by defeating fascism rather than protecting one nation. I've also focussed on the strategic assertion that by deserting to fight, the Irish soldiers did more to protect Ireland from German invasion than remaining in Ireland.

On closer inspection, however, we must ask how much of my judgement and following choice of supporting arguments are more influenced by my local context than an objective view point? How much of the value I place on the positive contribution to fighting alongside the British is done so because I am British and it is the army I once fought for? If the nation in question was my nation rather than Ireland, how much more would I value the negative contribution to the country's defence and how easy would I find it to focus on the more strategic viewpoint? Maybe the reaction of some in Ireland was also more about the values they held, too. If the deserters had not joined the British Army, a country and army that has a long and also recent history of conflict with the Ireland, would they have found it easier to see the value in their countrymen's contribution to the war against fascism?

Chapter Ten
Duties and Rights

England expects that every man will do his duty.
>Vice Admiral Horatio Nelson
>on the eve of the battle of Trafalgar, 1805

Bowe Bergdahl claimed his desertion was to highlight issues of poor leadership within his command chain.[300] The suggestions in the media that he had deserted to join the Taliban, and had converted to Islam, have both been unsubstantiated and (Serial concluded) were very likely untrue. Serial also wasn't convinced any US soldiers lost their lives on direct missions to try and find Bergdhal - serial further concluded these assertions were either false, or outright questionable.[301] Furthermore, political issues beleaguered his case, a key catalyst of which was a clumsily conceived portrayal of Bergdhal as hero by the US President, in a White House Rose Garden briefing. If we accept the aforementioned factors, his motivation seemed, if to be believed, a selfless one and the act done out of a sense of duty to his comrades and the mission. Bergdahl could not have believed that he had more of a chance to survive his tour by going it alone. By leaving camp in hostile territory, he placed himself in great danger, something he claims he was very aware of.

I found it difficult, however, to view Bergdahl in the same light as the Irish deserters. This may have been because the act seems disproportionate (he could have raised his concerns through the command chain rather than taking such a risk as a first action). It may have been because there is so much so much confusion as to why he let his post and the doubts of others as to whether the reason he gave was the real reason he left. My impression is that Bergdahl was more the Walter Mitty than the

Walter Purdy,[302] that he has been portrayed by some. This may also be because he was deserting from a coalition partner, one that I fought alongside, as opposed to the Irish deserters who were deserting to the British Forces.

With Bergdahl there is something else that struck me as important (but did not when thinking of the Irish deserters) and that was the fact that he was a volunteer, contrasted against many like Alan who in the Second World War who were conscripts. In today's US and UK Armed Forces you voluntarily sign up. There have been some in the US in particular that have pointed out that if some in society have no other options in employment, those who chose to enlist may not be doing so as freely as is suggested by the term "volunteer army"—claiming that young people from low to middle income neighbourhoods without college education make up a disproportionately high percentage of active service recruits in the US. The figures however do not seem to back this claim up, as Stephen J. Dubner's *Freakanomics* blog discussion of Heritage Foundation's Center for Data Analysis' report "Who Serves in the U.S. Military? The Demographics of Enlisted Troops and Officers"[303] discusses. Regardless, it is not conscription as experienced in the Civil War (where the rich who were conscripted through the lottery could buy someone to take their place[304]), Vietnam or both world wars. When you sign up you make the commitment and take up those associative duties. You are agreeing that there is no prisoner's dilemma—you voluntarily commit to keeping the bond. Alan was not a volunteer, he did not ask to be put in the situation he was put in and be given the responsibilities he was given. At the time though this did not make any legal difference; the country needed him to fight and he was expected to do his duty. From a moral perspective as well as we have seen with Lazar duties are non-voluntary.

Interestingly though if Alan had volunteered for another army - not the British, signed up as a mercenary and then deserted, then I suspect people would feel differently about his desertion, even though the associative duties taken on should in theory remain the same. My perception when serving in the military was when you sign up and become a mercenary it is just a job and very different from military service for your country. I saw military service for my country as more than a job, but also a form civic duty. To not perform your civic duty you are not just breaking a bond with those with you serve with, but with the whole of civil society. At that point in the Second World War the country needed people to do their civic duty more than any other time in recent history, the very existence of British civil society was threatened.

The term civil society goes back to *Politics* by Greek Philosopher Aristotle.[305] In *Politics* he refers to a "community"—a city-state characterized by a shared set of norms and ethos, in which free citizens were equals under the rule of law. In return, they accepted political duties—such as military service. The state would issue such equipment to citizens who could not afford a set of their own. Richer citizens who owned their own horses would join the cavalry. In today's British Army, some cavalry regiments still expect young officers wishing to join to have an independent income, although they are not expected to own their own tank. A significant difference from then to now is that the leaders of the past fought at the frontline. Leaders for the most part would fight alongside the people (for very different rewards). If those in today's political class who make the decisions to go to war or not, had to also fight on the frontline alongside their own sons, then maybe some decisions would be made differently.

The lack of rotation policy in the Second World War meant that it was not just the political leaders who were not at the frontline, but the vast majority of the population and even the vast majority of soldiers. It was a small percentage of the army that fought at the front line in multiple theatres, the civic burden of fighting the war was not shared equally, but quite the opposite. As Charles Glass noted it was often those not at the front line, those not taking up their share of the fighting, who judged those deserting from the front the harshest.[306] Maybe this was just down to the lack of appreciation of what it was like on the frontline (not true for all, as many senior commanders who were sceptical of psychological injuries, had fought in the Great War themselves, maybe for these it was a failure of memory). Maybe for some in the rear, their reaction was motivated more by self-preservation, as every deserter increased the chance of the frontline coming to them. Are those who loudly decry the actions of deserters are trying to drown out internal voices that question their own ability to cope with the dangers of battle? It may be that they are equally driven by fear of how they would perform in a hypothetical battle rather than the actual battle experienced by those deserting the frontline. Or maybe they just lack the imagination to properly understand that war, for the most part, is hell.

Though the concept of civic duty was taken on by Roman writers, it later entered into Western political culture following translations of Aristotle's works by late medieval and early Renaissance writers. A government green paper entitled *Rights and Responsibilities: developing our constitutional framework* presented to Parliament in 2009 had at its heart the key constitutional question of the relationship between the citizen and the state.[307] The paper traces the history of the idea of citizens having both rights and responsibilities (and therefore corresponding duties) from the classical times, through to liberal thinkers in the nineteenth century where in *On Liberty*, the English philosopher John Stuart Mill noted that "there are many positive acts for the benefit of others which [anyone] may rightfully be compelled to perform."[308] From there it traces ideas on the subject on to philosophers from the time of the American and French revolutions. The paper quotes Thomas Paine, an English political philosopher whose thinking influenced both revolutions, declaring that "[a] Declaration of Rights is, by reciprocity, a Declaration of Duties, also. Whatever is my right as a man, is also the right of another; and it becomes my duty to guarantee, as well as to possess."[309] It goes on to cite *The Social Contract* by French political philosopher Jean-Jacques Rousseau.

Rousseau argues the ideal form of political organisation was based on a contract between all citizens that would ensure everyone would be free as they all forfeit the same amount of rights and impose the same duties on all.[310]

The paper, after highlighting the development of similar thoughts in both socialist and free-market politics and across other world cultures, went on to note that "[r]esponsibilities have often been a poor cousin to rights in our national discourse, and yet they are deeply woven into our social and moral fabric" and expressed concerns that "an over-emphasis on rights, to the exclusion of notions of responsibility, can lead to a 'me' society rather than a 'we' society, in which an unbridled focus on our own individual rights and liberties risks overtaking our collective security and wellbeing, and respect for others."[311] There is no mention of the most extreme duty of going to war for our country, for the authors of the paper and I would suggest that for most citizens of the UK this would be a responsibility not considered today. At the time of writing, the bill has still yet to be enacted. Generations of military leaders though have appealed to the civic responsibilities and duties of the men and women under their command.

One of the most famous British military figures in history, Vice Admiral Horatio Nelson, reminded his men of this sense of duty, when sending a signal from his flagship HMS Victory as the Battle of Trafalgar was about to commence on 21 October 1805: "England expects that every man will do his duty."[312] Less than fifty years previous to Trafalgar, all Royal Navy officers and seamen had been given an added incentive to do their duty to the best of their abilities, when in 1757 Admiral John Byng was shot by firing squad for failing to relieve a besieged British garrison during the Battle of Minorca[313] (although 22 years after the event, the Articles of War were amended to allow "such other punishment as the nature and degree of the offence shall be found to deserve" as an alternative to capital punishment). At the outbreak of the Seven Years' War against the French, Byng, after he was refused more men for his undermanned ships and received orders he felt were unclear[314], sailed for Minorca. He fought an inconclusive engagement with the French off the Minorca coast, and then decided to return to Gibraltar for repairs after consultation with his other captains.

Upon return to Britain, Byng was court martialled and found guilty of failing to "do his utmost" to prevent Minorca falling. He was sentenced to death and shot by firing squad on 14 March 1757. Despite the severity of the penalty and the suspicion that the Admiralty sought to protect itself from public anger over the defeat by throwing all the blame on the admiral, which had led to a reaction in favour of Byng in both the Navy and the country, King George II chose not to exercise his prerogative to grant clemency. Byng's execution was satirized in *Candide* by the French Enlightenment writer, historian, and philosopher Voltaire, who met Byng and vainly tried to intercede on his behalf.[315] In Portsmouth, the eponymous Candide witnesses the execution of an officer by firing squad and is told that "in this country, it is good to kill an admiral from time to time, in order to encourage the others."[316] In 2007, some of Byng's descendants petitioned the government for a posthumous pardon. The Ministry of Defence refused. Members of his family continue to seek a pardon, along with a group at Southill in Bedfordshire where the Byng family lived.[317]

During the Second World War, an Admiralty propaganda poster intended to increase industrial production on the home front, carried the slogan; "Britain expects that you too, this day, will do your duty." Nelson's flag signal was hoisted by the Royal Navy monitor, HMS Erebus at the start of the bombardment for the Normandy landings on 6 June 1944.[318]

Churchill's most famous speeches all suggested that all of nation was involved in the fight against fascism together, all fighting to save our mutual existence. It was always "we will fight" them never "they will fight." In all the varying concepts of civic society and civic duty across time, one of the constants has been the notion that the civic burden should be shared equally amongst the citizens. For some, who do not know the context of Alan's desertion, for him to desert when he did was to neglect his civic duty. He was therefore not just letting his unit down, but all of civil society, and not just any civic society but *British* civil society. All those in that civil society could feel cheated by his actions.

Even seventy years later, a very different British society still wants to feel a continuity back to the society that held out and defeated fascism, and that continuity can include a continuity of feeling to those who back then were judged to have not "done their bit." The enduring myth of Britain standing alone against fascism is a defining one in the modern British society. We tell ourselves we lack the sophistication, or maybe pretentiousness of our continental neighbours, but we can be relied upon to keep fighting when our backs are to the wall, us brave 'happy few.' There is an ugly patriotism that can sometimes define 'us' by contrast with the foreign 'them,' who surrender at the first sign of a fight and more generally cannot be trusted. In *England: An Elegy*, English philosopher Roger Scruton claims, "[t]here thus grew on English soil a patriotism not unlike that from which the word patriotism derives—the patriotism of the Romans, in which the homeland, rather than the race, was the focus of loyalty."[319] From Shakespeare, we hear that ours is a "blessed plot, this earth, this realm, this England,"[320] and William Blake explores the myth that a young Jesus, accompanied by Joseph of Arimathea, a tin merchant, travelled to what is now England and visited Glastonbury during his unknown years, founding a new Jerusalem.[321] Ours is a sacred land whose inhabitants understand the great privilege granted to them by being born British and therefore accept the great responsibility each and every one of us has to defend that land. The idea that some of our soldiers deserted threatens this defining myth.

Lazar argues that there is a value created by certain relationships and a failure to recognise this value as a factor in duty and following actions, is a moral wrong.[322] I believe this is where much of the emotional response around desertion comes from— it is the perceived failure to recognise the value of a relationship that people have with their community, perceived or otherwise.

There is an emotional response to the term deserter that is influenced by the relationship the individual hearing the term has with the nation state that the soldier is deserting from. For a British person, the act of deserting the British Army is a great treason, but when that same person hears of a desertion by another from a foreign army may see that act as a personal failing. Sandel claims that "[p]ride and shame are moral sentiments that presuppose a shared identity."[323] I feel more critical when it is a deserter from the British Army because it feels like an attack on my relationship with my country, my community, my relationship with my comrades and our shared values. I was less emotive about hearing about a US deserter, but as I feel I have a shared identity and a relationship of value with a country that has a special relationship with mine and with an ally there is a still a feeling of attack against that relationship. But my seeing it purely in these terms fails to recognise the other side of the relationship and duty equation, and that is one's duty to oneself.

Do all members of a society have a civic duty, simply by membership and not through a conscious choice, to give their life for the rest of the society, which is greater than the duty an individual has to themselves and their right to life? In the 1980s, in *A Theory of Justice,* American moral and political philosopher John Rawls describes a moral person as "a subject with ends he has chosen."[324] He would seemingly argue against the idea that membership of a society would imply a duty to be forced in to choices not freely chosen. To Rawls, the role of the state is to create a morally neutral environment (including an unrestricted as possible economy), where individual's rights are protected to allow them to pursue whatever life they so choose, unencumbered by ties we haven't chosen. In *Justice,* Sandel notes that these ideas taken together are "characteristic of modern liberal political thought."[325] Liberal here is used to mean Libertarian, rather than the opposite of conservative. The ideas remain powerful and influential today across the Western world and beyond. Most of us in twenty-first-century Western society believe we have a set of basic human rights that are owed to us, and this set is ever increasing to now include such things as the right to internet access.

Philosophers have debated the nature of human rights since at least the twelfth century, often under the name of 'natural rights.' These natural rights were supposed to be possessed by everyone and discoverable with the aid of our ordinary powers of our 'natural reason,' as opposed to rights established by law or disclosed through divine revelation. Much of what we take for granted now was only internationally enshrined at the end of the Second World War and because of said war. During the war, the Allies adopted the Four Freedoms—freedom of speech, freedom of religion, freedom from fear, and freedom from want—as their basic war aims. The United Nations Charter, signed in June 1945, "reaffirmed faith in fundamental human rights, and dignity and worth of the human person" and committed all member states to promote "universal respect for, and observance of, human rights and fundamental freedoms for all without distinction as to race, sex, language, or religion."[326]

When, however, the atrocities committed by Nazi Germany became apparent after the war, the consensus within the world community was that the charter did not sufficiently define the rights to which it referred. A universal declaration that specified the rights of individuals was necessary to give effect to the Charter's provisions on human rights. This became the Universal Declaration of Human Rights (UDHR), a declaration adopted by the United Nations General Assembly in 1948. It represents the first global expression of what many people believe to be the rights to which all human beings are inherently entitled. The Declaration consists of thirty articles which, although not legally binding, have been elaborated in subsequent international treaties, economic transfers, regional human rights instruments, national constitutions, and other laws.

Without considering if there are such things as rights that exist independently in the world, objective truths that are independent of law, most of us now believe, as Kant suggested, that each of us has the right to be treated as an end in ourselves and not as a means to something else. Indeed, some professional philosophers, such as the American philosopher Richard Rorty believe that the philosophical enterprise of attempting to give a rational justification for human rights is now unnecessary.[327] He claims that as human rights are such a deeply embedded fact of our culture, not just our law, that it renders this unnecessary. This is arguably challenged by increasingly pluralistic societies, the increasing popularity of more conservative interpretations of old religions and the rising authoritarianism of the 'post-truth' era. However, what does a society that does aspire to providing these rights do when its very existence is threatened, and threatened by an enemy so perverse that a negative value judgement of their proposed way of life is almost impossible not to make? It is not a thought many now of us now entertain (although we have seen in recent years that the perceived existential threat from Islamic extremism has led some to justify practices previously deemed unacceptable, such as torture, that treat people as means to an end).

In the Second World War, an individual's rights became secondary to the survival of the society. As we have noted the ends were seen to justify the means, civilians were not seen as ends in themselves, but means to achieve victory. Conscripting someone to go off and fight in a war, where the odds of survival were as low as they were in the desert at the time Alan was fighting, treated soldiers as a means to end. Many of Alan's most basic individual rights were removed when he was conscripted.

In *How to Live: A Life of Montaigne in one question and twenty attempts at an answer* by English philosopher Sarah Bakewell she quotes Leonard Woolfe's response to reading Michel de Montaigne, the French Renaissance essayist. Woolfe is reminded reading Montaigne as an adult of being asked as a child to drown some unwanted day-old puppies. He wrote the following:

> Looked at casually, day-old puppies are little, blind, squirming undifferentiated objects or things. I put one of them in the bucket of water, and instantly an extraordi-

nary, a terrible thing happened. This blind, amorphous thing began to fight desperately for its life, struggling, beating the water with its paws. I suddenly saw that it was an individual, that like me it was an 'I', that in this bucket of water it was experiencing what I would experience and fighting death, as I would fight death if I were drowning in the multitudinous seas.[328]

Woolfe went on to apply this insight to his memory of the politics of the 1930s. He observed that the world retreated into a barbarism that made no room for this small individual self. Bakewell notes that 'on a global scale, no single creature can be of much importance yet in another way these 'I's are the only things of importance.'[329] Without arguing either way regarding what means were justified to achieve the ends of stopping fascism, I think it is important to challenge the average person of today to think how they would feel if their individual rights, particularly their right to choose how to life their life and the right to be safe from physical harm, were removed for a greater good and they were thrown in the multitudinous seas of the war.

Sandel disagrees with Rawls, even before we get to such an extreme example as the Second World War. Sandel believes that as we live in increasingly pluralistic and interdependent societies, where the lives some choose come in to conflict with lives others choose. The state can only resolve these conflicts by taking a moral position and making a value judgement.[330] Furthermore, due to the fact we are rooted in a particular culture and have had particular experiences, we cannot help but do so. To Sandel, it seems impossible to remain neutral in terms of values and morals when faced with any number of issues, from abortion and stem cell research, to how we restrict radical imams from preaching what many in a society describe as not just offensive, but threatening to their way of life. More than this, Sandel believes we are not totally free to choice our own path. We have duties due to the past we inherit and the groups we belong to. He quotes from *After Virtue,* by British philosopher Alasdair MacIntyre, in which MacIntrye describes us as narrative beings, only capable of answering the question "what am I to do" by first answering the question "of what stories do I find myself a part."[331] For MacIntyre, the narrative aspect of moral refection is bound up with membership and belonging:

> We all approach our circumstances as bearers of a particular social identity. I am someone's son or daughter...I am citizen of this or that city...I belong to this clan, that tribe, this nation. Hence what is good for me has to be what is good for the one who inhibits these roles. As such I inherit from the past of my family, my city, my tribe, my nation, a variety of debts, inheritances, rightful expectations and obligations.[332]

Sandel notes that sometimes those who take pride in the past of groups to which they belong and feel a responsibility to continue the traditions and celebrate their victories do not realise that by the same logic they must also own the failures and mistakes of that past too:

> With belonging comes responsibility. You can't really take pride in your country and its past if you're unwilling to acknowledge any responsibility for carrying its story into the present, and discharging the moral burdens that may come with it.[333]

If Sandel is right, then we do have a commitment that we inherit through our circumstances rather than make by choice, but can anyone decide how great that commitment is? Those who give their lives for the country are held in a special esteem. If, however, they are just doing their duty, is that esteem deserved? Maybe it is because we feel that such a sacrifice is far more than just doing your duty, more than doing what you are civically obliged to do, and that what you are obliged to do stops short of the ultimate sacrifice. Surely there is a limit to the duty we all have to those with whom we have relationships? Maybe the relationship a mother or father has to child is limitless, but do we expect the duty to ones' country to be the same? In times of national crisis, we may need to rely on some, especially those in the armed forces, to make the ultimate sacrifice, but should we insist that all in the armed forces do? Maybe in a voluntary army we should, but when we begin to conscript, we are extending this to all (within some caveats—in the UK in the Second World War this included conscientious objectors, who were required to justify their position to a tribunal) in society.

Returning then to Alan II, a theoretical version of Alan who, whilst experiencing everything that Alan had experienced and placed in the same situation, did not suffer psychological injury. Lazar uses the following though experiment to examine the concept of associative duties, one that might have had literal relevance:

> Suppose A is at the beach and sees B struggling in the water. If A had no connection with B, then he might be required to take on x cost in order to save him. But if B is someone with whom A shares a valuable relationship— his son, say—then the cost that he ought to bear will be greater than x. So, suppose B is caught in a rip, and A judges he would be risking his life to save B. This would not be morally required were B a stranger (suppose), but may be required if A is his father, and they have a valuable relationship. This will of course depend on further details—A's prospects of saving B must be sufficiently high, for example—but the basic point should be clear.[334]

I believe there were two limits to Alan II's duty. The first is the physical and mental capacity he had. I think it is clear that Alan exceeded his capacity, but we are theorising that Alan II had not. The second is when the cost borne by him reached the value of any relationship he had with his community. Especially when the cost has not been borne equally. Going back to Lazar's thought experiment and placing Alan II as A, B becomes his comrades on the battlefield or in a more abstract way his family back home and beyond that his community and all his countrymen and women. This throws up an interesting question; should those troops whose families who were directly at risk from German aggression have a greater duty to fight than those whose families were not? The Tower Hamlets Rifles were described as "highly motivated,"[335] by Shipton, due to mainly coming from the East End, which was receiving the brunt of the German aerial bombing campaign. This risk could have arguably changed with the progression of the war, with a German invasion increasing the risk for many more.

If Alan II had deserted at the point Alan deserted it would have been at a point when, neither his comrades nor his family were being threatened. It is true that his comrades would again soon be threatened and would be one more soldier down, and his country was being threatened with potential invasion. I believe that Alan II had a duty and was obliged to take on x cost. The question then becomes—did Alan II pay that cost? Suppose Alan II is A, and B was caught in strong rip tide, but A had gone in to the water to rescue B every day for 551 days previously.

We are now on day 552. During this time, there were many other people—P—who knew B just as well, who were sitting back from the beach in a café, as many of the rear echelons of the British army inhabited the cafes and bars of Cairo, they had not entered the water once. On day 552, the rip tide seemed stronger to A than it had before, and the prospects of saving B seemed lower than any other time. Phrased this way, it seems clear that A had clearly got closer to paying x than P had done, and by not entering again he would still remain closer to paying x. Can A be blamed for not entering again? To me, it seems to hinge on how much you value the relationship between an individual and their country—if it is as valuable as father and son, then you may believe he should. If it falls slightly short of this, then you may not be so sure in your answer, especially if you yourself have never had to weigh up the value of you give your own life to the value you place on such relationship.

The accusation which to me is most difficult to defend when thinking about desertion has always been that—if others had done the same, it may have resulted in the Allies losing the war in North Africa at a vital time in the wider conflict. This is undoubtedly true. Without the sacrifice of so many who stayed to fight, the war would have been lost and a great evil would have won. The quote often credited to the eighteenth-century Irish statesman and philosopher, Edmund Burke (but unlikely to have been said by him in these words): "the only thing necessary for the triumph of evil is that good men do nothing" was never more true than in the Second World War.

But, despite of the difficult circumstances, some of which were the making of his own leaders, Alan II did not do nothing. He fought for a significant period (551 days). He fought on until he reached his limit, and is that not all we can ask? Many men did more and we should always be grateful to them—the war created many heroes, many who seemed almost limitless in their physical and mental abilities. But what of those who, for a multiple of reasons, and to varying degrees, don't reach the highest of standards or he reached their limit before others—are they all villains?

Not everyone behaves impeccably in war, and in many ways, war is an environment where normally admired virtues can be a disadvantage and some behaviours deemed immoral and even illegal can be praised. With each page of the war diary I turned, the harder I found it to condemn Alan or Alan II. The negative feelings I had around his desertion were steadily eroded by reading about the actions he had been a part of and the experiences he had to endure on our behalf.

Praise and blame are used to influence behaviour. We praise people for the good acts they do and we issue blame to create shame for the bad acts. To Kant, this black and white approach made sense. Kant saw us as having the potential to be rational agents if we check our subjective emotional impulses against the objective laws of reason. We each have equal access to reason, which can help us determine what this right course of action is, and we are each free to choose. We should aim to do the right thing, and to do it because it is the right thing, regardless of the end result or whether it is what we want to do. This approach does make some assumptions about the nature of free will, our capabilities to reason, and the nature of reason itself. It also places great demands on us as individuals.

Aristotle questions some of these assumptions and provides a potentially more realistic approach. He was not convinced that acts are entirely voluntary, or whether we should attribute them to solely a person or to also include other factors. He highlights various conditions that diminish our responsibility listing force of events, threats and coercion, ignorance, intoxication, and bad character.[336] Aristotle uses the example of a ship in a storm to demonstrate the force of circumstances. The sailors must throw the cargo overboard, destroying it, if the ship is not to sink causing their likely deaths. Aristotle argues that this action is not fully voluntary, and we would not blame the sailors for their actions. The loss of the cargo is blamed on an act of God, not the sailors or the storm. Aristotle uses this example to show the force of necessity under which we always live.

We are always constrained in our actions by circumstances, although it is often only in more extreme circumstances that notice this. Aristotle claims that interference from other people often has the greatest impact on how responsible we are for our actions. Looking at coercion and manipulation, Aristotle suggests that a central issue at stake in attributions of responsibility is the expectations that people have of one another.[337] The level of expectation we set for whether we give praise or blame is important. The standard must be set to a level that we can reasonably expect most people to be able to reach. As we will hear in the next chapter, and as one could see on social media during the trail of Marine A, there are some who believe that the expectations we set for those in the storm of the battlefield cannot be set by those who have not experienced the conflict.

In 1942, in the desert of North Africa what should we have expected Alan II to do? A sense of controllability, which Hamner believes was proved critical to soldier's combat effectiveness when it aligned their desire to stay alive with military useful actions, would have been almost non-existent. They had then been fighting for well over a year, well past the recommended

200-250 days,[338] exposed to relentless artillery barrages, dive bombing from enemy aircraft, and minefield crossings that made survival seem like a matter of random chance. They had also been living in harsh and alien conditions that took a constant physical and mental toll. Many were in a constant state of confusion around their own side's strategy devised by far off senior commanders, and lacked confidence in their own inexperienced and undertrained officers. The officers of the Tower Hamlets Rifles' were mostly bank clerks, office managers, teachers, and other such professionals, no doubt doing their best, but certainly not fulltime professional soldiers. There were many who also thought they were facing what seemed like a superior and better commanded enemy, and who would most likely have struggled to see any way in which a decisive victory could be won in North Africa, let alone beyond.

Then for Alan, sitting there in a bunker in the chaos of an earth-shaking bombardment, not knowing when the shell would detonate, knowing that it was all down to luck whether he survived or not. He had done nothing wrong to be in that position; he had done what he was trained to do in a bombard-ment, yet his life was then out of his own hands. He would have known there was nothing he could then do in terms of skills or drills that would keep him alive. This must have impacted him massively—even if we concede that we cannot say for certain that this incident caused a psychological injury that would have been present at the time of desertion, it is hard to argue there would not have any impact on him. There are few better examples of "battle's randomness" deciding "who was hit and who was spared."[339]

For Alan and his fellow soldiers, it must have been hard not to see the war at that point as a battle with fate itself, rather as a series of rational choices within their control. It would have been hard not to feel like the crew of ship battling a storm in rough seas with no land in sight. For nearly all these soldiers, they at some point, for one reason or many, would have asked themselves the question: why carry on fighting? For those who believed victory was out of sight, the only ways out would have appeared to have been death, serious injury, capture, or desertion. I would say that you could make a very strong case that both Alan and Alan II did what can be reasonably expected of them. There should not be shame associated with reaching your mental limit after enduring the experiences Alan endured under the circumstances that Alan endured them, and maybe the same is true for Alan II too?

What did some of those who fought on to the end think about those who left them— did they think they should be ashamed? In the diary of R L Crimp of the Second Battalion, the Rifles, he describes another member of his platoon, "Squirts," an "Old Soldier" as in one who was serving as a regular before the war started, as being "bomb-happy," which seems to be the colloquialism used by the Crimp and his comrades for shell-shocked. It apparently most obviously manifest itself in Squirts always wearing his helmet (he is rumoured to sleep in it) when no-one else ever bothers, and always digging his trench a foot deeper than everyone else. Just before a "big push" (which would have been the 2nd Battalion's action in Operation CRUSADER) he recounts, on 17 November 1941:

> This morning, a minor sensation. Squirts Mulberry has deserted! Two days ago he and another chap went in a truck to Mersa Matruh on an errand for the Company Commander. They were expected back the same night, but nothing's been seen of them since. Everyone's mildly surprised (it's an unheard of thing for an Old Soldier). 'Fancy Squirts bucking off! Didn't think he had the guts. Of course he was always ticking, but that was just natter. The other bloke must have out him up to it.' But no-one seems to bear him any rancour. 'Good luck to them both,' is the general sentiment.[340]

Whilst from the description Crimp gives of Squirts, it is highly possible that he was suffering from what we would now diagnose as PTSD (but obviously no attempt was made to diagnose at the time despite his behaviour been widely observed) it was not necessarily this that caused the other soldiers in the battalion to bear him no rancour. This did not seem to be considered and luck was wished to them both.

Alan was to have little luck in what came next for him and very little control. It is highly unlikely that a very strong case was made for Alan during his court-martial. Berghdahl spent five years in Taliban captivity, which is described in *Serial*,[341] and many would argue that served as more than enough of a punishment for any crime committed. At the time of writing, he is still waiting to hear whether he will be found guilty of any charges. From 29 July, Alan was held on close arrest until 2 September. There is no record of the trial other than the fact he pleaded not guilty, but was found guilty—which is on his service record. From his plea, the suggestion is that Alan himself did not feel he was guilty, but we will never know why he felt this. He may have believed he was going to come back so was only in fact guilty of AWOL; he may have seen himself as a psychological casualty; or he may have believed that he had in fact more than done his bit and should have been rotated out of theatre negating the need to desert himself. He may have just wanted to try and avoid the shame of the label deserter and the severity of punishment it would bring. We will never know; Alan never to spoke to his family about any of this.

In Glass's *Deserters*, he describes the trial of Steve Weiss, a US infantryman, who had enlisted aged seventeen in 1942.[342] Weiss had fought through Italy before being his unit was posted to the invasion of southern France. In France, he became separated from his unit in fierce fighting and was rescued by the French Resistance. He spent a time fighting with them and then the American OSS (a wartime intelligence agency of the US and a predecessor of the Central Intelligence Agency formed to coordinate espionage activities behind enemy lines), but he eventually had to return to his old unit, which had fought almost every day without rest during the month he was gone. When he re-joined his unit, only two men remained from the group that had been saved by the resistance. One told him he was a fool to come back.

Weiss deserted twice, returning once before leaving for good and turning himself in. His defence counsel Major Wilson did not ask him why he deserted while preparing his case; neither Wilson nor the divisional psychiatrist, who spoke with him briefly in the open and noisy medical post that was receiving casualties at the time, asked him why he would not go back to the front, but would risk the firing squad. The fact that he had fought on two fronts and that he volunteered to parachute into Germany with the OSS did not seem to count. When asked by the prosecution why he left his post for the first time, Weiss stated that "I broke down inside; the artillery shells were coming in and I shook all over and just went to pieces." When asked why he deserted for the second time he stated; "intensified artillery barrage. I went to pieces again."[343] The fact that it was likely he was suffering from battle fatigue was not explored by either the defence or prosecution. The nineteen-year-old Weiss later said he was too depressed to make his condition clear to the court. He was found guilty of desertion.

Les Pearce, the Regimental Secretary of the Military Provost Staff Association, told me that because of the Rehabilitation of Offenders Act they were not allowed to keep "Servicemen under Sentence" (SUS) details for longer than is necessary under the Act, which meant that they would only be kept for a maximum of five years.[344] This being the case, the MPS have no records or archives of the trial or that can confirm or deny the sentence. At the National Archives, I found Alan's court-martial record. Whether Alan should have been found guilty, the record states that he was, and it states that he was sentenced to death.

Chapter Eleven
The Glass House in the Sand

They're not shooting me for deserting the United States Army, thousands of guys have done that. They just need to make an example out of somebody and I'm it because I'm an ex-con. I used to steal things when I was a kid, and that's what they are shooting me for. They're shooting me for the bread and chewing gum I stole when I was 12 years old.

Eddie Slovik, January 1945,
near the village of Sainte-Marie-aux-Mines.

And what are you supposed to be - a brave man in a permanent base job?

Squadron Sergeant Major Roberts (Sean Connery), *The Hill*

There was just one soldier executed for desertion in the Second World War across the British and US armies. His name was Eddie Slovik and he was the first US soldier to be executed for desertion since the American Civil War. After initially being deemed unfit for duty in the US military due to his criminal record (built up over his youth in Detroit), Slovik was reclassified as fit for duty and drafted in 1943. In August 1944, he was dispatched to join the fighting in France. While on route to his unit, the 109th Infantry Regiment, the 28th Infantry Division, Slovik and another private he met during basic training became separated from their detachment when they took cover during an artillery attack and then failed to join the rest of the unit as they then moved out. The next morning, they found a Canadian military police unit and remained with them for the next six weeks. Slovik's buddy wrote to their regiment to explain their absence and their intent to re-join before he and Slovik reported back to their unit on 7 October. The US Army's rapid advance through the French countryside had resulted in many replacements having trouble finding their assigned units, so neither of them received any charge.

The following day, however, Slovik informed his company commander, a Captain Ralph Grotte, that he was "too scared" to serve at the front-line with a rifle company and asked to be reassigned to a rear area unit.[345] He told Grotte that he would run away if he were assigned to a rifle unit, and asked if that would constitute desertion. Grotte confirmed that it would and refused Slovik's request for reassignment. On 9 October, Slovik deserted. He walked several miles to the rear until he found a headquarters detachment, where he handed a handwritten note to the first person he came across, a cook. The note explained the situation:

> I, Pvt. Eddie D. Slovik, 36896415, confess to the desertion of the United States Army. At the time of my desertion we were in Albuff [Elbeuf] in France. I came to Albuff as a replacement. They were shelling the town and we were told to dig in for the night. The following morning they were shelling us again. I was so scared, nerves and trembling, that at the time the other replacements moved out, I couldn't move. I stayed there in my fox hole till it was quiet and I was able to move. I then walked into town. Not seeing any of our troops, so I stayed overnight at a French hospital. The next morning I turned myself over to the Canadian Provost Corp. After being with them six weeks I was turned over to American M.P. They turned me loose. I told my commanding officer my story. I said that if I had to go out there again I'd run away. He said there was nothing he could do for me so I ran away again AND I'LL RUN AWAY AGAIN IF I HAVE TO GO OUT THERE.
> —Signed Pvt. Eddie D. Slovik A.S.N. 36 896 415[346]

The cook summoned his company commander and a military policeman, who both read the note and urged Slovik to destroy it before he was taken into custody. Slovik refused. He was brought before the Lieutenant Colonel commanding the HQ, who again offered him the opportunity to tear up the note and return to his unit, promising no further charges if he did so. After Slovik again refused, the colonel ordered Slovik to write on the back of the note stating that he fully understood the consequences of deliberately incriminating himself and that the note would be used as evidence against him. Slovik was taken into custody. The divisional judge advocate offered Slovik a final opportunity to return to his unit in exchange for a suspension of charges. He also offered to transfer Slovik to a different infantry regiment where no one would know of his attempted desertion. Slovik, convinced that he would face only time in prison (which having already experienced jail time he considered it preferable to the frontline) declined both offers.

Slovik's court-martial was held a few weeks later on 11 November 1944. Slovik had to be tried by a court-martial composed of staff officers from other US Army divisions, because all combat officers from the 28th Infantry Division were fighting at the front. One of those staff officers, Captain Benedict B. Kimmelman writing some years later noted that, "[t]he trial took place during the worst time the division had endured, a stalemate in the Hürtgen Forest."[347] The Americans had been suffering heavy casualties as they tried to advance against a heavily dug in enemy. The site of the trial was a scarred two-story building in the village of Rötgen, Germany. It was a cold, grey day, with occasional snow showers, when the trial began at 1000.

Benedict noted that "the judges all were, like myself, staff officers. Up to that time none of us had truly served in the line or had had the job of commanding troops in actual combat. I was a dentist. Another was a lawyer in civil life...their appointments to serve on general court-martial were not unusual."[348] Slovik's defence counsel, a young staff captain, was not a lawyer, but he had served on previous court-martials. Benedict recalled that five witnesses were heard and that the cross-examinations were perfunctory. Captain Woods, announced that Slovik had elected not to testify and the defence made no closing argument. One hour and forty minutes after the start of the proceedings the verdict and the sentence were announced: Slovik was to be dishonourably discharged, to forfeit all pay and allowances due, and to be shot to death with musketry. The sentence was reviewed and approved by the division commander, Major General Norman Cota. General Cota's stated that; "Given the situation as I knew it in November, 1944, I thought it was my duty to this country to approve that sentence. If I hadn't approved it—if I had let Slovik accomplish his purpose—I don't know how I could have gone up to the line and looked a good soldier in the face."[349]

On 9 December, Slovik wrote a letter to the Supreme Allied commander, General Dwight D Eisenhower, pleading for clemency, but none was granted. Desertion had started to become a systemic problem in France, reaching levels seen in North Africa when Alan deserted. The Battle of The Bulge, the surprise German offensive through the Ardennes, began on 16 December causing a high number of casualties and putting a great strain on the morale of the infantry.. Eisenhower confirmed the execution order on 23 December, stating that it was necessary to discourage further desertions. The sentence apparently came as a shock to Slovik, who had been expecting prison, the same punishment he had seen meted out to other deserters from the division while he was confined to the stockade. The execution by firing squad was carried out at 1004 on 31 January 1945, near the village of Sainte-Marie-aux-Mines.

Several of those involved in the case, Captain Kimmelman included, had been taken prisoner in the Ardennes that December—in Kimmelman's case, after actions on 19 December that would later qualify him for a Silver Star. Kimmelman found out about the execution following his release from a German prison camp in the spring of 1945, when a soldier, recognizing him, cried out, "Hey, Captain, you know they shot Slovik!" At the time, he was in a souvenir shop in Paris, looking for a wedding anniversary gift to send home to his wife. He claimed to have been shaken by "the bitter bad news." Kimmelman who had now witnessed combat first hand wrote the following:

> My experiences in the Battle of the Bulge had totally changed my mind about the sentence. Assign me to that court now, I maintained, and I would not vote the death penalty, knowing that among the thousands of soldiers engaged there had to be dozens or even hundreds who would fail. At the trial in November I simply had not had sufficient experience or understanding of that fact.[350]

Kimmelman came to believe frontline offenses ought to be judged only by frontline personnel, which none of the judges at the time were. Kimmelman later wrote, "I should always have known that there cannot be a fair trial under unfair circumstances. Our lack of first-hand, close-up battle experience disqualified us as a jury of Slovak's peers. The legal inexperience of his defence counsel amounted to a failure to grant him the full benefit of his day in court. He did not receive a fair trial."[351]

Kimmelman goes on to note that the month following the trial the assistant staff judge advocate, European Theatre of Operations, Major Frederick J Bertolet, who was even further away from the front line, claimed in his review that the death penalty should have been imposed, not as a punitive measure nor as retribution, but to maintain discipline. Major Bertolet approved the decision on the grounds of bolstering discipline, rather than the individual merits of the case. Kimmelman concluded that he believed the endorsements of the death sentence were beyond the knowledge and competence of the reviewers and "did not address Slovik's culpability and the appropriateness of the sentence."[352]

An official comment, undated, from C Robert Bard, a colonel in the judge advocate general's office, provides the following: "During the period 1 January 1942 through 30 June 1948, 2,864 Army personnel were tried for desertion.... Of these, forty-nine were sentenced to death. Only one was executed."[353] Over a six-and-a-half-year period, then, reasons were found by those in higher authority to void the death sentences of forty-eight men found guilty of desertion. Kimmelman notes though that only in Slovik's case was no reason found: "Slovik, guilty as many others were, was made an example—the sole example, as it turned out. An example is a victim."[354]

At the time Alan received his sentence, most initial sentences handed out to British soldiers were quickly reduces to three to five year custodial sentences. Alan was briefly sent to MPDB (Military Prison & Detention Barracks) number 51, which was located in Jerusalem, before being moved to MPDB 50 in Cairo after a month, a prison described in *Mutiny at Salerno 1943: An Injustice Exposed* by Saul David, as the "brutal 50th Military Prison."[355] There are very little surviving records of what life was like in a MPDB. They were designed to be tough environments that would dissuade troops from seeing them as an easier option than remaining at the front. They were tough places both physically and mentally. The majority of those sentenced to spend time in a MPDB would not have wanted to have publicised the fact. People in glass houses, as well as not throwing stones, tend not to pen memoirs.

The majority of those who ran the MPDBs, particularly those with the harshest regimes, were also be unlikely to have wanted to share their stories, even if they felt justified in their treatment of the inmates, due to the crimes they would have had to commit to have been sent there. Ultimately, they spent the war punishing troops on their own side, while elsewhere others were committing acts of bravery in the face of the enemy. We have not necessarily wanted to hear stories about how badly treated our troops, who themselves had not lived up to the ideal we have created around the Second World War Allied soldier.

In Rifleman Crimp's diaries (which his book was based on), he tells of his friend, a Corporal Furze, having to escort a prisoner, a Rifleman Randell, to MPDB 50. Furze described how Randell was made to double around the yard in full kit being screamed at by a sergeant. Furse claimed that prison staff were "[w]orse than the Nazi SS and that's what we're fighting the bloody war against!"

It is highly likely that the same sergeant also screamed at Alan. Rifleman Crimp went on to say the following:

> It makes your blood boil to think of Randell, a normal bloke not shirking his share of the shite, being kicked around by sadistic thugs whose only virtue is a brutality which is counterpart to the cowardice which keeps them out of the front line.[356]

The MPS provided a rough guide to what the routine at a MPDB would have been.[357]

0530hrs	Reveille
	Slop Out and Washing
	Breakfast
	Daily Cigarette
0830	Work Detail after inspection
1230	Lunch
	Afternoon Inspection obituary
1400	Back to work details
1630	Return to Accommodation at
	Wash up
1730	Evening Meal
	Clean up
1830	Last Cigarette and Tea
1900	Lock up

I was told that the day would also have included drill, weapon handling and physical training (apparently known as physical torture by the inmates in the heat of the desert). There were also many rules—such as no smoking and no speaking to other inmates at all except for on communications parade, which was once a day and ten minutes in duration. The 1965 film, *The Hill*, set in a British army prison in North Africa in the Second World War starring Sean Connery, is one of the very few tales of life in a MPDB.[358] Sometime cultures find it easier to deal with parts of their history through fiction first, before they are ready to admit the events to the reality of official histories.

The film was based on a screenplay by Ray Rigby, who wrote for TV and had spent time in military prison. During the Second World War, Rigby served as a private with the British Eighth Army in North Africa, but got into trouble due to various nefarious activities, and spent two spells in British field punishment centres. His experiences there would later form the basis for his award-winning novel, which was later turned into the film. The hill of the title is a hill of sand that inmates were forced to run up and down during drill and physical training. One of the few other accounts of life inside a MPDB is from Glass's book, where John Bain describes life in a MPDB in North Africa, not 50 MPDB but 55 MPDB, Mustafa Barracks, just outside Alexandria. It too contains a notorious hill of sand. Bain describes been told to strip on arrival at the barracks by a Staff Sergeant Henderson:

> When Henderson barked the order for the naked and sweating men to run back and forth across the parade square, humiliation gave way to physical pain. The weight pressing on Bain's arms was almost impossible to bear, although he was a physically strong twenty-one-year-old with a prize-fighter's physique. For those with less stamina, it was worse. Henderson shouted; 'Get them knees up! Straighten them arms! Left-right, left...Right... wheel!' This went on relentlessly until the sun had nearly set, when Henderson ordered a halt and marched them to their cell.[359]

The next morning Captain Babbage, the camp commandant, told Bain the following:

You're soft and you're yellow. If you weren't you would not be here. You'd be with your comrades, soldering, fighting. Well you listen to me. You thought you'd leave the dirty work to your comrades. You'd have it nice and easy here. In fact I wouldn't be surprised if you don't wish to god you were back with your units. Wherever they are. We're going to punish you.[360]

Six weeks into Bain's time in Mustapha Barracks, a truck delivered three loads of sand. The SUSs had to pile the loads onto a corner of the drill square. The following morning the SUSs were issued with two buckets each and told to fill them and run to the corner of the square diagonally opposite. They were to repeat until the hill of sand was moved in its entirety from one corner to the other. They then had to move it back again. This became a daily occurrence along with the drill and physical training. Glass noted that this came to "epitomised the Sisyphean absurdity of their daily tasks." Bain called it the "sheer lunacy of the regimen."[361] In Greek mythology, Sisyphus was punished for his craftiness and deceitfulness, which included tricking Death and placing him in chains, by being forced to roll an immense boulder up a hill, only to watch it roll back down again, repeating this action for eternity. In *The Myth of Sisyphus*, the 1942 essay by the French Existentialist philosopher Albert Camus, he claims that when Sisyphus acknowledges the futility of his task and the certainty of his fate, he is freed to realize the absurdity of his situation and to reach a state of contented acceptance.[362] It is very hard to imagine any of the inmates of Mustapha Barracks reaching a state of contented acceptance.

Alan never mentioned to his family anything about life in a MPDB. Stephenie remembers watching a sub-titled version of *The Hill* in Italy, probably not too long after it originally came out, with Alan. At the time, she had no idea he had been in a detention centre in Egypt just like the one depicted in the film and could not understand much of dialogue. She remembers Alan saying that it was an accurate picture of what it was really like and that the Military Policemen (MP)s were "tough bastards." Stephenie did not think too much of it at the time, and when he later commented again on the MPs as he watched a Remembrance Sunday Parade and some MPs were shown on the TV walking past the cenotaph. She said she thought he meant the MPs in the main army prison in Colchester, where she knew he had spent time after the war, but with what she now knows he could have meant the MPs from MPDB 50.

Overall, Alan remained very nervous of the police through-out his life. When Alan was in hospital towards the end of his life, he had a reaction to morphine, during which he began to hallucinate. He hallucinated that he was back in military prison and that the guards were going to experiment on him and beat him up if he didn't get away. He tried to escape the hospital, but realised the nurses and his family wouldn't let him. He eventually became compliant and just sat in his clothes, waiting to be discharged the next day.

We cannot say for sure what conditions Alan had to endure in the prisons that held him, but we can say that when they came round the prisons asking for volunteers to join the Italian Campaign, he decided he would rather go back to the frontline than stay in detention. On his release, he was sent back to the Rifle Brigade, but not to his original battalion. The 9th Battalion had been disbanded and the remaining member scattered across the rest of the battalions within the Brigade. Alan was sent to the 2nd Battalion, to join, amongst others, Rifleman Crimp, who since Alan had been in detention had had a busy time of it.

Chapter Twelve
Snipe

Now this is not the end; it is not even the beginning of the end.
But it is, perhaps, the end of the beginning.

Winston Churchill

During Alan's time in prison, the war in North Africa (in which many of his comrades were still fighting) turned in the Allies' favour. His comrades, however, were no longer fighting as the Tower Hamlets Rifles or as the 9th Battalion, the Rifles. The battalion had been disbanded and its members re-posted to the other rifle battalions still in the fight; namely the 1st Battalion, the Rifle Brigade, the 2nd Battalion, the Rifle Brigade, and the 7th Battalion, the Rifles Brigade.[363] On 31 August 1942 Rommel, despite being short of ammunition and fuel, made what was to be his last thrust at the Delta.

Ultra-intelligence (the designation adopted by British military intelligence for signals intelligence obtained by breaking high-level encrypted enemy communications at the Government Code and Cypher School at Bletchley Park) gave the Allies warning of the attack. According to Strawson, the Allies "succeeded in luring the Panzers on to lines of concealed anti-tank guns" and managed to "surprise Rommel with the depth and complexity of their defensive minefields."[364] Unable to outflank the British positions, Rommel's right-hook came up against the 22nd Armoured Brigade on the Alam Halfa Ridge.

At Alam Halfa, the British changed the tactic of confronting tanks with tanks and instead employed the tactics which Rommel had used so successfully at Gazala. Allied tanks were used to draw the enemy onto a line of well-sited anti-tank guns sited on the ridge. It was the new 6-pounder anti-tank guns (which had a much more destructive impact on German tanks than their 2-pounder predecessors) of the 1st Battalion, sited on the Alam Halfa ridge, supported by artillery, which, along with the attacks from the air of the RAF, were critical in bringing Rommel's advance to a halt. By 3 September, having failed to break through, Rommel withdrew. Realising that no further advance was possible, he now ordered an extensive minefield to be constructed, from the Qatara Depression to the sea. For the next six weeks, this minefield was strengthened to confront the offensive which he knew must come from the Allies.

By this point General Montgomery was now commanding the Eight Army. Strawson notes the following:

> Montgomery's extraordinary impact on soldier, commander and politician is well established. In its most plain form it was that he seemed to know exactly what to do, explained it in terms which made everyone both clear as to what was required and convinced that it was right, and then went on to actually do it.[365]

Before Montgomery took over, Strawson claims that the men of the Eighth Army were "puzzled and confused." After he took over, Strawson quotes Churchill noting "a complete change of atmosphere has taken place...the highest alacrity and activity prevails."[366] Montgomery was also a meticulous planner and had the strength of character to resist the political pressure his predecessors had faced and refused to commit to the offensive until he had the right plans, and crucially, the right numerical advantage. Following the halting of Axis forces at Alam Halfa, Montgomery spent nearly two months building up his own forces, stockpiling resources, training his forces, and resisting constant pressure from Churchill to attack. By mid-October he was ready to go on to the offensive. The Eighth Army at El Alamein now consisted of 195,000 men and 1,029 tanks, and it had a short line of communications (which as we have seen played such a key role in previous advances) and air superiority. They faced an over-extended Rommel with 100,000 men and 496 tanks.[367]

According to Strawson, the second battle of Alamein was quite different from any other battle that had been fought in North Africa up to that point. It was in his words a "set-piece conventional affair."[368] Montgomery's plan saw XXX Corps in the north breaking the enemy's defences, clearing two lanes through the minefields. Once the "break-in" was achieved, the tanks of X Corps would exploit, striking quickly through the lanes to attack the rear Axis positions. By the full moon at the end of October (necessary to allow the tricky task of clearing minefields at night), Montgomery was ready. He issued a note to be read to all troops in the Eighth Army (below). In the note, he told his men that the battle that was just about to commence would be "one of the decisive battles of history."[369]

Montgomery's Message to the Troops

Alan is unlikely to have received this note in his cell in the MPDB. Glass notes that in Mustapha Barracks, "no news reached the inmates, apart from what little seeped through in censored letters from their family."[370] Rumours of the assault would no doubt have reached the prison and when it was eventually launched at 2100 on 23 October 1942. He may even have been able to hear the massive artillery barrage that marked the opening of this decisive battle. The bombardment, which occurred along the entire front, was one of the greatest ever seen or heard, and the largest since the First World War. The night barrage consisted of over 1000 guns firing into the moonlit, bright and clear night. In *The Fusing of the Ploughshare: the Story of a Yeoman at War*, author Henry R. Ritchie describes the scene:

> In some outlandish and fanciful way it was like a great big dream, a dream that was diffused and had no core. With the increasing tremor that threatened to split the earth there seemed to be too much noise, too many gun flashes and too many hanging clusters of parachute flares for it to be well founded and real.[371]

Due to the scale of the bombardment, even though Alan's cell was back from the front line it would have shook as the attack was launched as planned. As used to hearing both incoming and outgoing artillery as Alan now was, he would have surely recognised the magnitude of this bombardment and would have known a significant assault was occurring. He would have hoped it was the Allies attacking rather than another Axis offensive, but it is entirely possible he would not have been sure.

The battle in the north proved harder than expected. The engineers tasked with clearing a path through the minefields struggled to move at the pace required under constant and heavy fire, despite the smokescreen provide by Ritchie and his fellow yeoman. For the first forty-eight hours of the battle, the task of the three rifle battalions was protecting these mine-clearing parties, and traffic-control. On 26 October, Colonel Vic Turner of the 2nd Battalion was summoned to Brigade HQ.[372] The battalion was given the task of taking and holding objective

Snipe, the south-west spur of Kidney Ridge. The 24th Armoured Brigade would then pass through them and drive deep into the German positions. Colonel Turner, after becoming aware of a significant dispute between several units as to where his accompanying artillery barrage would fall, gave orders to his battalion.[373] They were to move by night through enemy-held territory and secure Snipe. At 2300, the battalion set off, with scout platoons leading in their carriers, and the rest of the battalion on foot.

It immediately became clear that the barrage was on a bearing different from the battalion advance. The battalion moved to re-align. Colonel Turner had estimated that after 2000 metres they would have reached their objective, but after 3000, metres the barrage still continued. Becoming increasingly concerned, he told his Forward Observation Officer (FOO) to get the artillery to fire a smoke shell on the objective. This landed a few hundred metres to the south-east. Turner made the decision to dig in where they were and ordered the battalion to take up an all-round defensive position. The success signal was sent back to the 2IC (Major Tom Pearson) on the start line, informing them Snipe was secured. The 2IC's party had been under constant bombardment and had taken casualties. On receipt of the success signal, Major Pearson spent the rest of the night ferrying forward the heavy support weapons and other battalion vehicles.[374]

C Company's Scout Platoon, under Lieutenant Dick Flower, was sent out on patrol to the west of Snipe and discovered a German leaguer position consisting of approximately thirty-two tanks and support vehicles. Lieutenant Flower decided to attack, destroying numerous logistics vehicles before withdrawing. By 0400, the battalion identified two groups of advancing enemy tanks. The anti-tank guns had only just arrived on the position and had not been properly sited. The crews of guns waited until the tanks were metres away before engaging and destroying the first two. The remaining tanks withdrew. By first light, a larger group was sighted only about 700 metres away. However, the

FOO, who had gone to look for a good OP position, had got lost in the dark and had not made it back. The battalion therefore had no direct communications with the artillery.

The battalion could see that they were not in fact on top of the ridge, which had been their original objective, but were in an incline just to the south. When asked by the adjutant whether they were in the right place or not, Colonel Turner replied, "God knows, but here we are and here we damned well stay."[375] As soon as it was light enough, the yet to be identified anti-tank guns opened fire, and within a few minutes, sixteen enemy tanks and self-propelled guns had been knocked out.

The anti-tank gun fire resulted in Axis return fire, which caused several casualties and destroyed three guns. A second barrage followed, but this time from tanks of the 24th Armoured Brigade. British armour was meant to join the infantry at Snipe and a separate objective Woodcock, but the failure to take Woodcock had caused confusion. As the tanks drove over a ridge, they saw a post surrounded by German tanks, and assuming it was an enemy laager, they opened fire. The battalion dispatched the Intelligence Officer in an open topped vehicle across the 1,500 metres of open desert to politely ask them to stop. By approximately 0800, the first tanks of 24th Armoured Brigade arrived at Snipe. At the same time, twenty-five enemy tanks were seen taking up positions about 1,000 metres away. The battalion's anti-tank guns knocked-out another three and the rest withdrew. Following this the whole area came under heavy and prolonged fire—this time from the enemy. This resulted in the destruction of seven tanks and three guns. The 24th Armoured Brigade's advance was halted and the elements of the brigade which had arrived on Snipe now withdrew leaving the three hundred or so riflemen of the battalion on their own.

At 0900, Italian Infantry massed to the south. With no artillery support to call upon, Colonel Turner again dispatched Lieutenant Flower and his scout platoon to "see them off,"[376] which they did, inflicting many casualties. At 1000, thirteen Italian tanks moved to attack Snipe. The anti-tank gunners destroyed twelve of these tanks causing the rest to withdraw. By 1100, further enemy shelling had destroyed half of the anti-tank guns, and the battalion had received numerous casualties. The battalion position was now isolated and receiving accurate and sustained fire from the enemy, so much so it could not receive a resupply. By 1200, conditions inside Snipe worsened in the midday heat as the number of casualties increased. At 1300, eight Italian tanks and several self-propelled guns advanced on the position. There was only one gun in the C Company, manned by a Sergeant Charles Calistan, which was able to engage. The rest of his crew, however, had crawled away to get more ammunition, and had been unable to return due to the heavy fire. Colonel Turner stepped up as loader and his platoon commander, Second Lieutenant Jack Toms, stepped in as No.1 on the gun. Sergeant Calistan waited until the tanks were 500 meters away, before destroying five tanks and one gun.

The remaining three tanks continued to advance. Calistan was down to his last two rounds. Toms ran to his Jeep, drove to another gun, loaded up some ammunition and drove back all under intense machine-gun fire. His Jeep was riddled with bullets, and eventually caught fire about ten metres from the gun. Toms, Colonel Turner, and a Corporal Barnett, who had joined them, started to carry rounds over to Calistan, who waited beside his gun. Colonel Turner was hit in the head and had to sit down. By now the enemy tanks were just 200 metres away. Calistan waited until they were about 150 meters away, and then knocked out all three with three consecutive rounds. During the lull that followed the destruction of all eight tanks, Sergeant Calistan used the bonnet of the burning Jeep to make mugs of tea for all. Colonel Turner was later to say that it was the best brew he ever tasted.[377] The citation for Colonel Turner's Victoria Cross, which was later awarded for his actions that day stated that:

> From early morning until late in the evening the Battalion was subjected to repeated attacks by nearly 100 German tanks, which advanced in successive waves, all of which

were repulsed with heavy losses to the enemy, 35 tanks being burnt out and a further 20 immobilised. Throughout the action Lieutenant Colonel Turner never ceased to move in turn to each part of the front as it was threatened. All day long, wherever the fire was hottest and the fighting fiercest, there he was to be found bringing up ammunition, encouraging his men and directing the fire of his guns. Finding a six-pounder gun in action alone of its platoon, the others having been knocked out of action, he himself acted as loader and destroyed five enemy tanks at point blank range. While manning this gun he was wounded in the head by a machine-gun bullet, but he refused all aid until the last remaining tank had been destroyed, when only one round of ammunition was left. His superb personal bravery and complete disregard of danger resulted in the infliction of a severe defeat on the enemy armour in one of the finest actions of the war, and set an example of courageous leadership which was an inspiration not only to the whole Battalion, which fought magnificently, but also to the entire Eighth Army, in the critical opening days of the offensive.[378]

At approximately 1600, the 2nd Armoured Brigade appeared on the ridge to the north east. Like the 24th Brigade before them, they hoped to use Snipe as a launch-pad. And like the 24th Brigade, they also shelled the battalion at Snipe. Colonel Turner later described this in typically understated language of the time as "the most unpleasant thing that happened on a thoroughly unpleasant day."[379]

Rommel saw the fighting around Snipe from his HQ. It had become clear to him that the main attack was occurring in the north. He therefore redirected his amour and selected the area around Snipe to launch his counter attack. A group of approximately 40 tanks moved to attack the 2nd Armoured Brigade on the ridge to the north east of Snipe. They moved across the battalion position in front of A Company and the 239th Battery. Anti-tank guns from the company and battery opened fire, helped by the tanks on the ridge. Approximately twenty tanks were destroyed and the enemy withdrew. Shortly after, a second group of fifteen tanks charged the battalion.

The battalion managed to man three guns and engage the enemy destroying six tanks. The rest withdrew, but continued to engage the position with machine gun fire. By late afternoon, about seventy Axis vehicles littered Snipe, and the 2nd Battalion had lost sixteen Bren Gun Carriers and ten guns. At 1844, the battalion learned that armoured reinforcements would be sent, but none arrived. The battalion destroyed radio codes to prevent them falling in to enemy hands in the expectation that they would soon be overrun. However, despite the desperate state of the battalion, the counter-attack stalled. As the light began to fade, enemy tanks moved to the north east, where some tanks were silhouetted against the horizon and the last anti-tank ammunition was used up, hitting one of them. Survivors from all over the position began to move towards the command post. They dragged the wounded with them under constant machine gun fire, which would have created a storm of dust on the position and temporarily drowned out the moans of the injured. During the early evening, the remaining enemy tanks started to withdraw west, a withdrawal that did not end until the final surrender at Tunis, 1500 miles later in May 1943.

That night, what was left of the battalion withdrew. Seventy-two of the 300-strong force had been killed or wounded. At Snipe, the battalion gained one V.C. for Colonel Turner, who later claimed that it was in recognition of the performance of the battalion rather than his personal contribution, but also one Bar to the D.S.O., one D.S.O., one Bar to the M.C., four M.C.s, three D.C.M.s, one Bar to the M.M., and ten M.M.s.[380]

It can be argued that Snipe was the turning point of the Battle of Alamein, which itself can be argued as the turning point of the whole war. The actions of the battalion were unarguably heroic, and would have no doubt given the wider Eighth Army a morale boost, as well as preventing Rommel from seizing back momentum via the failed counter-attack. There was still a week of heavy fighting to go before the final break-through, but, after the defeat of Rommel's armour at Snipe by around three hundred riflemen from the 2nd Battalion and their accompanying support arms, Allied forces did not take another step back.

After Snipe, the 2nd Battalion joined the pursuit of Rommel's forces until they were held up in heavy rains (unusual for November), as they tried to flank them and cut them off west of Mersa Matruh. The 1st Battalion remained part of the pursuit and reached Benghazi by 22 November. As with Tobruk, and Msus before that, they found that the enemy had already moved through and continued on to the west.

By December, the Eighth Army had passed through Mersa Brega and taken Agheila. It was the furthest west Allied forces had reached in the desert. The Anglo-American First Army had now landed behind the frontline forces (Operation TORCH), and there was sufficient transport to ensure administrative backing that had been lacking in previous advances this far west. The advance continued, forcing the remnants of the Afrika Korps and Vichy French forces (who then changed sides) through modern day Libya, including involvement in the battle to take Tripoli, and into Tunisia, where they were involved in the battles at the Maruth Line, the main German defensive line just inside the border, where they first had to soak up German counter attacks before moving across the Tunisian plain with the First Army who had ridden out attacks on their beachhead and on to Tunis for the final battles of the war in the desert. The battalions of the regiment played a minor role in the hard battle against a cornered, but significant force of Germans and Italians in terms of the bigger picture of the Fall of Tunis, but Hastings claims that the closing stages of the war in North Africa were "full of incident for everyone who took part,"[381] as they were involved in some of the final acts of the desert war in the hills outside Tunis, where eventually:

> Amid scenes more remarkable than those that attended the end of the war in Europe the Afrika Korps, the German Tunisian Army and the whole of the Italian armies in Africa, with all their equipment...fell at one sudden, dramatic blow into our hands.[382]

On 16 May, a dinner was held in Tunis attended by sixty-four officers from the four rifle battalions. Hastings notes that, "with champagne at 2s. 6d. a bottle [the occasion] was celebrated in a suitable fashion."[383] For four months in the summer of 1943, no battalion of the regiment were involved in combat. Then on 22 September, the 1st Battalion shipped to England to prepare for D-Day and the invasion of North West Europe. The remaining three battalions waited in North Africa and the Middle East until they were gradually drawn into the war in Italy as Alan would be too. The 2nd Battalion, which Alan would join, would only do so after it first moved to Tripoli, the Delta, Syria, Palestine, the Delta again, Syria again, and the Delta again, where they moved from one camp to another until the Greek mutiny caused them to hurry to Alexandria on 8 April.

Chapter Thirteen
"E la Guerra"

It is humiliating to remain with our hands folded while others write history. It matters little who wins. To make a people great it is necessary to send them to battle even if you have to kick them in the pants. That is what I shall do.

Benito Mussolini

When Alan joined the 2nd Battalion, after he was briefly posted to the 10th Battalion, he joined a battle hardened and celebrated unit, as not only a replacement, but also as a deserter. It is unlikely that it was easy to win the trust of his new comrades. He may have recognised some men from his basic training or from his 9th Battalion service, but the attrition of the war in the desert would have made this unlikely, or at least limited it to only a handful of men.

Alan was also likely to have been in a weakened physical state after the prison diet and tough physical punishments. The battalion was in Alexandria dealing with the Greek mutiny. They were charged with guarding the mutinous Greek sailors and servicemen holed up inside the PKP Barracks and the Greek Marine Ministry. Not that anyone outside Alexandria would have known about the mutiny, as at the time strict censorship meant that no reference was made to it until a week after its outbreak. On 19 April, B Company "made a demonstration in front of PKP Barracks to impress those inside with the numbers guarding them."[384] They estimated there were 3800 Greek troops inside, 40 percent of which were mutineers and 60 percent loyalists. The latter were kept under guard by the mutineers. According to L S Stavrianos writing in 1950 in *The American Slavic and East European Review*, it was "a complex movement involving cabinet members, senior commanders in the Army and Navy, and, leftist elements in the rank and file."[385]

On 23 April, the battalion (less B and C Companies who remained in their OPs) moved to the concentration area for Operation RABBIT. From there, they launched an attack on the Greek OP, which is described as successful in the battalion war diary.[386] It, however, resulted in death of a Major Copeland. The following day, the Greeks asked for an Armistice and marched out of their camp. The battalion spent the day disarming and processing the surrendering Greeks. According to Stavrianos, although the mutiny was short lived, it had far reaching political repercussions. It resulted in the resignation of the cabinet, and via the Lebanon Conference, the formation of a national unity government. It was this government that would return to Athens in 1944 as the Germans retreated. By 26 April, the battalion had moved to transit camps in preparation for move to Italy, where they would re-join the war, again in a pursuit of retreating Germans, but this time over very different terrain in a new theatre of operations.

Hastings, writing in *All Hell Let Loose*, noted that as the end game in North Africa was playing out Churchill was very aware that it was still the ever increasingly resentful Russians fighting the Germans alone in mainland Europe.[387] He therefore began to push hard for an invasion of Italy. The US chiefs of staff were unhappy about diverting strength from the prospective French campaign, which they judged was the quickest way of winning the war, but in Washington they acknowledged that the Allied forces were not ready to commit to a landing in north-west Europe in 1943. Not wanting significant Allied forces to remain inactive in England until the preparations for D-Day were complete, and due to the lack of other credible objectives an Italian Campaign became the focus of the strategic planners after January 1943 when Churchill's delegation secured American agreement to a landing in Sicily, which would then be used as a jumping off point for an invasion of mainland Italy. The Italian commitment remained subject to an understanding that come autumn 1943, several divisions would be withdrawn, for redeployment to Britain to prepare for D-Day. The British planners assured their American counterparts it would be a quick victory.

The Allies had correctly assessed that a significant portion of the Italian population wanted Italy out of the war by early 1943. Hastings quotes Iris Origo, the American-born writer who occupied a castle in southern Tuscany in April, claiming:

> A marked change has come over public opinion. The active resentment and dismay which followed upon the Allies' landing in North Africa and the bombing of Italian cities has given place to a despairing apathy.[388]

The Allies were sure that Italy was close to quitting the war. Ultra Intelligence also indicated that the Germans did not intend to stand and fight in southern Italy, but instead withdraw to hold a mountain line in the north. As late as 27 July 1943, the British Joint Intelligence Committee correctly forecast an imminent Italian surrender, but mistakenly assumed (mainly due to Ultra Intelligence, who had stated as much, as well as their lack of appreciation of Hitler's tendency to frequently change his mind) that Hitler's forces would thereafter withdraw to a defensive line in the north. Churchill's chiefs of staff were more cautious, anticipating some German reinforcement of Italy. But Allied operations launched amid British assurances to the Americans of a swift victory, which later resulted in American bitterness when this did not materialise and heavy casualties were caused by the stiff German resistance.

It was originally hoped the invasion might take place in early summer 1943, but German resistance in the final battle for North Africa pushed back the Sicilian invasion target date to July 1943. The planning phase of the operation did, however, see one of the most successful deception operations of the war. In what was given the codename Operation MINCEMEAT, the corpse of a supposed Royal Marine Officer would wash ashore in Spain after a faked plane crash at sea, carrying faked secret documents suggesting an Allied invasion of Greece. The assumption was that the Spanish, although officially neutral, would pass the documents to the Germans.

On 19 April, the Royal Navy submarine HMS Seraph set sail, arriving at a point about a mile off the coast of Spain, near the town of Huelva, by 30 April. The British knew that there was an Abwehr agent (German military intelligence) in Huelva who was friendly with the Spanish officials there. In *Operation Mincemeat: The True Spy Story that Changed the Course of World War II*, author Ben Macintyre describes how on-board the submarine was the corpse of a 34-year-old Welsh man named Glyndwr Michael (acquired from a coroner in London on the condition that the man's real identity would never be revealed), dressed up as a Royal Marine.[389] Post-mortem Michael had become Acting Major William "Bill" Martin, born 1907, assigned to Headquarters, Combined Operations. As a Royal Marine, he could wear battledress rather than a naval uniform (uniforms were tailor-made by Gieves of Savile Row, and they could not have a Gieves tailor measure a corpse). The rank of acting major made him senior enough to be entrusted with sensitive documents, but not so senior enough that anyone would be expected to know of him. The name Martin was chosen because there were several Martins of approximately the same rank in the Royal Marines. Inside his coat carried a snapshot of Pam, his imagined fiancé (actually a clerk in MI5), two love letters, and a jeweller's bill for a diamond engagement ring, a letter from his father, a letter from the family solicitor, and a letter from the joint general manager of Lloyds Bank demanding payment of an overdraft. There were other items, including a St. Christopher's medallion, a used bus ticket, ticket stubs from a London theatre, a bill for four nights' lodging at the Naval and Military Club, and a receipt from Gieves for a new shirt (this last item was an error; it was for cash, and officers never paid cash at Gieves, but the Germans did not notice it). His dog tags were marked RC (indicating he was a Roman Catholic), to deter the Spanish authorities from conducting a proper autopsy. This was before DNA testing and other biometric techniques were available.

These days such an operation would not be possible. In the world of biometrics pretending to be someone else in person is much more difficult.

Martin was then given a briefcase containing the key faked secret documents. The main document of these was a personal letter from 'Archie Nye' (Lieutenant-General Sir Archibald Nye, Vice-Chief of the Imperial General Staff) to 'My dear Alex' (General Sir Harold Alexander, commander of 18th Army Group in Algeria and Tunisia). Nye was asked to draw up the letter himself to ensure authenticity. The letter covered several sensitive subjects, to explain why it was being hand-carried rather than sent through regular channels. On the Allied plans in the Mediterranean, the letter referred to Operation HUSKY as the invasion of Greece by troops from Egypt and Libya under General Sir Henry Maitland Wilson (Commander-in-Chief, Middle East). Two assault beaches and some of the assigned units were named. The letter also mentioned a second planned attack, Operation BRIMSTONE, for which the cover target was Sicily. This implied that Alexander's forces in Tunisia would invade Sardinia, as this was the only other plausible target.

In the early hours of 30 April, the HMS Seraph surfaced off Spain. The body was held in a steel canister, which had been filled with dry ice and sealed up. When the dry ice sublimated, it filled the canister with carbon dioxide and drove out any oxygen, preserving the body. The Seraph's commander, Lieutenant Bill Jewell, had told his men that the canister contained a top secret meteorological device. Jewell had the canister brought up on deck, then sent all his crew below except the officers, who were then briefed on the secret operation. They opened the canister, fitted 'Major Martin' with a life jacket, and attached his briefcase with the papers. Jewell read Psalm 39, although a burial service was not specified in orders; the body was then gently pushed into the sea for the tide to carry it ashore. Half a mile to the south, a rubber dinghy was thrown overboard to provide additional evidence of a plane crash. HMS Seraph then continued on to Gibraltar. The body was found that morning by a local fisherman and taken to Huelva.

The body was handed over to the British Vice-Consul, and 'Major Martin' was buried in a cemetery in Huelva. A Major Martin appeared in the list of casualties published in *The Times*. By coincidence, the names of two other officers who had died when their plane was lost at sea were also published the same day, giving credence to the story. The Admiralty also sent several messages to the naval attaché about the papers that Martin had been carrying. The attaché was urgently directed to locate the papers, and to recover them at all costs, but at the same time avoid alerting the Spanish to their importance. The Germans' most senior Abwehr agent in Spain became aware of the papers, and although they were briefly lost in the Spanish system, the Germans got hold of them and accepted them as genuine.

Hitler himself became convinced by the fake documents, which reinforced his own concerns for the region. He disagreed with Mussolini, who believed Sicily would be the most likely invasion point, and insisted that any attack against Sicily would be a feint.[390] Resultantly, the Germans diverted much of their defensive effort from Sicily to Greece. Rommel was sent to Greece to assume command. The Germans transferred a group of 'R boats' (German minesweepers and minelayers) from Sicily and laid additional minefields off the Greek coast. They also moved three Panzer divisions to Greece. The Italian navy was also moved to cover the anticipated upcoming Allied invasion of Greece.

Operation HUSKY was eventually launched on 10 July 1943 when 2590 warships and transports began to disembark 180,000 Allied troops on the coast of Sicily, the British in the east and the Americans in the south west (even at this point, the Germans remained convinced that the main attacks would be in Sardinia and Greece).[391]

The Combined Chiefs of Staff appointed General Eisenhower as Commander-in-Chief (C-in-C) of the Allied Expeditionary Force, with General Alexander as his deputy with responsibility for the planning and execution of the invasion. Strong winds wreaked havoc with the airborne plan, causing many gliders to fall into the sea—sixty-nine out of 147 that took off from Tunisia were lost, drowning 252 paratroopers. Four Italian divisions offered little resistance on the beaches, which was lucky, as many troops were put ashore in the wrong places. Hastings notes:

> [E]ven some Germans showed little fight: an American paratrooper who landed helpless and alone amid one of their units was amazed when three enemy soldiers approached him. Their leader said in perfect English, 'We surrender. For three years and eight months we've been fighting all over Europe, Russia and North Africa. That's long enough in any army. We're sick of it all.[392]

Mussolini had insisted that an Italian, General Alfredo Guzzoni, should control Axis forces in Sicily (the German General Kesselring commanded in the rest of Italy). Hastings concludes that it was a command that Guzzoni was not capable of. There were, however, two German formations on the island, who were reinforced by elements of a third. They committed themselves to the fight and fought determinedly. Ultimately Axis counterattacks, notably against the American beachheads, were easily repulsed. Even the German units, however, were not immune to panic and wide-scale dereliction of duty. Hastings notes that the commander of the Luftwaffe division, General Paul Conrath, wrote furiously on 12 July the following:

> I had the bitter experience of watching scenes during these last few days which are unworthy of a German soldier... Personnel came running to the rear, crying hysterically, because they had heard a single shot fired somewhere in the landscape... 'Tank panic' and the spreading of rumours are to be punished by the most severe measures. Withdrawal without orders and cowardice are to be dealt with on the spot, if necessary by shootings.[393]

The German withdrawals were dwarfed, however, by the large numbers of Italian troops surrendering to the Allies. There were widespread reports of Italian officers abandoning their troops and those men handing themselves over to the Allies on mass, often celebrating as they did as if it was the end of term before the summer holidays.[394]

Some Americans responded brutally to this, and in two separate incidents on 14 July, an officer and an NCO of the US 45th Division extra-judiciously executed large groups of surrendering Italians. One, Sergeant Horace West, who killed thirty-seven with a sub-machine gun, was convicted by a court-martial, but later granted clemency. The other, Captain John Compton, assembled a firing squad that massacred thirty-six Italian prisoners. Compton was court-martialled but acquitted. Fearing reprisals against Allied prisoners, General Eisenhower suppressed disclosure of both incidents. Hastings notes that if Germans had been responsible, they would have been indicted for war crimes in 1945, and probably executed.[395] It appears these were relatively isolated incidents, and it is not difficult to imagine (but in no way condone) that, seeing the enemy who had very recently killed one's comrade laughing and joking, someone suffering from the impacts of conflict or a pre-existing disorder could have been provoked to violence.

On 24 July, Mussolini summoned the Fascist Grand Council, which then passed a no confidence vote in him. The following day, King Victor Emmanuel, who had summoned Mussolini to become the country's youngest Prime Minister, ordered his arrest. In the end, Mussolini, Europe's first fascist leader, went quietly seemingly more concerned to save his own skin than continuing the fight or preserving any legacy for his National Fascist Party (*Partito Nazionale Fascista*). *Fascista* is derived from the Italian word *fascio*, meaning a bundle of rods, and it was Mussolini's use of it that gave us the word fascist. The fascists came to associate the term with the ancient Roman *fascio littorio*—a bundle of rods tied around an axe, which was used as a symbol of Mussolini's party.

According to Hastings, the ex-Duce spent the ensuing weeks of captivity eating prodigious quantities of grapes, reading a life of Christ, and attending mass for the first time since childhood. Hastings suggests that it is doubtful that he much relished his "rescue" by Otto Skorzeny's Nazi paratroopers on 12 September at Gran Sasso.[396] The operation, named Operation OAK, was described by Churchill as "most daring." While the airborne operation was personally ordered by Hitler, and Mussolini was notionally restored to power in German-held northern Italy, it is likely that both Hitler and Mussolini knew that Italy was a lost cause by this point. By the time the axe was taken from the bundle, the rods were already scattering.

The political upheaval in Rome persuaded Hitler to order the evacuation of Sicily in early August after US forces had missed an opportunity to cut off a Panzer division that was withdrawing eastward and the British had been held up by intense fighting at Primosole Bridge, where the Durham Light Infantry incurred 500 casualties in repeated attempts to take the bridge. The Germans withdrew eastwards, fighting a succession of further delaying actions. On the night of 11 August, the Germans began to ferry their forces across the Straits of Messina to the Italian mainland. Although Ultra flagged the enemy's intention, neither the Allied air forces nor the Royal Navy intervened effectively to prevent the Axis from withdrawing 40,000 German and 62,000 Italian soldiers together with most of their tanks and supplies. By 17 August, the Germans completed their withdrawal from the island in what must be seen as a missed opportunity by the Allies and a great success for the German naval planners.

Due to their naval supremacy, the Allies were able to land wherever they wished. The deciding factors included needing a landing site that could be supported by air from Sicily and needing a landing site that would allow the Allies to quickly move on to seize a major port south of Rome to then use as a supply base. This meant that the landing would be around Naples. The challenge initially came from the physical geography of southern Italy rather than the enemy. Throughout the campaign, the Allies would battle the terrain and the weather as much the German defenders.

The southern Italian coast consists of shallow beaches covered by steep mountains. The only beach wide enough to land two army corps (British X Corps and US VI Corps) together was at Salerno, whose plain was bisected by two rivers (which was at the time recognised as being a potential issue, but the assumption was that the Germans would not make a stand south of Rome, so a significant counterattack that could use exploit these features to split Allied forces was not assessed as likely). Therefore, the Allied assault on the Italian mainland would comprise of a main landing at Salerno on the west coast in Operation AVALANCHE, and two supporting operations in Calabria and Taranto, where the 2nd Battalion would land later (Operations BAYTOWN and SLAPSTICK).

The invasion began on 3 September, when the Canadians of the Eighth Army landed in Calabria without meeting resistance. Kesselring, commanding the German defence, had decided to fight his first engagement further north. Five days later, on 8 September, Marshal Badoglio's new government in Rome announced Italy's surrender. This raised hopes that there would be a quick conclusion to operations in the south of Italy,[397] hopes that would soon be dashed.

On 9 September, the main body of Lieutenant General Clark's Fifth Army landed at Salerno. There was initial success on the extreme left of the landings, where US forces cleared the vertiginous and ruggedly beautiful Amalfi coast resort villages and secured the Chiunzi pass. However, elsewhere, Kesselring chose to launch a series of counter-attacks with the experienced Panzer division charged with defending Salerno. The landed forces found themselves penned in four small beachheads, under intense fire from artillery located on higher ground at the rear of the beaches. The Germans were reinforcing from elsewhere in in southern Italy quicker than the Allies were landing and soon had a significant numerical advantage.

On 13 September, Kesselring's forces did what the Allies hoped they would not and drove a wedge between the two corps, exploiting the gap created that by the two rivers. The advance reached a mile and a half from the sea and within a short distance of Clark's HQ before it was halted by heavy bombardments from Allied guns. Clark, fearing disaster, proposed re-embarking his forces, but he was overruled by Eisenhower and Alexander. For hours, chaos dominated the beachhead, especially after darkness fell. "In the belief that our position had been infiltrated by German infantry, [American troops] began to shoot each other," wrote a British eyewitness, who then further elaborated:

> We crouched in our slit trench under the pink, fluttering leaves of the olives, and watched the fires come closer, and the night slowly passed... Official history will in due course set to work to dress up this part of the action at Salerno with what dignity it can. What we saw was ineptitude and cowardice spreading down from the command, and this resulted in chaos.[398]

The Scots Guards official history acknowledged "a general feeling in the air of another Dunkirk.[399] It was a combination of naval gunfire and intense bombing from the air that turned the tide on the beaches of Salerno, allowing the Allies to survive the initial German onslaught long enough to land enough forces to gain the advantage. Hastings notes that once again, Allied firepower had turned the scale.[400] Every movement by Kesselring's forces was met by a storm of shelling and air attacks. The poor Allied showing at Salerno, however, convinced Kesselring that his forces could use terrain ideally suited to defence to fight a significantly long delaying action in the Italian peninsula, longer than perhaps he had thought before the landings. Hitler agreed, and scrapped his earlier plan for a strategic withdrawal to the northern mountains. Churchill's goal of dragging German troops away from the Eastern Front and reducing the number of forces available for the defence of France was achieved by the opening up of the Italian front, but the

Allied planner's assessment of a quick and relatively straight-forward advance up the soft scenic underbelly of Europe was woefully over optimistic. Hastings notes:

> The stage was set for eighteen months of slow and costly fighting in some of the most unyielding country in Europe. Kesselring settled himself to conduct a series of defensive battles, which the Allies found painfully repetitive. At each stage they bombed and shelled the German positions for days before their own infantry advanced into machine-gun, artillery and mortar fire. After days or weeks of attrition, the Germans made a measured withdrawal to a new mountain or river line, protected by demolition of bridges, rail links and access roads. Everything of value to the civilian population as well as to the Allies was pillaged or destroyed. It was estimated that 92 per cent of all sheep and cattle in southern Italy together with 86 per cent of poultry were taken or killed by the retreating army. With the malice that so often characterised German behaviour, Kesselring's men destroyed much of Naples's cultural heritage before abandoning the city, burning whole medieval libraries, including the university's 50,000 volumes. Delayed-action bombs were laid in prominent buildings, where they inflicted severe casualties after the city's liberation.[401]

It was into this costly fighting that the 2nd Battalion would shortly be thrown. Much of this fighting was overshadowed by events elsewhere in Northern Europe, after a further amphibious landing occurred in Normandy, but what is discussed even less is the plight of the Italian people, who now found themselves on the receiving end of brutal treatment from their former ally and being liberated by former enemies. This situation caused severe material hardships for everyday people and created a confusing and uncertain environment, with Italians now fighting on both sides, or fighting for neither, seeking instead retribution and power in the vacuum of the collapse of Mussolini's reign. In *Naples '44*, Norman Lewis' brilliant memoir of his time in a Field

Security Section of the British Intelligence Corps in Naples in-between September 1943 to October 1944, the author captures, often with great compassion, the reality of life in Italy as the Germans withdrew, including the personal impact it had on him. Writing on witnessing a group of starving blind orphans entering a restaurant in Naples, Lewis claims:

> The experience changed my outlook. Until now I had clung to the comforting belief that human beings eventually come to terms with pain and sorrow. Now I understood I was wrong, and like Paul I suffered a conversion—but to pessimism. These little girls, any one of whom could be my daughter, came into the restaurant weeping, and they were weeping when they were led away. I knew that, condemned to everlasting darkness, hunger and loss, they would weep on incessantly. They would never recover from their pain, and I would never recover from the memory of it.[402]

Reading Lewis's descriptions of his attempts to mediate in local power struggles and how he would often end up the pawn in historic arguments he was unaware he was part of reminded me of our attempts many years later to unsuccessfully untangle the resurfacing grievances and local politics in post-Saddam Iraq. Reading Lewis should have been required reading before deployment, rather than stumbled-upon reading afterwards. Alan would not only briefly experience intense fighting in little known battles, but would, like Lewis, also witness first-hand the impact of the final years of the war on the people in one village in Italy, just from a different viewpoint. Alan would cross the Rubicon that Lewis never fully did and become one of them.

By the end of September, as Norman Lewis was arriving in Italy, thirteen Allied divisions had started to move up Italy slowed—at several points to a complete standstill—by German delaying operations. One of the first major obstacles faced was the Gustav line, which ran across Italy from just north of where the Garigliano River flows into the Tyrrhenian Sea in the west, through the Apennine Mountains to the mouth of the Sangro

River on the Adriatic coast in the east. There were also two subsidiary lines, the Bernhardt Line and the Hitler Line. These ran much shorter distances from the Tyrrehnian Sea to just north east of the town of Cassino, where they merged into the Gustav Line. The centre of the Gustav line crossed the main route north to Rome at strategically crucial Highway 6. It followed the Liri Valley and was anchored around the mountains behind Cassino. Above it stood a hilltop abbey of Monte Cassino, founded in AD 529 and lying in a protected historic zone, which dominated the valley entrance and gave the defenders clear observation of potential attackers advancing towards the valley mouth. It was to be the scene of what became known as The Battle of Monte Cassino. *Monte Cassino*, Matthew Parker's book covering the battle opens with the following:

> Not since Belisarius in AD 536 had anyone successfully taken Rome from the south. Hannibal even traversed the Alps rather than taking the direct route from Carthage. Napoleon is credited with saying 'Italy is a boot. You have to enter it from the top.' The reason was the geography south of Rome. High mountains are bisected by fast-flowing rivers. The only possible route to the Italian capital is from south is up the old Via Casilina, now route six. Eighty miles south of Rome, this road passes up the valley of the Liri River. This was where the German commander, Kesselring, chose to make his stand. Towering over the entrance to the valley was the monastery of Monte Cassino.[403]

Parker goes on to describe in great detail the costly series of four major assaults that began after the Allies had reached the Gustav Line in December. The first assault was launched on 17 January and the last, involving twenty divisions attacking along a twenty-mile front, on 18 May. In between the first and second assaults there was the controversial bombing of the abbey. The Germans had manned some positions set into the steep slopes below the abbey, but had claimed that they would not occupy the abbey.

Repeated accurate artillery attacks on Allied assault troops caused senior Allied commanders to conclude the abbey was being used by the Germans as an OP. If they were not, it seemed inconceivable to the Allied commanders that if the next assault was successful the Germans would be able to resist using it as part of their defences. If occupied, it would be incredibly difficult to shift the defenders from inside the abbey's thick stone walls. The high tonnage of explosives that would be needed could only be dropped from the air, which would be too inaccurate to have Allied troops anywhere near (when it occurred some bombs landed several miles away from target close to Clark's HQ). So, it was marked for destruction, the Allies citing 'military necessity.' For the Allies, the principle of military necessity effectively justified any damage to cultural heritage, except that which offered no distinct military advantage. Weighing up the loss of an historical building or the potential loss of further Allied lives if it were to be used by the enemy, the Allies made the decision to destroy it.

On 15 February, US bombers dropped 1400 tons of high explosives on Monte Cassino. The abbey was levelled; however, German forces then proceeded to occupy the ruins and establish strong defensive positions in them. Over 200 Italian civilians were killed who were sheltering within the abbey. There were no Germans soldiers among the dead. The destruction of the abbey was met with criticism from the Vatican, and the debate around how necessary the bombing was remains controversial today.

The First World War had seen wide-scale destruction of the cultural heritage of Europe, so by the beginning of the Second World War there had been several international laws and treaties introduced attempting to avoid this in future conflicts. However, despite these, the Second World War saw more destruction on the world's cultural heritage than any other war in history. Much of this was due to the use of air power on both sides to an extent not seen before in history. The principle of military necessity was arguably stretched to a much greater degree with the development of 'area bombing,' which instead of targeting specifically identified strategic targets, such as military forces, armament factories or railyards, targeted whole cities. Wide-scale cultural damage, as well as loss of life, was wrought on historic cities in the United Kingdom, France, Germany, and Japan. Officer Commanding-in-Chief RAF Bomber Command during the height of the Allied strategic bombing campaign against Germany, Arthur Travers Harris, widely known as 'Bomber' Harris, was clear about what he was trying to achieve, even if politicians, including Churchill, were uncomfortable with openly admitting to it:

> [T]he Combined Bomber Offensive...should be unambig-uously stated [as] the destruction of German cities, the killing of German workers, and the disruption of civilised life throughout Germany.... the destruction of houses, public utilities, transport and lives, the creation of a refu-gee problem on an unprecedented scale, and the breakdown of morale both at home and at the battle fronts by fear of extended and intensified bombing, are accepted and intended aims of our bombing policy. They are not by-products of attempts to hit factories.[404]

To Harris, there was no German cultural artefact or building that was worth the life of one British soldier:

> To my mind we have absolutely no right to give them [the area bombing raids] up unless it is certain that they will not have this effect. I do not personally regard the whole of the remaining cities of Germany as worth the bones of one British Grenadier.[405]

In a 2013 speech, Irina Bokova, director-general of United Nations Educational, Scientific, and Cultural Organisation (UNESCO), when speaking about the destruction and looting of cultural property in Syria, argued the importance of attempting to protect a country's cultural heritage:

> I am keenly aware that in the context of a tragic humanitarian crisis, the state of Syria's cultural heritage may seem secondary. However, I am convinced that each dimension of this crisis must be addressed on its own terms and in its own right. There is no choice between protecting human lives and safeguarding the dignity of a people through its culture. Both must be protected, as the one and same thing—there is no culture without people and no society without culture.[406]

As the Allies advanced through Italy, Eisenhower issued an order to all commanders:

> Today we are fighting in a country which has contributed a great deal to our cultural inheritance, a country rich in monuments which by their creation helped and now in their old age illustrate the growth of the civilization which is ours. We are bound to respect those monuments so far as war allows.[407]

The US military also established the American Commission for the Protection and Salvage of Artistic and Historic Monuments in Europe to coordinate protection of works of cultural value in 1943 for the advance through Italy. This unit, depicted the George Clooney film *The Monuments Men*,[408] was formed of a group of officers whose job was to advise commanders about cultural heritage sites, and argue the case for protecting such sites when the military argued there was a necessity of possible destruction. It was an argument won by military necessity at Cassino, but continues today, where whether the bricks and mortar or the abbey should have been destroyed is a bigger debate as to whether the flesh and bones of all those thrown at the slopes of Monte Cassino should have been destroyed.

The line was finally broken after the fourth assault, but at great human cost. The capture of Monte Cassino resulted in 55,000 Allied casualties, with German losses estimated at around 20,000 killed and wounded. It had now become clear that the Italian Campaign would be a long and difficult conflict, where victories would often be hollow when the cost of victory and the proximity and difficulty of the next defensive line was considered. It was not just the major defences that caused the Allies difficulty either. The Germans used every available means to stall the advance from cutting down trees to block roads, laying extensive minefields and rigging everything they could with improvised booby traps. "All roads lead to Rome," said Alexander ruefully, "but all the roads are mined."[409]

According to the Imperial War Museum, in an attempt to break the deadlock at Cassino, the Allied High Command had been planning another amphibious operation, codenamed Operation SHINGLE, which would take place alongside a renewed offensive on by the Fifth Army.[410] The objective was to land further up the coast behind the Gustav Line, compelling the Germans to pull troops back from Cassino. Churchill was a keen supporter of the plan, but his commanders were less keen on attempting another risky amphibious landing, especially after the near disaster of Salerno. The original plan anticipated landing only one division, but General Clark demanded the invasion force be doubled in strength. Churchill insisted that British forces be involved as well. For a location, they chose the resort town of Anzio, some 30 miles south of Rome.

The plan was shelved in December 1943, but Churchill pushed successfully for it to be reinstated. General Sir Harold Alexander stressed the need to strike out from Anzio to capture the strategically important Alban Hills, which dominated Highway 6 and Highway 7. These were the main German supply routes to Cassino and the western end of the Gustav Line. Clark, no doubt influenced by his experience at Salerno, was more concerned with establishing a bridgehead that could withstand the inevitable counterattacks. Major General John Lucas, the man entrusted with tactical command of the operation as officer commanding the US VI Corps, advocated a cautious approach. The landing was finally launched on 22 January, four days after a new US Fifth Army attack on the Garigliano and Rapido rivers near Cassino. They achieved tactical surprise, and the landings were virtually unopposed. Many German units had been deployed further south to counter the attack on the Garigliano. By the end of the day 36,000 troops and 3200 vehicles had been delivered ashore.

A US reconnaissance jeep patrol found the way open to Rome, but the cautious mind-set of the commanders meant the opportunity was missed. Instead, the Anglo-American Corps confined itself to a narrow perimeter (approximately seven miles deep), dug in and waited for the counter attack. The Germans obliged and which the Germans fiercely attacked repeatedly.

Kesselring redeployed the 14th Army from its bases near Rome and summoned reinforcements from northern Italy, France, Germany, and, from the Gustav Line. By 25 January, 40,000 German troops had surrounded the Allied beachhead. It was only on this date that Lucas attempted to push out from the beachhead; his lack of drive in these first days was to become the cause of subsequent controversy. But the Imperial War Museum notes that the cautious approach may not have been entirely misplaced, as the Garigliano-Rapido offensive had by now been halted.[411] Lucas believed that if his forces pushed on to the objectives at the Alban Hills they would be isolated and risk destruction, rather than causing a German withdrawal from the Gustav Line they would still holding. A week after the landings, the Germans had amassed approximately 71,000 troops versus 61,000 Allied troops. As well as numerical disadvantage, the Allies were exposed on a low-lying marshland with sparse vegetation, which offered little cover from the extensive German barrage.

On 30 January, Lucas again attempted to break out. After days of intense fighting resulting in heavy losses, all the Allies had to show for their losses was a narrow, two and a half mile salient into the German lines, which they nicknamed 'the Thumb.' Over 700 US troops were killed or captured on the offensive on the right flank, whilst on the left flank, in the attack that created the Thumb the Sherwood Foresters took 70 percent casualties and lost all their officers. On 7 February, the Germans launched a major counterattack against this salient. After suffering 1400 casualties, Allied forces withdrew from the Thumb. By 10 February, all the gains that the Allied break out attempts had managed were lost.

During the rest of February, the Germans launched two massive counter-attacks. The assault cost the Germans 5400 casualties. Some Allied units broke, streaming in flight towards the rear—and so too did several German ones, in the face of epic Allied artillery fire (the Allies expended 158,000 rounds defending the first counter-attack alone). Both counter-attacks failed to drive the Allies back into the sea, and the losses the Germans endured forced them to eventually return to the defensive.

The fighting in March and April became restricted to tactical level skirmishes, artillery exchanges, and night patrols in no-man's land. The similarities to the fighting on the Western Front during the First World War was not lost on the troops who had to endure it. The number of non-combat injuries began to steadily rise as the trenches dug in the low lying marsh land filled with water and caused trench foot, while mosquitos spread Malaria and other diseases, which would be a feature of the whole campaign. Alan himself would suffer from Malaria later on.

As preparation for the fourth and final battle was underway at Cassino, the battalion war diary notes that on 29 April the 2nd Battalion embarked in two halves for Italy.[412] B and S and half of HQ Company went on the SS Derbyshire and A and C and the other half of HQ Company went on the SS Circassia. In the Imperial War Museum, there is a war diary of one R L Crimp who was in B Company, the 2nd Battalion, entitled *The Overseas Tour of a Conscripted Rifleman - Italy 29th April to 17th March 1945 R L Crimp*. On 30 April, Crimp describes his feelings about leaving the desert behind:

> Away at dawn [30th April] and it's a relief to get out on the open sea. Watch the yellow strip of Egyptian shore reced-

ing astern, trying to make a complete cognition of the fact we're leaving the Middle East for good st last. No more sand and mirage, no more leaguers and columns, no more burgoo and pawny rations, no more tarantulas and scorpions, no more gazelles, jeboahs and shit-beetles, no more Cairo and Alex, no more bints and wallahs, no more ackers and bucksheesh. Farewell Capuzzo, Maddalens, Mechili! Goodbye Tobruk, Benghazi ad Mersa: and so long, all you lads on the Blue, under your lonely desert mounds![413]

The crossing lasted four three days, and the 2nd Battalion the disembarked at Taranto on 4 May and moved to a transit camp. Crimp notes that "everyone is thrilled with the European freshness of and familiarity of things" but, "immediately on arrival there are rumours of action within three weeks." Between the 5-6 May, the CO took a party of nineteen officers and seven ORs to Gissi, where they would join standing parties of the 11th Battalion KRRC on the front line and also arrange for billets for the Battalion HQ and C Company at Gissi, A Company at Furci and S Company at San Budno. From 5-14 May, the rest of the battalion remained at Taranto to draw up with stores and vehicles. Parties went to Naples and Bari to do this. Crimp notes that on 7 May the battalion was re-equipped with new 15-cwt trucks. He also reports that the "manpower state is being remedied likewise. Just before leaving Alexandria a sizeable draft fresh out from England came in, and another batch arrived yesterday."[414] Crimp notes that most of the officers changed too resulting in "a garnish of brightly green pips." The battalion trained with route marches and range shoots, acclimatising themselves. By the 14 May, Crimp claims the battalion is ready and that they were told that they would be "moving up tomorrow." The question they asked themselves at this point was to where; "to which Front/ The Eight Army's or the American's Fifth's?" To begin with, during the 15-16 May, the main body of the battalion moved up to Guglionesi. On the way, B Company passed Serracapriola, which Crimp describes as "one of the most perfectly sited villages imaginable (at least from an aesthetic point of view)."[415] Numerous accounts of the war in Italy note the beauty of the scenery between the violence of the fighting. In Albert Camus' *The Myth of Sisyphus*, he tells us that, "[i]n Italian museums are sometimes found little painted screens that the priest used to hold in front of the face of the condemned men to hide the scaffold from them."[416]

For Camus, the use of the small screens depicting religious scenes, known as *tavolettes*, held at the end of a black sleeve, was an analogy that described the way we hide from ourselves the absurd nature of all our fates. For soldiers like Crimp and Alan, the beauty of the scenes in front of them may have offered them moments of brief distraction, but mostly the beauty of the Italian countryside in moments between the shelling and death would have seemed incongruent with the violence that was always round the corner.

Between 17-19 May, they undertook training at the boating and rafting school, which would provide them with few useful skills for the fighting in the hills of central Italy that was to come next. Contained within the war diary is a Training Instructive (No.4) from 15 May, which states that there were; "two main roles the battalion which the battalion will be required to perform at any time in Italy:—

a. The holding of a sector of the front during a static period or in pauses during the general advance.

b. Participation in an armoured pursuit force in which elements of the battalion will almost always be included in the vanguard as the infantry component.[417]

On 21 May, the battalion received orders to move to an area five miles north of Capua, which they reached on 23 May. At Capua, a new brigade was formed, consisting, for the first time in its history, of the three battalions of the regiment all together (the 2nd Rifle Battalion, the 7th Rifle Battalion, and the 10th Rifle Battalion). It was to be called the 61st Infantry Brigade, commanded by Brigadier Adrian Gore and part of the 6th

Armoured Division. On the same day, Crimp at the more tactical level was pleased to note the return of an old friend:

> [T]his evening a surprise: Randell, hot on our heels (or wheels), returns to the fold. Laden with kit, up he comes 'with the rations,' all the way from the Egyptian Glasshouse. As customary, part of his sentence was remitted for good behaviour. Just in time for the Push, in fact, and some say he should have played his cards a bit more cleverly. But he reckons he's lucky to catch us up at all.[418]

However, as some soldiers re-joined, some left.

The Recollections of Rifleman Bowlby by Alex Bowlby is a first hand account of life in D Company, in a third battalion of an unnamed rifle regiment moving through the Italian Campaign.[419] Its title a nod to *Recollections of Rifleman Harris,* a memoir published in 1848 of the experiences of an enlisted soldier in the 95th Regiment of Foot in the British Army during the Napoleonic Wars.[420] The book provides the viewpoint of one of Wellington's foot soldiers at a time when so many were illiterate (Harris dictated it to a former officer as he himself could not write). Harris mentions dozens of men whose history is no longer remembered and whose names would otherwise be lost, and records the details of daily ennui in the language used by the soldiers of the time. The author, Bernard Cornwell, used the memoir as a source for his "Sharpe" series, which was serialised for television by ITV in the UK and starred Sean Bean. Bowlby's obituary in *The Daily Telegraph* revealed that the 3rd Battalion was actually the 2nd Battalion, the Rifles, Alan's battalion in Italy, with whom Bowlby, an ex-public school boy serving as soldier, also served.[421] He begins his account in April when Alan would have also joined the battalion. In the last weeks of May, as the battalion prepared to move up into the line he recounted the first time, but not the last time, that some of his colleagues deserted:

> He [O'Connor] ran back shouting 'They buggered off! Ernie Cross and Joe Bates. Them and three others!'

O'Connor enjoyed the incredulous shouts of 'No!' (Cross had been my section commander, and Bates had also belonged to it) the added 'They took a three-tonner full of food and petrol with them!'

Everyone laughed except Baker [Corporal Baker - section-commander]. When Rifleman Cooper shouted 'Good luck!' Baker snapped his head off.[422]

On the 24 May, the CO held a conference on the re-organisation of the battalion. Due to the mountainous nature of the country now in front of the Allies, it was infantry battalions that were going to be the key to the advance with armour playing a supporting role. They hoped that the advance would be rapid requiring the infantry to be mobile; however, if there was a hold up like there already had been at Cassio, the vehicles of a motor battalion would quickly become a liability. The formation of the new brigade was therefore going to be a compromise. The key compromise was that the 2nd Battalion's troop carrying vehicles that carried the motor platoons, such as the one Alan had driven in North Africa, were replaced by a smaller number of three-ton vehicles driven by the Royal Army Service Corps drivers. One carrier platoon would be retained with one anti-tank platoon, and one mortar platoon would be formed. Together with the other remaining heavy weapons these would join HQ Company. R Hasting's notes that this entailed a fundamental change in outlook.[423] Alan would have had to face the fact that what he had been trained, and mainly learnt through experience in the desert, to do, would no longer be his role.

The battalion spent between the 25-28 May re-organising along these lines. After hearing the good news on the 25 that "the Brits, French, Indians and New Zealanders are cracking Cassino and the Gustav Line," Crimp heard about the changes on 26 May, noting "nasty rumours that most of the company vehicles are going to be taken away, likewise those of other companies. The battalion is losing the greater part of its transport." He records on the following day how unpopular the changes were:

Nearly all the vehicles go today. The most disgruntled people are naturally the drivers, who've gained their jobs mainly by long service and now must revert to ordinary infantry duty. The prospect now of an entirely new set up - footslogging, fixed sword foolery and the like— comes as a shock, especially as we will be up to our eyes in it presto poco. Told by company commander that contact with the enemy is going to be 'a good deal closer than on the Desert.[424]

The battalion moved out on the 29 May in their new formation to join the 10th Battalion in the Liri Valley. That evening the battalion received the task of picqueting the hills east of Acre to prevent the enemy infiltrating the Corps main axis. On 30 May, the CO ordered them to take over positions held by the 1st Guards Brigade and the 17th Indian Brigade. The war diary notes that the battalion moved off along Route 6 in heavy traffic, completing the relief by 1630. Crimp, however, gives a more vivid description of the journey, which took the battalion through Cassino. He describes "a sickening sight of shattered houses and splintered trees."[425] Bowlby describes how in the late afternoon:

We passed through the outskirts of Cassino. Tanks and carriers lay around like burnt tins on a rubbish heap. A row of black crosses, topped with coal-scuttle helmets, snatched our pity. The smell— the sour-sweet stench of rotting flesh— cut it short. Instinctively I realised I was smelling my own kind, and not animals. I understood what they must feel like in a slaughterhouse. These dead were under the rubble. If we could have seen their bodies it would have helped. The unseen, consecrated dead assumed a most terrifying power. Their protest filled the truck. We avoided one another's eyes.[426]

For those like Bowlby and Alan driving through the ruins, it must have been difficult not to feel that civilisation was collapsing around them. Crimp goes on to describe how the battalion sets up camp that evening under the monastery which stands "without a sign of life on its hill, an impervious sentinel at the entrance to the Liri Valley."[427] The diary notes that clearance patrols were sent out as the enemy was still retreating along Routes 6 and 82 and odd pockets of para troops remained in the hills around Santo padre. One patrol returned the following morning bringing five escaped POWs or deserters they had met.[428]

While this was happening, one of the decisive battles of the campaign was being fought. The Anglo-American Corps were finally breaking out from the Anzio beachhead. Operation BUFFALO was launched on 23 May. The US 1st Armoured Division drove a hole through the German defences, while other Allied formations staged diversionary attacks. The town of Cisterna fell on 25 May, and by the end of May, VI Corps was in the Alban Hills, threatening Valmontone and Highway 6. The US advance was now in significant enough numbers to threaten the rear of the enemy opposing The Eighth Army.

At this point, Clark controversially decided to change the main axis of his advance.[429] Instead of advancing north towards Highway 6, he advanced towards Rome via Highway 7. He ignored orders from his senior commanders, who wanted him to cut off the retreat of the German 10th Army from the Gustav Line. The 10th Army, aware of the danger, sped up their withdrawal as Clark fought his way through the Caesar Line on the left flank of the Alban Hills. Clark was determined that the US Fifth Army, and not the British advancing from the south, should be first into Rome. The US 45th Infantry Division, supported by the 1st Armoured, battled its way towards Campoleone, but by 31 May, the advance had stalled. It was then left to the US 36th Infantry Division to exploit a lightly-defended route through the centre of the Alban Hills near Velletri. This then allowed US forces to cross over the hills and outflank the Caesar Line.

Clark ordered the advance towards Valmontone and Highway 6 to resume. On 1 June, Valmontone was captured by and Highway 6 was secured. By now, a link-up had been made with

US II Corps troops advancing from the Garigliano. They had breached the German defences, and the road to Rome, which was soon after declared an open city by Kesselring, was open for Clark to march in unopposed 22 years after Mussolini and his National Fascist Party and his 'blackshirts' had done the same at the end of their March on Rome to seize power. The 10th Army escaped to take up positions on the Gothic Line, ready to fight another bloody battle at great cost to Allied and Axis lives.

On the same day that Highway 6 was cut, the CO of the 2nd battalion held a conference on the points raised by administrative and transport problems in the mountains at Coldragone.[430] By 3 June, the battalion has passed through the 7th Rifle Battalion, who had taken casualties during their advance, and established a line at Trevigliano accompanied by the Engineers to deal with demolition and mine clearance. Crimp recalls hearing a church bell ringing, which he believed was the work of fifth columnists (meaning at this point fascist sympathisers). Shells followed the ringing. One landed on a house in the village and "begins burning amid sounds of lamentation from women's voices."[431] This would have most likely been the first time Alan heard the terrifying noise of enemy shells falling since his time in the desert. We cannot know what memories and feelings this would have triggered in him.

The next day, it was the 2nd Battalion's turn to lead the advance to contact, but as they formed up ready to push off the Divisional Commander changed the plans after hearing the enemy had rapidly withdrawn. The commander, General Vyvyan Evelegh, decided that it was the time to put the Armoured Brigade in the lead. The battalion's task was now to mop up behind the armour, which meant clearing villages on the high ground one side of the axis of advance, beginning with Trevigliano, where B Company was greeted briefly by Spandau fire. A Company leapfrogged B Company on to Fiuggi, which they cleared quickly with limited opposition. They took approximately thirty prisoners, including some rounded up by the military police and the field security section (similar to the one Norman

Lewis would have served with), who were with the leading troops.

Hastings notes that the job of mopping up now became more difficult due to a build-up of traffic on the narrow and cratered road.[432] He describes how S Company was involved in the clearing of the village of Piglio in the afternoon. The war diary reveals that by the early evening, A Company had reached Piglio where they were held up by "increased opposition" when the tanks of the 26th Armoured Brigade had by-passed and that after that passed through the village the battalion HQ, B Company and S Company moved up and set up a patrol harbour.[433] According to Hastings, the enemy troops opposing the battalion at this point were Austrians from the 44th Division, who did not fight with much determination; however, as they withdrew, they moved on to high ground overlooking the road. The 2nd battalion's transport and Reserve Company attracted the attention of an enemy OP and suffered two spells of "very accurate shelling." The diary notes that as C Company were then sent out on patrols the diary notes that B and S Companies were then shelled in their harbour location "at first moderately and then severely."[434] This resulted in multiple casualties, including the deaths of Captain P C Brealy at the scene and a Capt. C H Blackham, Royal Army Medical Corps, who subsequently died of his wounds and according to the diary "five ORs." In total, seven were killed and eighteen wounded. Hastings points out that this occurred when the leading tanks were now some twenty miles ahead and one was understandably lulled into a false sense of security.

Alan would have been reminded that as in North Africa there was never anywhere that they were safe, even away from the frontline. Crimp describes the shelling in more detail:

> The next few hours are extremely unpleasant. Jerry be-
> gins by systematically plastering the whole area,
> obviously trying to whack the vehicles, then rumbling our
> hide-out, concentrates on the ditch. Wherever he spots
> any movement, over comes a box-salvo, and the ditch is

writhing with a daisy chain of chaps crawling backwards and forwards to empty the part on which he's dropping...practically all the shells fall on either side of it [the ditch], but it is nerve-wracking enough to hear them scream over and crash nearby. Our knees are sore through constant crawling, and our clothes rough with sweat and dirt. One officer and three men killed and ten wounded. There was a direct hit on a Red Cross ambulance killing the Red Cross orderly—a quiet chap, belonging to an ambulance unit, composed, before the US entered the war, of American volunteers wanting to help the allies in the only way then possible.[435]

That night, A Company were heavily mortared. Then the following morning, on 5 June, the battalion received orders to move north east of Rome along the 6th Armoured Division's main axis of advance. When the lead elements of the 2nd battalion had passed Serrone, the battalion hit a delay. During this delay, a party of around twenty enemy soldiers tried to mortar the road from an area to the north of Serrone. The battalion returned fire until civilian sources informed the battalion that the enemy had retreated. During the action, one of the battalion's carriers overturned and a Lieutenant D F Ware was killed along with one OR.[436] In the first pages of *Recollections*, Bowlby describes how he lands up in a Mr Lane's platoon. He describes him as having "warmth, dash, and his sense of humour made itself felt in whatever the platoon did. We loved him."[437] On 5 June, Bowlby describes the same events as the war diary:

> As we stepped on to the road we heard the roar of Bren carriers. Mr Lane was in the leading vehicle. We had hardly any time to remark on his arrival when a white-faced mortarman rushed out of the lane.
> 'Mr. Lane is dead!' he gasped.
> The platoon stood very still.
> 'He's dead?' said O'Connor at last. His voice sharp with disbelief.

'Carrier overturned - crushed 'im. The signaller's 'ad it, too. Young Knocker White was driving. 'e went into a skid-'

The mortarman's voice cracked. Meadows stepped forward, and put an arm around him.

'Easy, lad, easy,' he said.

'What happened to Knocker?' Someone asked.

'Thrown clear. When 'e saw what 'ad 'appened he near went off his nut. Started blubbing, then scarpered. Two of the lads are trying to find 'im.'

The platoon still hadn't moved. They looked like figures carved in stone.[438]

Mr. Lane of Bowlby's account was Mr. Ware (Bowlby did not use the real names of the fellow members of his battalion). According to the Commonwealth War Graves Commission, Lieutenant Derick Flowers Ware, was 27 years old when he was killed. He was the son of Walter Flowers Ware and Ethel Marguerite Ware of Twickenham, Middlesex. According to the London Gazette of 5 February 1943, he had originally commissioned into the Essex Regiment. He is buried at the Cassino War Cemetery along with 4,270 other Commonwealth servicemen of the Second World War, 289 of which are unidentified.[439]

The advance then resumed and slowly proceeded throughout the night. Bowlby describes sitting on the tailgate of the truck as it moved through the night and smelling the wildflowers of the Italian countryside until the smell suddenly changed to one of decay. When the smell reached a pitch that made him want to vomit, the convoy stopped. On debussing, Bowlby found "two bodies puffed up like Michelin men."[440] Turning away from the bodies, he found a pile of unsent letters, sealed and addressed in German. Bowlby recalls that "their poignancy struck me like a blow,"[441] even more so than the bodies lying all around. He kept three of the letters, written by those who had been trying to kill him and had killed some of his friends, with the intention of trying to post them on. It is not clear if these were letters were just normal letters home from the front or the last letters, those missives soldiers write in case they do not make it home that say all things they never said when alive.

The following day, 6 June, Crimp's entry in his diary records news of one of the events of the war: "great news today! A second front has opened with an invasion of Normandy. At last."[442] After this date, known to the operational planners and now in the history books D-Day, the focus would be on North West Europe, even though the fighting in Italy would continue on. After spending the day of 6 June in harbours conducting maintenance, Crimp's company received news on 7 June of a pocket of enemy resistance firing onto the road and causing a traffic block at Lunghezza. Platoons from S Company were sent out to investigate, but identified no German troops after patrolling throughout the night. The battalion was now in sight of Rome. Crimp describes his irritation at being so near and yet so far from the great city, that Clark had entered unopposed three days previously.[443]

After spending another day in maintenance on the evening of 9 June the CO gave orders for advance behind 26th Armoured Brigade towards the Divisional objective Terni. Crimp tells us that the general outline of pursuit was now clear to all, that being the Fifth Army up the west coast, the South Africans on their right, the division that the battalion was part of moving up through central Italy, with the Polish Corps holding the right flank.[444] The battalion moved out on 10 June, but the advance did not progress at the intended speed, meaning that the battalion had to harbour in positions that left their vehicles too close to the enemy.

Bowlby writes of being caught in a private battle as a single German gun shelled the battalion, increasing its rate of fire as the three Priests (US self-propelled artillery vehicles) thirty yards behind their harbour returned fire. He describes the guns of the Priest's making a noise like the "crack of doom."[445] While the shelling dragged on throughout the afternoon, hour after hour, Bowlby watched two ants struggle with each other and the ledge of his shell scrape. He also heard Baker yelling at Coke, and when he looked over to the trench where the shouting came from, he saw Baker sitting on Coke's chest, waving his fist under his nose, telling him, "No one is going to fuck off from my section!"[446] Bowlby confesses that if he had known the shelling duel would have gone on for a further five hours at that point he would have wept.

At 1700, the CO gave provisional orders for night operations or the night 10-11 June.[447] The battalion was to move through the 1st Guards Brigade after they had captured their objective, securing the high ground at Cantelupo, which would protect the flank of the advance and the give the 8th Indian Division a jumping off point for their advance north on the following night. The Guards did not manage to secure their objective until 0130. As Bowlby's company formed up at 0230 by the three tonner trucks, he heard Baker reporting that Coke and Cooper were missing. Sergeant Meadows quietly stated that they could do without Coke, but Bowlby notes that he was worried about Cooper as he "been blown up in the desert" and would have "hated to think of him being court-martialled."[448]

They set off in the trucks, but mines and demolitions prevented the battalion debussing where they had planned, resulting in them being dropped further away from their objective than they hoped. The leading company (S) eventually lead off around 0330. The advance was unopposed, and S Company reached their objective by 0800. B and C Companies moved through and captured the village of Cantelupo again without opposition. Bowlby's company passed through the guards around dawn. The guards confirmed they had not seen any Germans, but had a lost a few men in the barrage. Bowlby remembers the guardsman nodding towards a stretcher. He recalls seeing a leg sticking out from under a blanket.[449] The road leading to Cantelupo was heavily cratered and mined, which prevented the battalion and its supporting detachments' vehicles following up the infantry advance closely. The war diary notes under the circumstance that it was fortunate the infantry was able to look after itself and take the final objective taken unopposed.[450]

R Hastings notes that an uncomfortable day was spent in Cantelupo.[451] The war diary, however, notes all was quiet until around 1200, when they were heavily shelled by enemy guns of all calibres. This included *nebelwerfer* (smoke mortar) fire.[452]

The nebelwefer were a series of weapons given their name as a disinformation strategy to mislead the League of Nations observers (who were observing any possible infraction of the Treaty of Versailles) into thinking that it was merely a device for creating a smoke screen, although a high-explosive shell was developed for the Nebelwerfer from the beginning. Troops in Sicily had nicknamed them 'Screaming Mimi' and 'Moaning Minnie' due to the loud and unnerving noise they were designed to make in order to explode. Crimp describes the being shelled by multi-barrel mortars on the same day, but call them "sobbing sisters."[453] Bowlby describes them as "Moaning Minnies," recalling how the rattle turned into a moan and the moan "changed to a deafening roar" and confesses, "I think I screamed."[454] Considering the intensity of the shelling, casualties were light, although, as usual, the psychological toll on Alan and the other troops remains unrecorded outside of the few comments from Bowlby and Crimp.

By around 1500, the road had been cleared and traffic was moving. Further shelling hit the village around 1900. When the barrage ceased at last, "the absence of sound [was] almost painful."[455] The battalion was slowly relieved over the next few hours, S Company being the last to go around 0400 on 12 June. During the day, three ORs were killed and one officer and three ORs were wounded, one OR seriously. Five POWs were captured. A check of the Commonwealth Graves Commission reveals the likelihood that the three ORs referred to were Douglas Robert Goulden, James Henry Sawyer, and Joseph William Weetch.

The next morning, Bowlby tells, as his company was enjoying a late breakfast Coke and Cooper re-join them from Battalion HQ (they had handed themselves in shortly after going AWOL).

They had been let off with a warning, along with some other part-time deserters. Coke spoke with Bowlby later on that day, saying:

'I wrote 'ome and told me girl I'm no good,' he said. 'Told 'er I was yellow.'

This touched me.

'You'll be all right, Cokey,' I said, wishing I could sound more convincing.[456]

Bowlby notes that it was different with Cooper. He told Bowlby that he "got a bubble on" and said to himself, "Sammy, me lad, you've 'ad this trip'."[457] It seems common that soldiers would, often for superstitious reason, feel certain operations somehow had it in for them and would opt to miss them out, often then returning and fighting on after that specific operation finished.

The Brigade, with the exception of the 7th Battalion, was behind the main advance. The next few days, they spent the time enjoying the benefits of hot showers from the mobile shower units that had been brought forward and replacing lost equipment. Bowlby notes that this actually gave the soldiers the chance to get something for nothing, as they claimed for various lost bits of kit that had not been lost at all. Extra rations and khaki drill trousers were the most claimed for items. They had discovered that the trousers fetched a higher price from the locals than anything else. Bowlby believes the number of trousers claimed as lost in battle must have run into the tens of thousands. He claims they created much more goodwill with the locals than the Allied propaganda leaflets "written *in English*, telling the Italian peasants 'What Liberation means to *you*'."[458]

In the desert, Alan and the other soldiers of the Eighth Army had little contact with locals. Italy was very different. There was regular interaction between the liberating army and the locals, and by now Alan and the battalion were starting to understand the hardships the local population were enduring.

There is little of note in either the war diary or Crimp's diary covering the next week. Bowlby notes that his company was briefed three times for an attack, but that each time "the Indians go there before us" and that "we loved them for it."[459] The biggest threat to the health of his company during this period was "gippy tummy" from the fruit acquired from orchards they passed through. On 19 June, the battalion received a resupply of rations and more equipment that they could use to trade with the locals. Bowlby recounts setting off with a couple of others to a nearby farmhouse to trade cigarettes for wine and a good meal. They were welcomed in and welcomed to the family dinner table. At the end of the evening, he retired outside with the old man of the house for a cigarette. Leaning on gate outside the house, he had the following interaction:

> Over cigarettes the farmer told me that his three sons had been killed in North Africa. When I tried to convey our sympathy he smiled sadly.
>
> 'E la guerra,' he said.[460]

He would have known that he could well have been speaking with the soldiers who had killed his three sons. Despite this, he did not see these British soldiers as anything other than fellow human beings who had been caught up in the same horrendous circumstances in which his sons had been caught up. He did not see them as 'British' or representatives of an enemy. He saw past the uniform and foreign accents and saw them as individuals, victims of their circumstances as much as we all are. He was not alone in doing so. In *All Hell Let Loose* Hastings notes the following:

> Italy's surrender precipitated a mass migration of British prisoners of war, set free from camps in the north of the country to undertake treks through the Apennines to- wards the Allied lines. A defining characteristic of these odysseys, many of which lasted months, was the succour such men received from local people. Peasant kindness was prompted by an instinctive human sympathy, rather than enthusiasm for the Allied cause, which deeply moved its beneficiaries. The Germans punished civilians

who assisted escapers by the destruction of their homes, and often by death, yet sanctions proved ineffectual: thousands of British soldiers were sheltered by tens of thousands of Italian country folk whose courage and charity represented one of the noblest aspects of Italy's unhappy part in the war.[461]

When a war begins, humanity has failed. In amongst the failure though humanity can at times shine in the darkness. He had invited them into his house and fed them. The man's comments had a profound impact on Bowlby, saying "[h]is lack of bitterness left me numb with compassion and guilt." Bowlby then notes that, "the next morning the war caught up with us."[462] That "us" would have included Alan.

Chapter Fourteen
Behind the Tavolette

If the capture of Perugia had not followed so soon after the political excitement of the fall of Rome and had not coincided with the most critical days of the French invasion, the fame of the 61st Brigades capture of the hills to the north-west of the town must have reached a larger public.

The Rifle Brigade 1939-45, R Hastings

You ask, always in friendship, Tullus, what are my household gods, and of what race am I. If our country's graves, at Perusia, are known to you, Italy's graveyard in the darkest times, when Rome's citizens dealt in war (and, to my special sorrow, Etruscan dust, you allowed my kinsman's limbs to be scattered, you covered his wretched bones with no scrap of soil), know that Umbria rich in fertile ground bore me, where it touches there on the plain below.

Elegies (Book I.22:1-10), Sextus Propertius

The path of the Brigade's advance had veered towards the centre of the country since bypassing Rome, and they received the objective of the high ground to the north west of Perugia, between the town and Lake Trasimene.[463] This was part of the wider battle for what was known as the Trasimene or Albert Line, a line of German defences stretching east to west through Lake Trasimene and to both coasts. Alan's brother Ken would also be involved in this wider battle, as his regiment would be fighting its way up the west side of the lake.

Alan, however, would be fighting on the east side for the high ground that would make it impossible for the enemy to hold Perugia and therefore the junction of several major roads of which Perugia sits astride. At some point, most likely during the build up to the attacks on the Trasimene Line, Alan and Ken would march past each other, having not seen each other for years, but they could not stop for a greeting. This would probably have been a bittersweet experience for them both. They would have known that their brother was alive, maybe for the first time in a significant amount of time. The feeling of seeing a reassuring face may have been a source of strength, but it may also have brought back homesickness and been a reminder of better times. For Alan, it may have also been desperately frustrating to see maybe the one person in the world he thought would understand how he felt and been able to help him, go marching past tantalisingly out of reach, reminding him he was not in control of who he could see and speak with, reminding him that he was part of a bigger machine that had its own priorities to which he was subservient.

The Battle of Perugia, a town described by Crimp as he approached from the south as "an imposing city on a hill to the north, reddish hued in a watery sunset,"[464] consisted of four successive night attacks in mountainous country. Some enemy who were passed over in the night would then engage from the rear at daylight. During the four nights, there were many "sharp engagements"[465] on a company scale, often for individual hills or even defensive strong points located in single buildings. The history notes that tanks were not much use, but mortars and mines were used to great effect. It claims that above all, the swift counter attacks by German infantry were often harder to repel than taking the ground in the first place.

The first night attack was led by the 10th Battalion on night of 18-19 June and had the object of capturing Monte Lacugnano, a large hill to the south of Perugia, on which the small village of Lacugnano is sited. It was a fairly insignificant village in the wider context of the area, but one that came to have an immense significance in Alan's life. A Company of the 2nd Battalion was involved, while the rest of the battalion was still harbouring further back (and in Bowlby's case building relations with the locals). These locals may have been the very same locals that Alan would later come to know, and it may have been at this point that he met some friendly faces that he deliberately tried to seek out again later. It is not clear how far back the rest of the battalion was and whether Alan was with the companies in the rear or with A Company. According to the war diary, A Company had a subsidiary role, to the south covering a field squadron constructing bridges that would provide a route that would allow troops to by-pass Perugia.[466] The attacks went in on a dark night with steady rain throughout. The 10th Battalion reached their objectives after a long march relatively unopposed. A Company was held up by snipers, small arms, and mortars whilst trying to support the Royal Engineers repairing demolitions on the Division's main axis road (Route 75).

This would have been one of the first times the battalion would have come across a sniper; the use of snipers was much more limited in the wide open spaces of the sand deserts of North Africa. Members of the battalion who had fought in the closer country of Tunisia after Alan had deserted would have been more familiar with the threat. One etymology of the term sniper claims it originated in the British Army in 1824, when the verb 'snipe' was used by British soldiers in India to refer to accurate shooting from a hidden location—an allusion to hunting the game bird called the snipe. Those skilled in this type of shooting became referred to as 'snipers.'

Snipers create a different fear to that of artillery. If you are hit, it is likely you will not hear anything. If you hear the crack, then the round has already passed you. You may hear the faint sound of the round cutting blades of grass metres away and feel the energy as it passes. It is more personal than artillery, mortars or even normal small arms or machine gun fire, which will be either fired at a location or at your general area. A sniper is looking directly at his victim. He chooses him specifically. When you know there are snipers operating in the area, you are aware that at any moment you may unknowingly be between someone's sights.

I have never been shot by a sniper, but on the helipad in Iraq I saw the aftermath. As we debussed from one helicopter, another was arriving from al Amara. A stretcher was carried off the other helicopter on it, covered with a blanket, was the body of Lance Corporal Allan Douglas, 65122, son of Walter and Diane and brother of Donna. He had been shot by a sniper whilst out on patrol. His left boot was poking out from underneath the blanket. It was a boot just like mine. It is the little details that you remember, and the little details reveal so much.

A company abandoned the attempt to repair the road demolitions early in the morning on 19 June, but elements of the battalion continued to come under fire from enemy shells for most of the rest of the day (from the lack of any mentions of enemy contact this day by Crimp and Bowlby we can assume this did not include B Company). At the same time, daylight had revealed that the 10th battalion had bypassed significant numbers of enemy in the dark. The early morning was spent mopping up the enemy whilst being sniped at from numerous positions. Reserve companies came to help in the mop up, and by the afternoon the situation was quiet. Hasting claims that the capture of Lacugnano was likely to be the deciding factor in the German decision to pull out of Perugia on the night of 19 June.

By the evening of the 19 June, the 7th Battalion received orders to capture Monte Malbe. In another dark night, the attack went well, with most companies reaching their objective with little incident. The morning brought what is described by Hastings as "some unpleasantly accurate shelling of their positions,"[467] but much worse was to come in the afternoon. At 1500, the first counter attack was launched from the north west. The battalion repelled it with relative ease. This was followed up, however by a much more significant attack from both the north west and the north east simultaneously. This resulted in an enemy penetration on the east side of the hill, which threatened the Battalion HQ. The battalion held it off for a couple of hours and dealt with largely by a force described by Hastings as "an assortment of signallers and others not usually concerned with firing their weapons."[468]

After some confused fighting, a squadron of Lancers turned up and managed to convince the remaining enemy to surrender or hastily withdraw. It was now the 2nd Battalion's turn, but not straightaway. There was a twenty-four-hour pause first. On 20 June, Crimp's diary entry for that day notes in his diary that "tonight there is a do on."[469] Orders were issued for an attack in the early hours of the following morning. B Company received orders to occupy the ring contour at 588939, C Company was sent to the Mt Rentella feature, S Company was to occupy the high ground immediately south of Corciano, and A Company were to be held in reserve. Before this was to happen, the battalion was to first clear some enemy positions that had been harassing the Lothians advance along Route 75 the previous night, providing cover for a field squadron who would clear a series of demolitions. So, as Bowlby noted, it was the early hours of 21 June when the war caught up with them.

At 0030, the leading companies left the debussing areas. S Company met stiff opposition during the night, but were successful in surrounding a house from which they took eighteen prisoners. Subsequently, they did not manage to reach their objective, owing to enemy opposition, and spent the day under enemy observation. They were subjected to considerable enemy fire during the afternoon of 21 June. They laid out a plan to capture the final objective, but put it aside when they learnt that the 10th Rifle Battalion would pass through and take the objective during the hours of darkness later that day. C Company met heavy opposition during their approach march and did not successfully reach their final objective, which was a dominating feature held throughout the day by the enemy, who, with commanding observation made life very unpleasant for the remainder of the battalion. A Company reached their objective, but had considerable difficulty establishing themselves due to well-placed enemy positions in their immediate vicinity and the fire from the Rentella feature. They laid out a plan to mop up the south end of the Battalion position with the support of tanks, but these were withdrawn for another task before the plan could be put into action. Tactical Battalion HQ was established, as was the Commanding Officer's recce party. Any movement around this position attracted immediate reaction from the enemy in the form of mortar and artillery fire.

B Company obtained their objective without serious opposition. Crimp describes a pitch-dark night and appreciated that they were fortunate that "Jerry [was] not in possession, as moving up in growing light would be no picnic."[470] Although B Company were able to dig in without enemy attention, Crimp could hear the "sounds of strife... down in the valley a rattling of machine guns and further west a couple of explosions."[471] News of their situation was, however, vague due to the breakdown in communications. Counter attacks came three times during the day. Two of those attacks they withheld, but the third eventually drove them off their feature in the late afternoon. Crimp describes the day in more detail:

> After a while we hear twigs cracking and somebody plodding up our hill. It's a Jerry, as soon he begins calling out in German. We lie dog, ready to put him quietly in the bag. But suddenly his voice and footfalls cease, no doubt he's got wind of us and blown the gaff. By 0900 the mist has yielded to bright sunshine. Suddenly from a hill on the left rips the rapid metallic splitting of Spandau's. Silence for an hour - just as beginning to relax the stinging clatter of Spandau's, obviously re-enforced breaks out again and from the far side of the hill mortar bombs begin sailing over: small phut of firing, a few seconds of silence a gentle swishing, insidious descent and tremendous brutal crash on landing. One after the other they come with pauses only to vary flight. This last about ten minutes and is extremely unpleasant. The chaps up in the platoons up on the brow have it worse than us in HQ about 30 yards down as they're under full observation by the Spandau gunners. We cannot see Jerry. All we can do is lie in our holes and smoke and sweat and hope for the best.

Hour later the next dose— company commander worried about lack of relief. Mortar fire more concentrated and crept nearer. The platoons have a very rough time of it. If only they could see something to have a pot at, retaliation would ease matters. Cannot get through by radio and half an hour later battery dies. After a third bash about 1300hrs in which several platoon chaps wounded company commander decides to withdraw. By the time HQ company moves mortared again have to retreat now company split. Lie in holes all afternoon. Hear and see artillery coming and going in both directions over the hill. By 1800 "the concert begins" ear-splitting clatter of Spandau's opens up followed by the sinister hissing of mortars and their earth shaking crashes, and for good measure a new joker is introduced - a smart succession of powerful explosions from the summit, probably caused by the 88-mil of a Tiger tank firing point blank or a self-propelled gun. This lasts several minutes and when it stops the company commander decides it is useless to hang round and gives order to go.[472]

Bowlby describes in the first barrage how he became convinced that a German mortarman was after his trench in particular. The idea terrified him. He yelled to his mate O'Connor, who was in the trench with him that he was getting out of there; it was only O'Connor's firm instruction to stay where he was that kept him there.

He describes being "hypnotised with fear" as a German Tiger tank used a tree behind his trench as aiming post in the next attack.[473] Bowlby describes withdrawing from the trenches during a particularly intense barrage, to then return to them. Withdrawing a second time, Bowlby left his rifle on the parapet of his trench. He was sent back to get it from a clearing they had reached half-way down the hill. After sneaking back to the position, he ran back to the clearing to see the last of company disappearing down the hill. Crimp recalls how they set off down the slope at speed and become scattered.[474] As Bowlby ran after them, the guns opened up and shells began to burst between them as they ran across an open field. He expected to be blown to bits at any moment and asked himself how he could survive shells bursting at his feet?[475]

Bowlby ended up in what sounds like the same ditch Crimp and some of the stragglers, including the company commander, landed in. They soon heard Spandau fire and voices in field they had just left. According to Crimp, one chap then saw a German in a tree not 20 yards off—it was an OP missed in the dark of pervious night.[476] Bowlby, unaware of the German OP, describes the tension in the ditch as they decided to wait the three hours until dark to make a run for it:

> As I sat in the ditch I was ware of a creeping fear. The longer the silence the worse the fear. I longed for a noise, any noise, even the noise on the hill. In lieu of it I began praying, a stream of promises of what I would do if God would let me leave the ditch alive
>
> 'And if I do get out,' I thought, 'I'll desert. Anything's better than this'.[477]

It is very possible Alan was somewhere in that same ditch, thinking the same thing. It is very possible many more in the ditch were thinking the same thing. Moments later, Bowlby heard footsteps approaching and then the unbuckling of a belt. The German only a few feet away from him, was, in his words, "having a shit."[478] Bowlby grinned at his platoon commander, who just stared back straight through him. Such are the extremes of combat, where all of human nature is present. They finally made a run for it, dodging German sentries, Spandau fire, and mortars.

Bowlby's trousers gave way and his pants fell down his ankles tripping him over as he ran through a cornfield with rounds impacting all around him. He sobbed with rage as his trousers kept tripping him until they finally reached safety. When they arrived, Bowlby saw the haunted look of men going into a big attack as he passed them forming up from what he calls the 5th

Battalion.[479] This was most likely the 10th battalion, as it was the 10th that, according to Hastings, during the following night relieved the 2nd Battalion. This withdrawal was described in Hasting's history as having gone "quite smoothly."[480]

According to the war diary, the casualties during 21 June for the 2nd Battalion were six ORs killed, Lieutenant J E Wright, Lieutenant NWN Naper, and twenty-three ORs wounded (two ORs later died of wounds), and six ORs listed as missing.[481] During the day, thirty-three PWs, including one officer, were taken and a considerable number of enemy accounted for in action. On the relief, the whole Battalion was concentrated in an area. Major Reader Harris (known as Major Dunkerley in Bowlby's recollections), who was wounded with the Battalion on 4 June, re-joined the Battalion during the afternoon and assumed command of B Company. Information from the Commonwealth Graves Commission reveals the likelihood that the six ORs who died on 21 June were John Stanley Lobar, Lawrence Nedas, Maurice Rampley, Ernest William Severn, William George Wells, and John Worley. There were no more deaths of soldiers from the battalion listed in the following week, so it is not possible to identify the two ORs who died of their wounds without knowing when they died.

Bowlby eventually found out from O'Connor that at his end of the ditch there was a German up a tree.[482] All he had to do was look round, and he would have seen the lot of them. To O'Connor, surviving the ditch meant he could survive anything. To another, it could very easily have felt like it was an extraordinarily lucky escape that might have used up all remaining luck. In war, it is easy to become suspicious and to develop a complex relationship with luck and fate, where dues are accrued, debts paid, and limits perceived. Bowlby also discovered that what he thought were cuckoos calling to one another were actually Germans.[483]

There were more discoveries for Bowlby too, in the days after the battle. The men that Bowlby passed who had been forming up to relieve them were unsuccessful in their attempt to hold the ground that the 2nd should have occupied. They suffered heavy casualties. When Bowlby heard of the losses the 5th (10th), he had "an immediate and overwhelming sense of horror—and guilt." Bowlby saw the attack in his head, hearing the screams. He asked himself, "[h]ad they been killed because of us?"[484] He concluded that they'd had their share and it was just their bad luck. He briefly felt better when he heard that their withdrawal had been ordered by the company commander and the company had not cut and run as he had thought at the time.

Not long after hearing this, the company received demoralising news. Bowlby told of the NCO's returning from the Battalion HQ, "[t]he CO's called us lot gutless swine." To Bowlby and the company, it was "like a blow in the face."[485] They were initially speechless, but then let rip. Alan had experienced many defeats in the desert and missed the key victories others in the battalion had gone on to have. This victory, described by Hastings as one deserving of fame, must have felt hollow if he too had heard the CO's description of the battalion.

On 22 June, the Battalion remained in a harbour area and received intelligence that they had been opposed by enemy forces considerably greater than first thought. They were told that the combined efforts of their battalion and 10th Battalion had also inflicted considerably more casualties on the enemy than was previously thought and forced them as a result to withdraw to fresh positions without further pressure from our troops. Crimp notes that whilst Perugia was now taken, the Germans were "still on the hills to the north throwing muck at it."[486] He also notes that a few chaps still hadn't returned.

By 23 June, it was clear that the Germans had withdrawn. On the same day, Medway, one of the missing has been found. The 10th Battalion found his body, riddled with bullets, in a cornfield. Crimp reckons it might have been the field in which the Spandau sprayed them as they lay in the ditch. Crimp remembers that it was Medway who said when they reached Taranto that "one could easily die in a land like this—its halfway to heaven already" and then more lately in a quietly depressed tone, "you know, I feel that if I got my lot it wouldn't matter."[487]

There then followed a week where the battalion remained in same area. There was a training programme in mornings and trips into Perugia in afternoons and evenings to watch the mobile cinema and take in the town, a routine only interrupted by Medway's church service. Crimp notes that—"It [Perugia] is a fine picturesque place, spread over several hills, full of stately buildings and steep lanes."[488] By 26 June, though, Crimp notes that he "[felt] rather depressed; portents point to action again soon."[489] On 29 June, the battalion saw enemy aircraft, such a regular feature of combat in the desert, dropping bombs for the first time.

On 30 June, the battalion finally moved again and harboured near Lake Tresimene. They spent the next three days practicing stalking in the mornings. Then, according to Bowlby, they spent the next day covering 20 miles. On the same day, Meadows, returning from leave, managed to catch up with them despite the distance travelled that day. He told of meeting 'Topper' Brown, who was sitting down to dinner with the family at the house he was billeted at. Meadows told them "e's on the trot!"—(slang for deserter).[490] They all sat down for dinner together quite happily. At the end of the meal, they wished him good luck as he departed, but then received a shock when he stole their jeep with all their equipment and rifles:

> The wild Italian countryside and the hospitable customs of its inhabitants prompted desertions from the Allied armies on a scale greater than in any other theatre. The rear areas teemed with military fugitives, men 'on the trot'—overwhelmingly infantry, because they recognised their poor prospects of survival at the front. Thirty thousand British deserters were estimated by some informed senior officers to be at liberty in Italy in 1944-45—the equivalent of two divisions—and around half that number of Americans. These are quite extraordinary figures, which deserve more notice in narratives of the campaign,

though it should be noted that official histories set the desertion numbers much lower, partly because they omit those who, by a technically important distinction, were deemed merely to be 'absent without leave.'[491]

The first three days of July were some of the hottest of the year. Hastings notes these days were rest days. The war diary notes that other than receiving information on 1 July, they would likely relieve a battalion of 78th Division north west of the lake on the night of 3-4 July. They spent the days training and going on leave parties. There was not much shade to take advantage of where they were harboured. Even if Alan had not gotten a fear of water, the south shore of Lake Tresimene was not suitable for bathing due to the reeds and slippery mud. As the battalion began to move again, Bowlby makes mention of the numerous times they were shelled, none of which make Hasting's account. Bowlby describes driving through a "fog of cordite" left from a shelling minutes before.

I clearly remember the smell of cordite from the first time I was rocketed in Iraq. It was a single Katusha rocket that landed on the house I was in at the time in Baghdad's Green Zone. It was nothing compared to a sustained bombardment of heavy German artillery, but the acrid smell of cordite still takes me back to the strange moment of quiet after the rocket. For Alan, every bombardment, every lingering cloud of cordite, must have taken him back to the hell of the bunker as well as create a new hell to endure.

During these first days of July, Crimp read an article in the Eighth Army News, which he says "got our backs up another way." The article reports that Roosevelt had suggested to Churchill that the United States should provide all the land forces for the Pacific sector. Churchill had turned this down. "We can't let you chaps have all the fun," he had said. According to Crimp, "[t]his infuriated us. War may have been fun for him; it wasn't for us."[492]

The divisional axis was now Route 71 heading to Arezzo through the Chiana Valley. The valley, as described by Hastings, was thickly cultivated with vines and orchards and interlaced with irrigation ditches.[493] The right flank of the valley was mountainous. Clearing enemy positions in these mountains was to be the brigade's next, by no means unformidable, task. There were three key features that needed clearing, all three of which were complex features with no clearly defined summits, covered with scrub and in parts with trees and with dug in German positions.

By 4 July, heavy rain had made conditions difficult. The war diary notes that the battalion received reinforcements, including a small number of officers and twenty-six ORs.[494] The first attempt to clear the area happened on the evening of the following day by the 10th Battalion, who again suffered casualties. The 2nd Battalion received orders to relieve a company of the 10th on a feature on the Ligacuro the following day. According to the war diary, the battalion moved off at 2130 on 5 July in order to be in a position to execute their orders on 6 July.[495]

Alan, however did not move off with them.

Bowlby notes that as the battalion prepared to move, Coke disappeared, and when they did move off an hour later, Sullivan has also disappeared. Sullivan returned, having had "second thoughts about deserting."[496] He was left off with a warning from the platoon commander. In Alan's war record, it states that on July 5 he went AWOL from approximately 2100.[497] Crimp notes that the next action was on 6 July, and both he and Bowlby record another intense and bloody battle.

The war diary includes a rare additional summary note covering the period 6-8 July as well as the detailed diary entries for each individual day. The summary states the following:

> The Battalion worked under trying conditions for a peri-od of two and a half days. The enemy had well sited OPs and was able to bring down effective artillery and mortar fire not only on forward positions, but all along Route 71, which was the main axis as far back as Castigione. Opera-tions during this period once again proved that it is

necessary to the high ground on the flanks of any axis of advance or at least prevent the enemy from obtaining observation. The Brigade was extended over a five mile front and was not under the circumstances strong enough to prevent the enemy from obtaining observation. The approach to Mt Ligacuro was not easy and supplies had to be portered up each night in the absence of mules. Between 6-8th July casualties were six killed and 26 wounded. Owing to the lack of good observation casualties inflicted on the enemy cannot be estimated but it is considered that our arty fire on the enemy positions was effective and accurate.[498]

On 9 July, as the battalion recovered from the fighting in a harbour area, Crimp notes the following:

Two chaps who disappeared on the eve of our recent dabble have returned to the fold. They claim of course to be bomb happy, hoping for a MOs grading as unfit for service in the front line. Even the chance of a court-martial doesn't daunt them. A military nick breaks no bones and a term inside has the edge I suppose, on getting squashed like flies under an iron flail. But the method of treatment currently in force is keeping them under open arrest, which means they stay with the company and most of its rigours until the Battalion's withdrawn and they can be put on the pegs. Some chaps, of course, don't reappear.[499]

Alan was one of those chaps. He had had enough. He would tell Stephenie years later that he just couldn't do it. He could not go back. He had again reached his limit. It sounded like Alan thought he had no choice. The next entry on his war record is on 13 July, which notes that he "still is absent."[500] On August 7, he was declared deserter by court of inquiry in his absence. It was, however, not until 24 October 1945, after the war in Europe was over, that he was apprehended for desertion by MPs.

Where Alan went between these two dates shaped the rest of his life, and in many ways saved it.

Alan, a broken man, was lost in a war zone. He was lost in a foreign country whose language he did not speak and whose people he had been at war with until very recently. Most Italians he had met before had been shooting at him, and he had shot back at them. The Italian people were now caught between two great foreign armies and struggling to survive, as those armies destroyed their ways and means of life as they swept through.

Chapter Fifteen
Lacugnano

First you must realise that a defeated people has no loyalties. Their leaders have failed them. Their sons have died in a lost cause. They believe in no-one not even themselves.

It was a full summer in a world without men. Hot mornings and blazing moons, and nights when the clouds rolled in, sweating, over the valley and then moved on unspent of rain. Tempers were high, and vitality was low, because the armies were like locusts, eating out the land, and there were no men in the beds—except the old ones, who were a nuisance, and occasional visitors, like the polizia and the carabinieri and the agricultural inspector and the requisitioning officers from the Army. These were a nuisance, too, because when they were gone there were quarrels in the houses and bloody faces and torn skirts in the fields.

The Devil's Advocate, Morris West

Lacugnano is a fraction of the municipality of Perugia. Lacugnano (or Lacugnana) lies on the southern side of a hill called Mount Lacugnano, located south west of the Umbrian capital. According to Wikipedia, it now has a population of 1122. Despite being bigger in size now, Stephenie tells me it is still a very close-knit village, where the families all know one another. Stephenie believes that village started because of a nearby quarry, which would have provided jobs for the first residents. In the early days of the village, most men would have worked there, but that was by this time closed. At one point, there was a cottage industry making up the boxes for the chocolate factory in Perugia, which is now owned by the multinational company

Nestle. The women of the village would sit together in their garages and make up the boxes for the Baci chocolates by hand.

The village doesn't have a main square, but the main road, the only way in and out, called the Via Antonio, goes through the bottom of the village and widens at the church. This is where the people used to gather, to sit and chat, and maybe later on to drink wine and sing, accompanied by an accordion in the soft light of long evenings. They would gather on a terrace which belonged to the Cesarini family, then later built a terrace for the whole village to use for *festas*. But, as the village has grown over time, they have now built a community centre higher up the hill with a bar, a large community room, and the garden in front of it. The bar replaced the one bar the village used to have. It has never had any shops. There was, however, a large statue of Jesus in the Parco de Lacugnano on the top of hill. Stephenie remembers going to the *festa* they had when they brought it down, and remembered seeing the bullet holes in it from the war.

The church in Lacugnano

At the time of the war and up until the 1970s, the village consisted only of houses built on the Via Antonio and on the land up the hill from that road, with some built onto the rock face in places. There were plenty of angles to capture the perfect postcard picture. All the buildings that have now been built below that road have been built in the last thirty years. Therefore, at the time of Alan's battalion's arrival in the area, if you stood on the main road, you would have been able to see all the valley right back to the railway and station in Ellera and the house across from the station where Vivi Batani and her mother lived at the time and to the sunset beyond. Vivi, a resident of Lacugnano and Ellera for over sixty years, gave Stephenie an insight to what life was like in the village under Mussolini in a series conversations and also appears in the film *Corciano 44*, made by the nearby commune of Corciano in 2004 to celebrate sixty years since liberation.[501] The majority of what follows was relayed to me by Stephenie from discussions she has had over the years with friends in the village and from sections of the film, which she has translated.

Vivi went to school in Lacugnano for the first three years of her schooling, but then in years four and five, when she would have been a teenager, she went to nearby San Mariano, a few miles to the west. She recalls that the teachers were all fascists. One of them would get the children to climb the stairs of the school, marching them to the top where they would have to yell "Long live the Duke."

During the war in Africa, every morning after an Italian victory, the teachers would get the children to move flags representing the Italian formations around, plotting their movements on a large map of the continent. When there was a defeat, however, the children were not asked to move the flags. From the time Alan deserted until the end of the war, there would not have been much contact between the children and the flags. Dust settled on those flags like the layers of sand on the burnt-out Italian tanks in the North African sand.

Vivi recalls that the teachers in Lacugnano were just as bad as those in San Mariano. She remembers them as "fanatics," who would come to school dressed like *"Massaie Rurali."* Mussolini was an advocate of Futurism, an artistic and social movement that originated in Italy in the early 20th century, which glorified themes associated with contemporary concepts of the future, including speed, technology, youth, and violence. It worshipped objects such as the car, the airplane, and the industrial city. It glorified modernity and aimed to liberate Italy from the weight of its past *The Futurist Manifesto* had declared "we will glorify war—the world's only hygiene—militarism, patriotism, the destructive gesture of freedom-bringers, beautiful ideas worth dying for, and scorn for woman."[502] At the same time, though, the fascist government was interested in the Roman history and especially Roman military prowess—a source of disagreement with the Futurists who refer to a "useless admiration of the past"[503]—and in the countryside both materially and symbolically.

The *Massaie Rurali* was an organisation that grew out of the national union of rural housewives and rural women workers. In *Peasant Women and Politics in Fascist Italy: The Massaie Rurali*, author Perry Wilson notes that by 1939 it had over a million members and was controlled by the central party authorities in the same way they controlled the urban based mass organisations of fascist Italy.[504] Propaganda in the form of pamphlets, films, and festivals was distributed centrally down to the small village, idolising the ideal of the rural peasant women, attaching a status akin to that of a pagan earth goddess. In German fascism, there also seemed to be a strong link to a folksy past underpinning the steel and concrete vision of the future.

Accounts from the village speak of the teachers coming to school with a coloured handkerchief round their necks and large crisped skirts, the unofficial uniform of the *Massaie Rurali*. They would take the children to political rallies dressed in the uniform. One time, Vivi remembers being taken us to the town hall of nearby Corciano in a small lorry, where they were made to listen to what Vivi describes as "absurd conversations that meant nothing to us." They told the children that they would get a nice lunch, but Vivi told Stephenie instead they had to wait three hours until they were starving when they received instead of the promised nice lunch they got two rolls of bread.

Wilson argues that, for the rural women, membership often meant something less than a whole-hearted embracing of the Fascist cause. According to Wilson, women joined the *Massaie Rurali* for a variety of material and immaterial reasons.[505] It is impossible to know whether the residents of Lacugnano and the surrounding villages wholeheartedly embraced the fascist cause or not, but Vivi certainly was not impressed. She also remembers that there were a significant number of communist sympathisers in the area by the end of the war, the political party that the fascists originally defined themselves by their opposition.

The author Jay Griffiths writing about Italian fascism claims, "It champions 'might is right', a Darwinian survival of the nastiest, and detests vulnerability: the sight of weakness brings out the jackboot in the fascist mind, which then blames the victim for encouraging the kick."[506]

Fortunately, this was not the attitude of the people of Lacugnano, and as we have heard from Hastings, much of the rural Italian population. The church had been there much longer than *Il Duce*, had been around and was infused by even more ancient pagan traditions and codes. The patron saint of the village is St Christopher, the patron saint of travellers, who, the legend goes, after learning of Christianity from a hermit, dedicated himself to helping travellers across a dangerous river. One day, he helped a small child across the river. As it swelled dangerously, he struggled across, not understand how such a small child could be so heavy. When they got to the other side the child revealed himself as Christ and then disappeared.

Vivi recalls that life was not too bad when the Germans came. She remembers that as they were fighting on the side of the Germans, for the most part, people did what they were told by the German troops based locally. She recalls that the everyday troops were nice to them, but "the SS Troops and Officers were awful. Brutal and would not hesitate to bully and hit them." The residents of the area fared better than the residents of Rome as depicted in the film *Rome, Open City*. Directed by Roberto Rossellini, filmed in 1944, and released in 1945, it mostly used ordinary people who had lived through the hunger and oppression that Lewis described in *Naples '44*, as well investigating the tension between collaboration and resistance.[507] The latter led to torture, imprisonment, and for some, death at the hands of the former ally.

Whilst there was little conflict in Lacugnano, it was only approximately 30 miles north of the village that a tragic murder would occur in August 1944 as the Germans withdrew, highlighting the brutality of the time. In the autobiographical novel *The Sky Falls*, Lorenza Mazzetti describes the murder of her aunt and two young cousins by SS Officers.[508] Her uncle Roberto was not present at the time, but killed himself less than a year later, overcome with grief. He was not present, as he had been advised by the partisans to hide away from his villa because Robert was the cousin of the physicist Albert Einstein and was sought out by the SS on the orders of Hitler himself as a way of either punishing his famous cousin or to act as a bargaining chip, depending on which story you believe.

Albert Einstein was now in the US, having briefly spent time in Italy before the war began, and was a vocal critic of Hitler and the Nazi regime (as well as secretly working on the Manhattan Project). Prosecutors opened a war crimes investigation in 2007 to try and identify the officers behind the killing, but have yet to identify anyone they can place charges against.[509] It was likely that it was not just the communists in the wider area around Perugia would have been keen to see the Germans leave.

Before the war, Vivi lived in the house in front of the nearest station in Ellera, in the valley just below Lacugnano, whose bombing announced the arrival of the war to the residents of the village who would become Alan's hosts. As the war in Africa ended, it headed north and crossed the Mediterranean Sea to Italian shores. The foreshocks of the war reached Lacugnano on

2 May 1944, while Alan and his battalion were halfway through the sea crossing from North Africa to Taranto. Vivi Batani remembers a train with Red Cross markings arriving at the station:

> We all thought it was coming to take the injured away. It stayed for three or four days, then the bombing started. It wasn't Red Cross, it was full of Germans or ammunition; we didn't know. We didn't know where the airplanes came from the direction of Perugia. They flew over then turned and came back. We heard them and we went and hid in the fireplace. It didn't give us much refuge but some from the falling debris.[510]

The shock of this sudden violence in their quiet valley must have been profound. These people were not soldiers. They were mostly children, women, and old men, people who had no training that could prepare for this terrifying experience.

During the bombing, the offices of the station were hit, and the head of the station, a man called Contini, was buried under the debris but survived. Vivi, who by now had just left school and started to train as a nurse, remembers that a lot of people ran to help get him out, but just as they had nearly got him out the Allied planes came back round again and everyone had to run and take cover, leaving him stuck under the rubble. Luckily, he wasn't hit again. Vivi claims that another man, who had been working at the station and staying with her mother due to the proximity of their house to the station was not so lucky. According to Vivi, he left straight after the bombings to travel to his home and was hit on the way. This was the village's first contact with Allied forces.

Another resident of Lacugnano, Maria Carletti, remembers that the station was bombed a few times, but the bombing on 2 May 1944 in particular is remembered in the village as it is written on the wall of the cabin by her brother that became the station office after the original station office was hit. She lived in the house next to the station offices and was six years old in 1944. She recalls her mother sending her out to find some rocket to make salad with in the fields. Her mother was working in the house and her father, who worked on the railway, had been sent to Messina for work.

She thinks it was about 0930 in the morning when the planes arrived. She remembers there being about five or six of them. She also recalls them bombing the Red Cross train, which she says had been in the station for a few days. She also remembers that the German High Command was not too far away from the station. Maria Carletti claims that the day before, there had been a train with bombs on board in the shunting yard next to the station. She maintains that if the Allied bombers had hit that, nobody would have been left. When the planes arrived, she was outside near the gate in between the station office and the woodpile on her way to collect the salad. She recalls that, "I was lucky that I didn't get hurt but the blast took me off my feet and threw me to the floor and knocked me out." One of the railway workers, who was running to take cover saw her, and managed to pick her up and run with her to cover. She believes that she was only out for a matter of seconds and saw it was only the first two planes that dropped bombs. She says that, "People said they thought the train wasn't Red Cross, but it was and it was the oxygen bottles that exploded."

The trauma of those days has stayed with her all these years. After that night, her mother wouldn't sleep in the house, so they went and stayed with a farmer's family. She remembers that they slept in the barn; "with the rabbits and drank the milk from the cow in the morning." They then moved over to Lacugnano. The bombing had a big impact on Maria: "After the bombing I couldn't stand the English. The bombing left me traumatise and I was afraid of the English."[511] When you are a soldier deployed to a war zone, no matter how horrendous the experience you can cling to an idea of home. The idea that there is somewhere you can return to that is safe and will be separate from whatever you are experiencing; it helps give you a sense that there will be an end to it. When the war comes to your home, it can feel like there is nowhere to go and it is easier to doubt if there will ever be an end to it.

Maria also remembers later on after the Allies arrived, Allied officers talking to her father and the Station Master, claiming they had a tip off, but afterwards they realised there was nothing to bomb. It is seems unlikely that the Allied army officers moving through the village several months later would know the intelligence that lead to an air force bombing mission several months previously, but it is possible that a record of the mission was accessible and they had the clearance to view the intelligence, or maybe the officers felt saying so would help them in some way mend the damage done.

During the battle of Perugia, Stephenie was told that the bombing was horrendous, especially on the station of Ellera and along the valley below Lacugnano. In the days leading up to the fighting and during, the Allies bombed the tracks and the trains coming and going on them, that the locals believed were mostly transporting prisoners in the cattle trucks to the north and then they assumed to Germany.

Stephenie was told by one villager how her mother had been killed while they were in the fields outside the village by Allied shelling. They were out taking biscuits and drinks to people in the fields as they had done so many times before when the shelling started. Her mother had stopped to help an elderly gentleman who couldn't stand straight, and she was hit by a shell as her children ran to safety inside the nearest building. We have already heard of the fighting on night of 18-19 June that captured Monte Lacugnano itself, which must have passed ground-shakingly close to the village.

Those in the village that Stephenie spoke to claim that the Germans had left by 24 June after the battle of Perugia had ended, but there were a few left still setting mines and blowing up the bridges and water ways after this date. There was then a gap of a few days before the Allies would arrive in the village. During those days of quiet when the Germans were leaving and the Allies arriving people had the chance to come out and try and find food. The Germans had left mines in the fields so they were worried of being blown up. Stephenie heard a story of four people who were killed on the 29 June by mines. One place in Capocavallo near the New Bridge where a man was killed and was for years called the Field of the Damned. As years passed and no one would go there because they still thought it was mined, it gradually grew into a wood. It is now protected because of the plants there.

After the Liberation, people started to get back to normal living and repair the damage done to their houses after the various bombardments. The fields and animals still had to be looked after even though it this was now a dangerous activity due to the mines. At some point, some of the men from the village who had been fighting at Cassino arrived home, some bare footed, having walked the whole way after having technically deserted. One of these men was Vivi's future husband. After the Allies arrived, they took over the German High Command and made it into their base. There were English Polish, Indians, Americans and Australians. There was a great deal of rivalry between the English and Americans. Maria remembers when her family moved back to their home she would have to walk past the English soldiers and she would cry and scream when she saw them:

> One day one Soldier who spoke a little Italian asked why I was crying and my mother told him. After that they used to try and be nice and give me things because they had children at home like me and understood. My father told me off because I wouldn't look at them and be nice. I became ill with a fever and my father took me to the English medic and he was very nice and change into civilian clothes so I wasn't scared. They gave me medicine. My father explained that there was good and bad in every nation, but the repulsion remained. They stayed for many months and would always give me chocolate.[512]

We think that when Alan first deserted in July through to August, he spent time hiding in ditches and storm drains and stealing food out of the fields. He told Stephenie about eating raw corn on the cob. Alan must have faced a daily tension between the fear of getting caught and satisfying the dull ache of hunger. Living like a wild animal, he must have reacted with similar cautious fear to every unfamiliar noise in the foreign land in which he was trying to survive. For these days and weeks, survival must have been his only thought. He eventually made it to the railway bridge, half a mile from the station in the valley below the village, which would have given him shelter from the rain when he slept at night. We think also the bridge had a small hole at the side in which a man could just have squeezed into if a patrol came close by. This could not have helped his fear of confined spaces we believe he had already got by this point after the bunker. Vivi remembers the following:

> Once the Germans had left we had to deal with the English. Poor Carletti our neighbour knew that my mother liked the English and one day came to tell her that two English soldiers that had run from the Front were hiding in Lacugnano. During the night when it rained they slept under the railway bridge. One night they brought one of them to us because they thought the other one had gone back to his command. Even though my father wasn't happy my mother allowed him to sleep at our house.[513]

There does not seem to have been any debate as to what to do with Alan, despite there been shortages of food and a risk of punishment from the authorities. At possibly the lowest point in his life Alan was shown compassion by people from a country he had recently been fighting against. "E la Guerra." Stephenie believes that the people of the village just saw a man at his limits, exhausted by a war that had also taken so many of their men. They saw past the tattered uniform and saw a man in need, and treated him just like they treated their own men who walked from the Battle of Monte Cassino back home to the village many without even boots on their feet. His future now lay with and in the hands of these people of Lacugnano.

The Ponte di S Sabina,
where Alan would sleep when he first arrived in the village

To begin with, Alan and the other deserter, who we believe was called Jonny, would stay between three families and the priest. They stayed with the families for one or two nights, depending on how many patrols there were. They would move him to another house when others would tell them the patrols were coming near. They hid them behind the wood pile in the bakery and in basements behind piles of wood or furniture. The three families were the Cesarini family, who lived in the centre of the village by the church, the Tenerini who lived at the entrance to Lacugnano, and the Micrea who lived just below the village in the valley in a farm house. The priest, Don Amadeo, became one of Alan's closest friends until he died in the 1960s. Alan would help him tend to the grape vines around the church and help ring the church bell to call people to mass. Alan would often sit in the evenings and listen to him play the organ.

It seems that Jonny started to see one of the daughters at the Tenerini house (they were a family of five daughters and seven boys, but some were born after the war). One of the younger daughters, now in her nineties, told Stephenie that she made a bet of 100 Lira with Alan that Johnny would come to their house one night when it was Alan's turn to stay. Alan, not knowing of the burgeoning affair, said he didn't think Jonny would come. She won her bet Alan had to settle for a 100 Lira, which was no small amount in 1944. One morning Jonny was no longer there in the village. The villagers later told Stephenie that they assumed that he decided that he was going to return to his unit and left to find them. It is not known whether an angry relative who had discovered the affair encouraged Jonny to do so or Jonny felt recovered enough to re-join the war, felt guilty about his actions, felt homesick, or was motivated by the fear of the shame or punishment he might eventually face.

Alan did not return when Jonny did, and gradually became accepted as part of the community. He settled into a routine of leaving early in the morning by 0600 to go and help the farmers of Lacugnano in the fields all day, and in that way, he would pay his keep, receiving food and lodgings in return. He would work all day and then in the evening, when not with Don Amadeo, play *boccia* (bowls) in the street with the young men of the village. They would go from house to house playing like on a pub crawl.

The villagers told Stephenie that he was loved by all as a very kind, loveable young man. The young women of the area liked him because he was fair haired and had a moustache like David Niven—probably without knowing that Alan had been trained by Niven all that time ago back in England, before he had come to know war.

Those who were young children at the time still remember him now, telling Stephenie of how he would laugh and play with them and bring them sweets. He always had a pocket full of them. At the end of the day, he would arrive at the house he was to stay in that evening about 2200 and remain there overnight before the next early start and another day in the fields. The family Micree had a farm and would hide Alan in his wood shed when the Allies were patrolling. There was a network of lookouts that would let them know if the RMPs were patrolling looking for deserters. It seems that while he was moving through Italy, Alan had picked up some Italian and after a short time in the village he could speak the local language well enough for the villagers to claim he was from the north of Italy (to explain his fair hair) if anyone started to ask questions.

Food was scare and rationing was in place, but what was there was shared. The things that they didn't have were clothes, blankets, shoes, socks, and petrol. This was where Alan really proved his worth to the village as winter approached and the work in the fields ceased. He would take an army issue kit bag and would put on a New Zealand officer's uniform that one of the families had managed to acquire from a dead soldier. The women patched the bullet hole, washed, and brushed the uniform. Alan would put it on and go to the stores at the nearest army base, which was located a couple of miles walk away, and steal whatever people in the village needed. It is an activity that Alan later told Stephenie he felt very guilty about.

Stephenie thinks he must have sold some of the items so he had some money to live off, but everyone she spoke to in the village told her that he gave them what they needed for free. He would regularly give food to the village priest so he would give it to the families that needed it most. This was obviously a highly risky operation for him to undertake and one that would have endeared him to the village, who would not have demanded he took such a risk on their behalf, but also shows how keen Alan was to give something back to the people who took him in.

One day a New Zealand soldier arrived in Lacugnano and somehow discovered Alan was in hiding in the village. The Kiwi soldier, instead of reporting him up the command chain, after spending some time with Alan agreed not to say anything. He was due to return home in a matter of days and was going through London to get back to New Zealand. He promised Alan when he was passing through London he would go to his mother's house and let her know that he was alright and would contact her as soon as he could, for at this point she had no idea whether he was alive or dead. The Kiwi kept both his promises and as well as not informing the authorities of Alan's presence he found his mother and passed on the message.

Stephenie tells me that for her grandmother, it was such a relief to know that her son was alive, as all she had was a telegram saying he was missing in action. Stephenie managed to acquire a photo from someone in the village that showed Alan, a number of villagers, and this Kiwi soldier. We decided to try and track him down. We approached a journalist in New Zealand who agreed to do a story in the on-line version of *The Dominion Post* in the run up to Anzac Day which would hopefully lead to the identification of the soldier from the photograph.[514] After the article went out, there were two families who came forward, both thought a family member who had now passed away was the unknown soldier. The family whose claim I think is the strongest sent me the photo of their dad William (Bill) Frazier, who they believe is our mystery man (taken a couple of years after the war and included below). Both his daughter Maxine and his son, Kevin, are convinced it is him. I gave the photo to a military intelligence imagery analyst whose assessment is that it is the same man in both photos.

Bill Frazier, 1949

Mystery Soldier (far right), 1944

Bill was born in the UK, but his father was a submariner killed in the First World War. He was first placed in an orphanage and then later sent to New Zealand, still as a young boy, to attend Flock House. Flock House was set up by the New Zealand Sheep Owners Acknowledgement of Debt to British Seamen Fund, which was set up by the New Zealand Farmers Union to acknowledge a 'debt' to the British Royal and Mercantile Navy, who had kept the shipping lanes open enabling New Zealand's wool-clip to be sent to England. From 1921, funds were distributed to dependents, of those seamen killed in the war, in England and by 1924, the Fund purchased Flock House Farm in Rangitikei, with the intention of bringing some of these dependents to New Zealand, to teach them the basics of farming, then get them placed on farms around the country.

Between 1924 and 1937, a total of over 600 dependents were brought over, trained and placed on farms, and Bill was one of these. He was, however, shipped out to New Zealand without his father's relations' knowledge; they only found out after he had left England— he was only able to meet up with some of them again when he visited London on leave during the war. Bill's early years were therefore spent working on farms in the North and South Islands. He then joined the army during the Second World War, going on to serve in the 2nd New Zealand Expeditionary Force (NZEF) as part of the New Zealand Army Service Corps (NZASC), which was later renamed the Royal New Zealand Corps of Transport (RNZCT). His service number was 82762, and he reached the rank of Corporal. Bill died in 1992.

The mystery man in the photos is a corporal, and this is the same rank that Bill reached. Bill's unit was in the area at the right time. He was part of the supply chain, so moved around in the convoys with general supplies for the troops, food, maybe munitions and also had his own driver so would have had a means and an excuse to visit local villages. He also travelled to London on his leave as the mystery soldier did. Maxine finishes one of her emails; "I'm sorry I can't provide better verification but both Kevin and I feel it is Bill in your photo and the story is the type of thing he would have done as he had seen life and always had a sense of fair play."[515]

As well as provoking the responses from the families at-tempting to help identify the soldier, there were also four comments posted beneath the request for help in *The Dominion Post*. One was a positive comment, but there were also three negative comments. One comment claimed it was "just as well the rest of the soldiers fighting his battle weren't so soft, or the world might be a different place"[516] another questioned why a Kiwi would want to help a deserter.

Vivi remembers that when Alan eventually moved in with her and her parents in October 1945, her mother would give Alan a glass of milk every morning "so that he didn't go out starving." From the conversations Stephenie had with people in the village, Alan was hidden by these three families and Don Amadeo for the first year, potentially a little less. He then moved into Vivi Batani's house in a more permanent arrangement for the last eight months. We think this was because Alan became ill and Vivi was a student nurse who could look after him. At some point, he seemed to have caught malaria, and as winter approached he became very seriously ill. Vivi had to steal medicines from the local hospital where she was working to nurse him back to health. After a tough time, he did recover and once again resumed his routine. This could not go on forever, though.

When Alan was returning home from the village back to Vivi's house one night as he was walking by the bridge he stumbled upon a married woman and the village milkman, who was also married, having sex. He tried to avoid them seeing him, but he saw them and they saw him. He went straight home and told Julia (Vivi's mother) what he had seen and confessed his worry that knowing this secret would only cause him a problem. As a precaution Orfeo, Vivi's brother slept on the floor that night so if the RMPs came for Alan they would assume it was Orfeo.

Nothing happened that night, but the next night, shortly after Alan had got back to Vivi's house, there was a banging at the door. Julia refused them entry, but the RMP officer told her they had good information that there was an English deserter hiding in the house and it was no good claiming otherwise. None of the villagers Stephenie is in touch with know whether or not it was a result of stumbling upon the affair, but the timings suggests a strong chance it was. They threatened to arrest them all if she didn't let them in and then managed to barge past her. Vivi ran up to the bedroom to warn Alan and Orfeo, but the MPs followed and on entering the bedroom asked which one was the Englishman. Orfeo stepped forward and announced that he was. As they started to arrest Orfeo Alan stepped forward and said told the RMPs that it was him that they wanted.

It was all over for Alan.

Vivi remembers; "There was nothing we could do; they held him and took him away."

His service record notes that on 24 October 1945, almost two months after the Second World War had ended, Alan was apprehended from desertion.[517] Alan told his family that he was court-martialled in Rome. His record states that he was tried on 28 November 1945 for absenting himself without leave in the field. This time, Alan plead guilty. He was sentenced to two years' detention in addition to the rest of his previous sentence that he had not served due to volunteering to fight in Italy. Alan told Stephenie that he was kept with hundreds of other prisoners of many different nationalities, all of them soldiers who had deserted. They were then loaded on to rail cattle wagons, so packed that they couldn't all sit down at the same time so had take turns to sit to sleep. They were moved to different barracks, Alan first to MPDB 32 and then back to the Glasshouse at Colchester, the only military prison now still in operation in the UK.

What Alan did not know at the time, however, and what Stephenie and the rest of his family did not know until much later, was that he was not the only member in his family to get arrested in the Lacugnano area. When Stephenie went on holiday in 1960 or 1961, her Uncle Ken and his wife Eileen and their two children Beryl and Phillip came with them. They all drove together, down to the south coast of England, the length of France, and through northern and central Italy in a Dormobile caravan, based on that same chassis Alan would have driven in North Africa. Stephenie remembers going to Lacugnano, and the family stopping off to go to see a gentleman called Vincenzo (Cesarini) who Stephenie knew was from one of the families that helped Alan.

Alan and Ken left the rest of their families and disappeared off to speak with Vincenzo. Even though Stephenie was very young at the time, only five or six years old, she remembers that the men were in the house for a long time. When they came back to the vehicle to get them, Stephenie's mother was annoyed and asked why they had been so long. Alan just said they were talking about the war. Years later, Stephenie spoke to Vincenzo's daughter Argene, who is now in her late 70's, and she was able to tell Stephenie what they had been talking about.

Argene told her that Ken had been arrested in a village called Olmo, about two miles away from Lacugnano, as he went AWOL to look for Alan. Vicenzo had been with Alan, and they had witnessed Ken being arrested. At the point of his arrest, he had only been AWOL for a couple of days, so when he was taken back to his regiment, the mitigating circumstances (and no doubt the fact that he had been mentioned in dispatches previously) resulted in Ken only getting a warning. Ken and Alan went to speak to Vicenzo, as he knew about this and they wanted to ask him if he would keep it quiet from the rest of the family, which he did. By the time Stephenie heard about this it was too late to speak to Ken, as he had passed away. From what she has pieced together from Ken's family and the villagers, she does not believe that they got to speak or indeed if Ken even knew how close he was to finding Alan. On hearing of this desertion, I only feel the same sympathy that it seems Ken's commanding officer must have felt that led him to let Ken off.

Argene thought that Stephenie had known what had happened. Unfortunately, Ken died when Stephenie was only a teenager and by her own admission, and quite understandably, at that time Stephenie wasn't interested in her father's war experience and had learnt it was it was not something that should be discussed anyway. Speaking to me now though Stephenie reflects:

> I realise now that he [Alan] obviously kept quite a lot of things from us and he never realised that I have spoken to people about that time... I have only spoken to my friends a few times about Dad and the war because once I knew he had deserted I kept quiet about it as well. Life is very strange how things are now being talked about when it is nearly too late to get the truth.[518]

In 1947, he was on parade at Colchester when he was seen by an officer from the Rifles who had fought with him in North Africa. The officer recognised Alan and told him that he would get him out of prison and back to his unit to finish his sentence with them. We think that after a few weeks, his unit was being sent out to Germany as part of the tidying up force. A different officer saw him who again he had fought under at some time and told Alan that he had seen too much action and did not need to be going away again. The officer signed his demob papers, allowing Alan to leave. He came out of the army with nothing. His brothers had to give him a suit to wear. His time in the military was finally over after six years, but for Alan, as with many others, the peace would be almost as traumatic as the war.

Alan had tried to write a different ending to his story, an ending that would not be an entry on the Commonwealth War Graves Commission archive. Briefly in Lacugnano, Alan was back in charge of his own narrative. The shame attached to desertion meant in the years after the war, Alan, and then his family, had to fall silent. He lost control of his own story. The family feared that when others heard the word deserter, they would have attached their own story to Alan, without stopping to hear what he had been through.

Chapter Sixteen
All Soldiers Run Away

And I retained the technique of endurance, a brutal persistence in seeing things through, somehow, anyhow, without finesse, satisfied with the main points of any situation.

Goodbye to All That, Robert Graves

I am tired and sick of war. Its glory is all moonshine. It is only those who have neither fired a shot nor heard the shrieks and groans of the wounded who cry aloud for blood, for vengeance, for desolation. War is Hell.

William Sherman

All soldiers run away. It does not matter as long as their supports stand firm.

Arthur Wellesley, Duke of Wellington

After Alan had deserted, a bout of jaundice took Bowlby off the front line, so he missed the attack on Lignano, in which the battalion lost so many men killed that it was disbanded. The ghosts of his dead comrades haunted Bowlby's dreams ever afterwards. After Bowlby left the Army in 1947, he found it difficult to settle down in to civilian life, and the following year he joined 21 SAS, the Territorial Army unit of the regiment. There then followed a variety of jobs including game keeping in Scotland; advertising copywriter in the UK, Sweden, and New Zealand; and lecturing at British Council summer schools. In the mid-1950s he had a breakdown. On 5 November 1957, exactly thirteen years to the day his section commander "Judge" had been blown to bits on a mine, Bowlby's grief exploded.

He tells us in *Recollections* how, after dreaming of walking up the hill where Judge died, he painted Judge as Christ hanging on a willow tree, the picture also had a nodding Easter hen, an infant Christ, and an old childhood toys in its branches, with Bowlby's tears rolling round it. He then walked the six miles from Notting Hill Gate to Swiss Cottage, "crying all the whole way."[519] As Bowlby's world broke up, he says he turned to the one thing he had left to hang on to—his book. During his breakdown, the dialogue of the time came back to him and he describes seeing the words in his head just as they had been spoken back in Italy.

He revisited the battlefields in 1959 for the first time, and then the next summer wrote the final draft. Seventeen publishers turned it down, the last for fear of libel (which may have been the point where the names were changed but he does not state this). He sent a new draft to Leo Cooper, the romantic novelist Jilly Cooper's husband, who had turned it down at Longmans and had just set up on his own as a military publisher. Cooper insisted that Bowlby's title be changed from *All Soldiers Run Away*, after a quote attributed to the British Army's most famous general, but brought the book out in 1969. It received critical acclaim when it finally reached an audience. Arthur Koestler, who had deserted himself, described the book as "a monument to the Unknown Soldier."[520] Bowlby wrote years later: "I discovered that peace can be a much more disturbing business than war and that the near-loss of one's own sense of self under pressure is more terrifying than fear of death in battle. I began retreating to memories of the war, and the happiness and security it had brought me." Alex Bowlby spent his last years in receipt of a pension for his shell shock. He ended his life residing at an alms-house in Holborn, where he died on July 1, 2005, aged 81.

Ultimately it is the commander's job to win wars; doing so requires that they lose some of their men. I remember a senior commander in charge of UK forces on the initial invasion phase of Operation TELIC, the 2003 invasion of Iraq, speaking to a group of us at a dinner for young officers telling us that, when asked if he could achieve the mission as given to his brigade, he made his calculations of what resources he had, both men and equipment, and what the intelligence provided assessed as the enemy's strength, capability, and intent, and then made an assessment of whether victory was possible and if it would fall within what were deemed acceptable levels of casualties, before committing to the politicians that he could achieve militarily what they were asking. He knew he did not have all the resources he needed, including body armour for all his troops, but this would not keep him from achieving the mission below that acceptable level of casualties. He agreed, achieved his mission and an acceptable number of troops were killed, some without body armour that would have saved them if they had it.

Being a senior military commander on operations is a job that comes with a heavy legacy. Since the Iraq war, there have been numerous enquires reviewing all of the decisions that led to going to war and the planning that went on beforehand. Some have dealt with the issue of body armour specifically. Commanders in the Second World War dealt with different scales of acceptable casualties. At points of the war, there were no limits to acceptable casualties, as operations such as the commando raid Operation CHARIOT demonstrated. In most statements of the traditional just war theory, reasonable hope of success is a requirement included among the principles of *jus ad bellum*. The satisfaction of which is held to be necessary in order for the war to be justified as to prevent needless slaughter. By this reading, many Allied action during this period would not have been classed as just.

In war, there will always be this conflict between the higher aims of the war and the aims of the individuals fighting the war. Commanders will, in extreme situations, resort to thinking that allows them to see their soldiers as means to end, even if they will keenly feel the loss of every individual end. This manifests itself in a variety of ways, such as the failing in the first years of fighting in the desert to provide Allied soldiers with adequate psychological support and rotation from the front. As Hamner points out, the military is very aware of this conflict, so it tries as much as it can to get soldiers to see that by sticking to their tasks and completing their mission they give themselves the best chance of survival. When the military fails to do this and it becomes clear for soldiers at the front line that their best chance of surviving is not to continue on with the mission, there is a need to for other factors to motivate soldiers to keep fighting. A desire for a glorious death that may have once motivated warriors in different ages is no longer enough for most. A belief in the just nature of the cause and the conduct of the war does in my experience play a role in motivation.

However, when the rounds start flying and the shells start falling, a more personal and local motivation is necessary, and a sense of duty to comrades and the communities from which soldiers come from provides this. In practical terms, this sense of duty also gives an individual the greatest chance of surviving when it becomes reciprocal. Maybe the strongest motivation though, outside of simply surviving, is the fear of disgrace and desire to be remembered positively as someone who did their duty. Soldiers have a fear of the disgrace that will be theirs if their duties are not done and a fear of being forgotten and not remembered. They fear their story never being told.

However, to just focus on the duties an individual should do neglects the other side of the equation. On this other side of the equation are the rights of the individual, the right to live and the right not to be treated as a means, but as an end in oneself.

Researching and writing this book I have come across two types of hero, one group more obvious and more widely regaled than the other. There are those who have received Victoria Crosses and other awards of bravery for their fearlessness, self-sacrifice and daring. Those like Jock Campbell, Henry Foote, and Vic Turner and his fellow riflemen at Snipe. There are then those like Bill the Kiwi, Alex Bowlby's Italian host, and the people of Lacugnano, who, despite the context of the time, saw another human being as just that. In amongst the failure of humanity that is war, they saw humanity still and treated another as means in themselves.

Alan did wrong his comrades by deserting them, but this wrong is more than excused by the fact that he was a psychological casualty who had been pushed past his limit by the service he had already given. There were many other men like him who were labelled cowards, who were just ordinary men who never asked to go to war and just couldn't take any more. Some would have fell on the wrong side of an arbitrary line that meant they were never given a diagnosis that could have given them some solace. The value of Alan's service up to this point is also significant. Further to that, the wrong (even if justified) done to him by his commanders and arguably the whole community by treating him as a means to an end is potentially greater even if they are fighting a just war.

None of us can say with any degree of certainty how we would react to similar experiences, especially over such a prolonged period. As the commentators under the article in *The Dominion Post* showed, however, this does not stop us criticising, and usually without any attempt to understand the wider context before we do so. I can say, though, that having traced Alan's journey, I sympathise with him and what he did. Like those soldiers that Bain met on the way back from the front who knew what Bain was walking away from, I do not blame him.

The British Government, however, still does. Despite his sacrifice, despite the 500-plus days he fought bravely for the country, he died 70 years later with the shame of being a deserter still hanging over him. It was an extraordinary time so we asked people to do extraordinary things, and in Alan and many others' cases without the training and support needed to have a decent chance of succeeding. The burden also was not spread equally— the brunt of the extraordinary demands fell disproportionate number of front-line troops. The fact that some of these incredibly brave men and women managed to get through it is not a reflection on those that didn't, but rather purely a reflection of their resolve. We should be asking how they managed it, rather than why some did not. We should also be conscious of what price they paid in later years because they did.

Stephenie is very conscious of this and is now a volunteer for the military charities SSAFA—the Armed Forces charity (formerly known as Soldiers, Sailors, Airmen and Families Association) and the Royal Marines Association. She is determined that we should not in 2070 be diagnosing those who fought in the last few years with PTSD like Alan was diagnosed 60 years after his service. Let us hope and insist that the Ministry of Defence and the UK Government more generally are as determined as Stephenie.

There are acts we see as inherently wrong that when we put them into an unfamiliar context suddenly don't seem so black and white. Different contexts we have not considered before can make us realise the subjective values that have influenced our thinking previously. Alan's story has forced me to look at different contexts and question some of my values. This, more than any other reason, is why we should remember. We should remember not to vainly imbue those we never knew with an immortality they never asked for, but to learn from those memories. We should remember them. We should remember men like Alan, not the national myths. Nations tell themselves stories as much as people do. The stories aren't necessarily a true reflection of events, but rather a reflection of how they would like things to be.

There are circumstances where all soldiers run away. There are circumstances where we all fail to be as brave as we would like, we are all at times intolerant of the actions of others more because in them we see our own worst faults. We should remember that, too.

Postscript

"Only the dead have seen the end of the war."

George Santoya

At the age of eighty-five, Stephenie describes Alan as going into "shut down with his PTSD." The family contacted the charity Combat Stress who came and helped with counselling and an official diagnosis. Due to this, Alan was given an official War Pension payment for his PTSD in 2004. The family were encouraged by the medical professionals that diagnosed Alan to request a pardon for him from the government. They spent two years writing to the Secretary of State for Defence and were eventual told that because there are no documents to substantiate his claim of having PTSD at the time of desertion, they could not give him a pardon.

Alan died on 7 February 2016.

I attended the funeral at Poole Crematorium a few weeks later and met his wider family for the first time. Many people in the chapel that day would not have been there if it was not for the compassion of the people of Lacugnano. The service was as joyful as a funeral service can be, and focussed on all the positive attributes Alan clearly had. Alan's grandson (Stephenie's son) gave a personal eulogy that described a man who was a big part in his grandchildren's lives, a man always on hand to play games with them and spend time doing things he once may have doubted he would ever get the chance to do. There was no mention of desertion. Alan had a full life, unlike so many soldiers who took part in the Second World War on both sides. It is with those that did not get the chance to have a full life that our greatest sympathises should lie. This does not mean we should not have sympathy for those who did return and tried their best to move on.

After he had served out his sentence back in the UK for deserting, he managed to find work, first as a groundsman for sports pitches and then on golf courses, always working outside, never comfortable inside in enclosed spaces, which would bring on panic attacks. Even a crowded bus or train was a problem to begin with. He had to gradually learn to control his panic, a process that would take many years. He met Stephenie's mother through Ken and her sister. Ken could not get to Alan in Italy, but was there for him when he returned. Two brothers and two sisters made for a close family. His family learnt to spot the signs of his panic attacks and supported him through the years, accounting for his fears and, often without noticing, making excuses for him.

The family travelled the world with Alan's job as he progressed to constructing golf courses and became in demand. In 1959, he decided to go back with his wife on holiday with two friends to see if the place was still the same. They were driving up a dirt road to the village and a man on a Lambretta stopped them when he saw Alan. He turned around and went back up to the village and started to ring the church bell. The bell was rung by standing up on the tower and ringing it with their feet. From the top of the church tower he shouted out "Alano is back!"

By the time Alan, his wife and their friends arrived the whole village had come out to greet them. There was one place they kept returning to and that was Italy, either to Lacugnano itself on holidays or elsewhere with work, including Sardinia to work on the Aga Khan's Pevero golf course when Stephenie was a teenager.

I was the last to leave the crematorium. I paused and looked into the kind eyes of the man in the photo resting on top of the coffin. For so long, Alan had been an unseen presence staring back at me from the diaries and the emails from Stephenie that shared her memories, just like he had been for Stephenie in the photograph of the Duchess of Atoll. Alan as an individual always remained tantalisingly out of view for me; his dementia was too severe by the time I met Stephenie for me to be able to meet him. Stephenie thought he would have panicked and assumed I was the RMP.

I was now standing alone in the crematorium, separated from him by the wood of the coffin and the more impenetrable barrier of death, looking at another image of the man, who was probably only now at peace for the first time seventy years after his war was meant to have ended. Hopefully for those that knew him he, has come in to clearer focus through this book, even if he remains slightly blurred and out of reach to me. None of us though, both those who knew him and those like me who have only the briefest of impressions, will never really be able to know what he experienced and what state he was in when he made the decision to desert. We can now at least maybe now begin to appreciate what he and so many others went through in North Africa, Italy and elsewhere outside of some of the lesser known battles of the war.

The Recessional music was "El Dorado Film Theme" one of Alan's favourite John Wayne films. The last lines are; "So ride, boldly ride, to the end of the rainbow, Ride, boldly ride, till you find El Dorado." As I left the crematorium, there was a wreath from the Rifles Brigade lying on the side of the hallway that leads from the main room back out into the sunshine. On the wreath there was a note. It said, "[w]e are sorry for what we put you through."

Alan would have one more journey to complete after this. A few months later, Stephenie took Alan's ashes out to Italy and scattered them in the garden at the community centre on the hillside in Lacugnano, the village that was Alan's El Dorado. I began trying to give Stephenie the book she wanted written, but I hope, in the end, that I have given Alan his story back to him.

Acknowledgements

I owe a great deal of thanks to many people who have helped in the research, writing and publication of this book. I owe special thanks to Cecile Fabre, who was immensely generous with her time and advice. I also owe a great thanks to Christopher H Hamner, Seth Lazar and Julian Shales for sharing valuable research with me and also giving me great advice. Thanks to R L Crimp and Alex Bowlby for sharing what it was really like for the men in a Rifle Battalion. Thanks to Wulstan Reeve, Harry Abdy Collins and Seamus Spencer for their encouragement, challenges and suggestions. Thanks to my publisher Jeremy Lammi for his sound advice and hard work on this project and his editor Karen Hann who pushed me for more and then more again. Both made this book more than it would have otherwise been. Thanks to the team at Smith Publicity, especially Sarah, Courtney, Mallory and Mike for all their positivity, hard work and support. Thanks to Paul Hewitt for putting Lacugnano on the map! Thanks to the Imperial War Museum, the National Archives and the Hampshire Records Office for the great services they provide and which I have taken advantage of. Thanks to Tommy Livingstone and the family of Bill Frazier for uncovering the identity of the mystery Kiwi. Most of all thanks to Stephenie, her family and the people of Lacugnano for their bravery in letting me tell their story. This book is dedicated to all those, who despite the context of the time, see other human beings as just that.

Endnotes

[1] "Source List and Detailed Death Tolls for the Primary Megadeaths of the Twentieth Century", last modified March 4, 2016, http://necrometrics.com/25m.htm#Second

[2] Royal Proclamation, carried in various press outlets, November 7, 1919

[3] Antony Beevor, "Europe's Long Shadow," Prospect, 27 November, 2012, www.prospectmagazine.co.uk/magazine/eurozone-democracy-antony-beevor

[4] Julian Clegg, "The family of a Poole man who deserted the battlefield during WW2 tell his story, seven decades on," *BBC Radio Solent*, November 26, 2015, , www.bbc.co.uk/programmes/p0396xqg

[5] "The passing of the WWII generation," The National World War Two Museum, New Orleans, accessed 1 January 2017, www.nationalww2museum.org/honor/wwii-veterans-statistics.html

[6] "Operations in Iraq, Fatalities," Ministry of Defence, accessed April 24, 2017, www.gov.uk/government/fields-of-operation/iraq

[7] Richard A. Oppel Jr, "Bergdahl, Called 'Dirty Rotten Traitor' by Trump, Seeks End to Charges," *New York Times,* January 20, 2017, www.nytimes.com/2017/01/20/us/bergdahl-called-dirty-rotten-traitor-by-trump-seeks-end-to-charges.html?action=click&pgtype=Homepage&clickSource=story-heading&module=span-abc-region&region=span-abc-region&WT.nav=span-abc-region&_r=1

[8] Sarah Koenig, "The Golden Chicken," Episode 2, Season Two, *Serial,* https://serialpodcast.org/season-two/2/the-golden-chicken

[9] Sarah Koenig, "Hindsight Part Two," Episode 8, Season Two, *Serial,* https://serialpodcast.org/season-two/8/hindsight-part-2

[10] "Pardons for servicemen executed for disciplinary offences: recognition as victims of First World War" Section 359, Armed Forces Act 2006, November 8, 2006, www.legislation.gov.uk/ukpga/2006/52/section/359/enacted

[11] "Shot at dawn, pardoned 90 years on," *BBC News*, 16 August, 2006 http://news.bbc.co.uk/1/hi/england/4798025.stm

[12] "Shot at dawn."

[13] "Shot at dawn."

[14] John Bingham, "Ireland pardons Second World War soldiers who left to fight Nazis," *The Telegraph*, 07 May, 2013,

www.telegraph.co.uk/news/uknews/defence/10041215/Ireland-pardons-Second-World-War-soldiers-who-left-to-fight-Nazis.html

[15] Arthur and Cynthia Koestler, Stranger on the Square (London: Hutchinson, 1984)

[16] Michael Scammell, Koestler: The Indispensable Intellectual (Faber, 2010)

[17] Jeff McMahan, Killing In War (Oxford University Press, 2009)

[18] Seth Lazar, "Just War Theory: Revisionists Vs Traditionalists," Annual Review of Political Science (2017)

[19] Michael Walzer, Just and Unjust Wars (Basic Books, fourth edition, 2006)

[20] Cécile Fabre, "War, Crime and Punishment," (Aeon Video, September 2016), www.youtube.com/watch?v=H6LU8N9NWzg

[21] Jeff McMahan, Killing In War (Oxford University Press May 2009)

[22] Also see: Cecile Fabre, Cosmopolitan War (Oxford: Oxford University Press, 2012), Cecile Fabre, "Cosmopolitanism, Just War Theory and Legitimate Authority," International Affairs 84/5 (2008) 963-976., Seth Lazar, "Just War Theory: Revisionists Vs Traditionalists," Annual Review of Political Science (2017).

[23] Fabre, "War, Crime and Punishment"

[24] 1 Tower Hamlets Rifles (London Regiment), War Diary, 1940 Nov.- Dec. 1941, November, File WO 169/367, The National Archives, Kew, London

[25] Lieutenant-Colonel E. A. Shipton, "Western Desert: account of action of 9th Battalion the Rifle Brigade during the withdrawal in Cyrenaica 1941 Mar. 31-Apr. 12," File CAB 106/617, The National Archives, Kew, London

[26] 1st Tower Hamlets Rifles, later to become 9th Rifle Brigade, File 170A12W/D/4059, The Hampshire Records Office, Winchester.

[27] Alan Juniper, Service Record - honest and hard working

[28] The London Gazette, September 5, 1933. p. 1978

[29] BBC America. "'Fleming': 10 Famous Brits Who Were Heroes In World War II." Last accessed July 27, 2017 www.bbcamerica.com/anglophenia/2014/01/10-famous-brits-heroes-world-war-ii

[30] Wikipedia. "David Niven." Last modified on July 4, 2017 https://en.wikipedia.org/wiki/David_Niven

[31] Captain Frisk

[32] Naguib Mahfouz, Midaq Alley (Beirut: Khayats, 1966)

[33] R L Crimp, The Diary of a Desert Rat, (Pan Books Ltd, 1974), 2.

[34] Shipton, "Western Desert"

[35] John Strawson, The Battle For North Africa, (Pen and Sword Military Classics, 2004), 32.

[36] Strawson, Battle For North Africa, 37.

[37] Strawson, Battle For North Africa, 4.

[38] Wikipedia. "Brega." Last modified on April 1, 2017
https://en.wikipedia.org/wiki/Brega#Battle_of_Brega_.281941.29

[39] Ian Hogg, Armour in Conflict, (London: Jane's Publishing, 1989), 98.

[40] Strawson, Battle for North Africa, 49.

[41] General Sir William Jackson, The North African Campaign, 1940-43, (Batsford, 1975), 100.

[42] Norman Kenneth Murphy, "The "lost" battle of Mersa el Brega, Libyan desert, 31 March 1941" (Phd diss. University Hull, 2011).

[43] Julian Shales, A Detailed Fighting Account of: 2nd Armoured Division 9th Australian Division, 3rd Indian Motor Brigade, 7th Support Group and 22nd Guards Brigade in Contact with the Afrika Korps and units from the February to May 1941 Infantry, Artillery and Tank Combat in Libya and Egypt, Volume One, (Armour Publishing, 2015).

[44] Shipton, "Western Desert"

[45] Major R.H.W.S Hastings, The Rifle Brigade in the Second World War 1939 - 1945, (Gale & Polden Ltd, Aldershot, 1950), 63

[46] Shales, A Detailed Fighting Account, 303.

[47] Shipton, "Western Desert"

[48] Shipton, "Western Desert"

[49] Shipton, "Western Desert"

[50] Shipton, "Western Desert"

[51] L E Tutt, The Private Papers of L E Tutt, 1985, File 3706, Imperial War Museum, London

[52] Hastings, The Rifle Brigade, 65.

[53] Albert Edward Handscombe (Oral history), 1996, File 16909 (Sound), Imperial War Museum, London, www.iwm.org.uk/collections/item/object/80016837

[54] Shipton, "Western Desert"

[55] Shipton, "Western Desert"

[56] Vernon Scannell, Baptism of Fire, Of Love and War: New and selected poems, (London : Robson Books, 2002)

[57] Shipton, "Western Desert"

[58] C Rae, A L Harris and R K Bryant, On Target - The Story of 2/3rd Australian Light Anti-Aircraft Regiment, (Victoria: 2/3 Light Anti-Aircraft Association, 1987)

[59] Spencer, Samuel Taylor Walker (Oral history), 2011, File 33359 (Sound), Imperial War Museum, London, www.iwm.org.uk/collections/item/object/80032311

[60] 2 Armoured Division: General Staff (GS), War Diary, 1941 Apr.- May, File WO169/1146, The National Archives, Kew, London

61 National Health Service. "Why lack of sleep is bad for your health.", Last reviewed June 15, 2015, www.nhs.uk/Livewell/tiredness-and-fatigue/Pages/lack-of-sleep-health-risks.aspx

62 3rd Armoured Brigade HQ, War Diary, 1941 Jan-Sep, File WO169/1278, The National Archives, Kew, London

63 2nd Support Group, War Diary, 1941 Jan-May, File WO169/1159, the National Archives, Kew, London

64 B/O Battery 1 Regiment Royal Horse Artillery (RHA), War Diary, Jan.- Dec. 1941 , File WO169/1436, The National Archives, Kew, London

65 Shipton, "Western Desert"

66 Handscombe, File 16909 (Sound), IWM

67 The Commonwealth War Graves Commission. www.cwgc.org/find-war-dead/casualty/2205937/NEWELL,%20VICTOR%20LEVI

68 2 Armoured Division, War Diary, File WO169/1146, The National Archives.

69 The Commonwealth War Graves Commission. "El Alamein War Cemetery." www.cwgc.org/find-a-cemetery/cemetery/2019000/EL%20ALAMEIN%20WAR%20CEMETERY

70 Ministry of Defence. "Operations in Afghanistan: Lance Corporal Mathew Ford killed in Afghanistan." First published January 16, 2007 www.gov.uk/government/fatalities/lance-corporal-mathew-ford-killed-in-afghanistan

71 Declan Walsh and Richard Norton-Taylor, "Strapped to Apaches and dodging fire, how troops recovered fallen comrade," *The Guardian*, January 17, 2017 www.theguardian.com/world/2007/jan/17/afghanistan.military

72 Strawson, Battle For North Africa, 59.

73 Strawson, Battle For North Africa, 59.

74 Strawson, Battle For North Africa, 60.

75 Strawson, Battle For North Africa, 60-61.

76 Strawson, Battle For North Africa, 61.

77 Strawson, Battle For North Africa, 62.

78 Shales, A Detailed Fighting Account, 517.

79 A Shales Detailed Fighting Account, 704-802.

80 Spencer, File 33359 (Sound), IWM

81 Spencer, File 33359 (Sound), IWM

82 Strawson, Battle For North Africa, 60.

83 Strawson, Battle For North Africa, 62.

84 Strawson, Battle For North Africa, 67.

85 Tower Hamlets Rifles, War Diary, June, File WO 169/367

86 Alan Juniper, Service Record

87 Crimp, The Diary of a Desert Rat, 9.

[88] Tower Hamlets Rifles, War Diary, August, File WO 169/367

[89] Tower Hamlets Rifles, War Diary, August, File WO 169/367

[90] Richard Humble, Crusader: Eighth Army's Forgotten Victory, November 1941 to January 1942 (Pen & Sword Books Ltd, 1987)

[91] Adrian Stewart, The Early Battles of Eighth Army (Pen and Sword Ltd, 2002), 15-16.

[92] Sir David Hunt, A Don at War (Abingdon: Frank Cass, 1990), 72-73.

[93] Strawson, Battle For North Africa, 76.

[94] Ken Ford, Operation Crusader 1941 (Osprey, 2010), 64-65.

[95] Stewart, The Early Battles of Eighth Army, 35.

[96] Desert War: The New Zealanders at Sis Rezegh. "The New Zealand Division in Operation Crusader," www.sidirezegh.co.nz/Operation-Crusader-An-Overview/

[97] Tower Hamlets Rifles, War Diary, November, File WO 169/367

[98] James Joyce, The Portrait of the Artist as a Young Man (Penguin, 1965)

[99] Hastings, The Rifle Brigade, 89.

[100] Tower Hamlets Rifles, War Diary, November, File WO 169/367

[101] The Commonwealth War Graves Commission. www.cwgc.org/find-war-dead.aspx?cpage=1

[102] Stewart, The Early Battles of Eighth Army, 37.

[103] W. E Murphy, The Relief of Tobruk: The Official History of New Zealand in the Second World War 1939-1945 (New Zealand Electronic Text Collection ed.) (Wellington, NZ: War History Branch, Department of Internal Affairs) Retrieved July, 30 2015

[104] Stewart, The Early Battles of Eighth Army, 37.

[105] Stewart, The Early Battles of Eighth Army, 38.

[106] Tower Hamlets Rifles, War Diary, December, File WO 169/367

[107] Jon Krakauer, Where Men Win Glory: The Odyssey of Pat Tillman (Atlantic Books, 2010).

[108] Tower Hamlets Rifles, War Diary, December, WO 169/367

[109] Tower Hamlets Rifles, War Diary, December, WO 169/367

[110] Stewart, The Early Battles of Eighth Army, 39.

[111] 9 Rifle Brigade (Prince Consort's Own), War Diary, 1942 Jan.- Sept., File WO 169/5057, The National Archives, Kew, London

[112] The Commonwealth War Graves Commission. www.cwgc.org/find-war-dead/casualty/2123014/KENNEDY,%20SYDNEY%20ALBERT

[113] Ford, Operation Crusader, 92.

[114] Strawson, Battle For North Africa, 81.

[115] Strawson, Battle For North Africa, 87-88.

[116] Stewart, The Early Battles of Eighth Army, 40.

117 Strawson, Battle For North Africa, 91.

118 Stewart, The Early Battles of Eighth Army, 42.

119 Stewart, The Early Battles of Eighth Army, 42.

120 Stewart, The Early Battles of Eighth Army, 45.

121 David Hume, A Treatise of Human Nature: Being an Attempt to Introduce the Experimental Method of Reasoning into Moral Subjects, Book III, Part III, Section. III. Of the Influencing Motives of the Will (Penguin Classics; New Ed edition, 1985)

122 Jonathan Haidt, The Righteous Mind: Why are good people divided by politics and religion (London: Penguin, 2013)

123 Strawson, Battle For North Africa, 95.

124 The Encyclopedia Britannica. "Al-Mu?allaq?t". www.britannica.com/topic/Al-Muallaqat-Arabic-literature

125 Crimp, The Diary of a Desert Rat, 23.

126 9 Rifle Brigade, War Diary, January, WO 169/5057

127 Stewart, The Early Battles of Eighth Army, 46.

128 Strawson, Battle For North Africa, 96.

129 Stewart, The Early Battles of Eighth Army, 47.

130 9 Rifle Brigade, War Diary, January, WO 169/5057

131 Strawson, Battle For North Africa, 96-97.

132 9 Rifle Brigade, War Diary, January, WO 169/5057

133 Strawson, Battle For North Africa, 97.

134 9 Rifle Brigade, War Diary, January, WO 169/5057

135 Stewart, The Early Battles of Eighth Army, 47.

136 9 Rifle Brigade, War Diary, January, WO 169/5057

137 Hastings, The Rifle Brigade, 106.

138 9 Rifle Brigade, War Diary, January, WO 169/5057

139 9 Rifle Brigade, War Diary, January, WO 169/5057

140 9 Rifle Brigade, War Diary, January, WO 169/5057

141 Strawson, Battle For North Africa, 99.

142 9 Rifle Brigade, War Diary, January, WO 169/5057

143 The Commonwealth War Graves Commission. www.cwgc.org/find-war-dead.aspx?cpage=1

144 9 Rifle Brigade, War Diary, January, WO 169/5057

145 9 Rifle Brigade, War Diary, January, WO 169/5057

146 Stewart, The Early Battles of Eighth Army, 50.

147 Stewart, The Early Battles of Eighth Army, 50.

148 Major-General I. S. O. Playfair et al. The Mediterranean and Middle East: British Fortunes reach their Lowest Ebb (September 1941 to September

1942). History of the Second World War, United Kingdom Military Series III (Uckfield, UK: Naval & Military Press, 2004), 197-198, 216-217.

[149] 9 Rifle Brigade, War Diary, February, WO 169/5057

[150] The Commonwealth War Graves Commission. www.cwgc.org/find-war-dead/casualty/2118993/ADLER,%20HAROLD%20JAMES

[151] 9 Rifle Brigade, War Diary, February, WO 169/5057

[152] The Commonwealth War Graves Commission. www.cwgc.org/find-war-dead/casualty/2206088/PRESTON,%20HUGH%20GRAHAM

[153] Ronald Lewin, Rommel As Military Commander (New York: B&N Books, 1998), 109.

[154] Strawson, Battle For North Africa, 104.

[155] Strawson, Battle For North Africa, 104.

[156] Stewart, The Early Battles of Eighth Army, 63.

[157] 9 Rifle Brigade, War Diary, April, WO 169/5057

[158] 9 Rifle Brigade, War Diary, April, WO 169/5057

[159] 9 Rifle Brigade, War Diary, April, WO 169/5057

[160] Alan Juniper, 6915504, Territorial Army Record of Service, Army Form B 200d

[161] The Commonwealth War Graves Commission. www.cwgc.org/find-war-dead/casualty/2768521/FOGARTY,%20JOHN

[162] Stephenie Stockley, e-mail to the author, March 24,2016.

[163] Alan Juniper, Record of Service

[164] Strawson, Battle For North Africa, 103.

[165] Stewart, The Early Battles of Eighth Army, 60-61.

[166] Stewart, The Early Battles of Eighth Army, 64-65

[167] Stewart, The Early Battles of Eighth Army, 60

[168] 9 Rifle Brigade, War Diary, May, WO 169/5057

[169] Strawson, Battle For North Africa, 103.

[170] 9 Rifle Brigade, War Diary, May, WO 169/5057

[171] Stewart, The Early Battles of Eighth Army, 73.

[172] Stewart, The Early Battles of Eighth Army, 75.

[173] 9 Rifle Brigade, War Diary, May, WO 169/5057

[174] The Commonwealth Graves Commission. www.cwgc.org/find-war-dead/casualty/2058240/TILLOTT,%20JOHN%20WILLIAM

[175] 9 Rifle Brigade, War Diary, June, WO 169/5057

[176] 9 Rifle Brigade, War Diary, June, WO 169/5057

[177] Stewart, The Early Battles of Eighth Army, 76.

[178] 9 Rifle Brigade, War Diary, June, WO 169/5057

[179] Stewart, The Early Battles of Eighth Army, 76.

[180] The Commonwealth Graves Commission. www.cwgc.org/find-war-dead/casualty/2096565/DREW,%20ALBERT%20EDWARD

[181] Playfair , The Mediterranean and Middle East, 235-236

[182] 9 Rifle Brigade, War Diary, June, WO 169/5057

[183] 9 Rifle Brigade, War Diary, June, WO 169/5057

[184] Playfair, The Mediterranean and Middle East, 237

[185] Robert Twigger, "The legend of the Legion," Aeon, April 10, 2017. https://aeon.co/essays/why-young-men-queue-up-to-die-in-the-french-foreign-legion

[186] Richard Mead, Churchill's Lions: A Biographical Guide to the Key British Generals of World War II, (Stroud: Spellmount, 2007), 298.

[187] 9 Rifle Brigade, War Diary, June, WO 169/5057

[188] Stewart, The Early Battles of Eighth Army, 79.

[189] S Mitcham, Rommel's Lieutenants: The Men who Served the Desert Fox, France, 1940 (Westport, CN: Praeger, 2007), 98.

[190] Alexander Clifford, Three Against Rommel: The Campaigns of Wavell, Auchinleck and Alexander (London: Harrap, 1944), 264.

[191] 9 Rifle Brigade, War Diary, June, WO 169/5057

[192] Stewart, The Early Battles of Eighth Army, 85.

[193] Hastings, The Rifle Brigade, 123.

[194] 9 Rifle Brigade, War Diary, June, WO 169/5057

[195] The Commonwealth War Graves Commission. www.cwgc.org/find-war-dead.aspx

[196] Stewart, The Early Battles of Eighth Army, 86.

[197] Hastings, The Rifle Brigade, 128.

[198] Hastings, The Rife Brigade, 128.

[199] Hastings, The Rifle Brigade, 129.

[200] Stewart, The Early Battles of Eighth Army, 91.

[201] Stewart, The Early Battles of Eighth Army, 92.

[202] Waller, Douglas (Oral history) 2002-2007, File 23447 (Sound), Imperial War Museum, London, www.iwm.org.uk/collections/item/object/80021973

[203] Max Hastings, All Hell Let Loose: The World at War 1939-1945 (Harper Press, 2012) Kindle Edition. Loc 2647.

[204] Hastings, All Hell Let Loose, 2657.

[205] Niall Barr, Pendulum of War: The Three Battles of El Alamein (Woodstock NY: Overlook, 2005), 1.

[206] 9 Rifle Brigade, War Diary, June, WO 169/5057

[207] Stewart, The Early Battles of Eighth Army, 98.

[208] Stewart, The Early Battles of Eighth Army, 99.

[209] 9 Rifle Brigade, War Diary, June, WO 169/5057

[210] Stewart, The Early Battles of Eighth Army, 101.

[211] Stewart, The Early Battles of Eighth Army, 105.

[212] Richard Toye, The Roar of the Lion: The Untold Story of Churchill's World War II Speeches (Oxford University Press, 2013), 143.

[213] 9 Rifle Brigade, War Diary, July, WO 169/5057

[214] Alan Juniper Service Record

[215] Enrich Maria Remarque, All Quiet on the Western Front (Vintage, 1996), 75-77.

[216] Jean Paul Sartre, The Wall (New Directions; 3rd Revised edition, 1969), 7.

[217] Remarque, All Quiet on the Western Front, 77.

[218] Chart of Court Martial Convictions For All Offences, provided by Assistant Curator, The Adjutant General's Corps Museum.

[219] Dr. Louise Walker, e-mail to the author, July 8, 2016.

[220] Glass, Deserters, xi

[221] Samuel A. Stouffer, The American Soldier: Combat and its aftermath, Studies in social psychology in World War II ?(United States. Army Service Forces. Information and Education Division, 1950), 203.

[222] Christopher H. Hamner, Enduring Battle: American Soldiers in Three Wars, 1776-1945 (University Press of Kansas, 2011), 218.

[223] Approved Judgment, The Lord Chief Justice of England and Wales, The President of the Queen's Bench Division, Mr Justice Openshaw, Mr Justice Sweeney, Between: Regina and Alexander Wayne Blackman, Case No: 2016/05551/B1 & 2016/05552/B1, March 15, 2017, Royal Courts of Justice Strand, London.

[224] Shephard, War of Nerves, 182-184.

[225] The American Psychiatric Association. "Diagnostic and Statistical Manual of Mental Disorders (DSM-5)." www.psychiatry.org/psychiatrists/practice/dsm

[226] American Psychiatric Association. "Diagnostic and Statistical Manual of Mental Disorders (DSM-5; 1)", 2013.

[227] Matthew Green, Aftershock: Fighting War, Surviving Trauma and Finding Peace (Portobello Books, 2015), 236.

[228] Green, Aftershock, 56.

[229] Green, Aftershock, 56.

[230] Shephard, War of Nerves, 182-184.

[231] Shephard, War of Nerves, 182-184

[232] Shephard, War of Nerves, 182-184.

[233] Green, Aftershock, 58.

234 Marie-Louise Sharp, Nicola T. Fear, Roberto J. Rona, Simon Wessely, Neil Greenberg, Norman Jones, and Laura Goodwin, "Stigma as a Barrier to Seeking Health Care Among Military Personnel With Mental Health Problems", Epidemiologic Reviews Vol. 37 (2015): 144, accessed July 29, 2017. www.kcl.ac.uk/kcmhr/publications/assetfiles/2015/Sharp2015.pdf

235 Shephard, War of Nerves, 211.

236 Green, Aftershock, 139.

237 Nafsika Thalassis, 'Treating and Preventing Trauma: British Military Psychiatry during the Second World War' (Phd diss. University of Salford, 2004).

238 Nafsika Thalassis, e-mail to the author, August 7,2016.

239 Approved Judgment, Regina and Alexander Wayne Blackman

240 Michael Sandel, Justice: What's the Right Thing to Do? (Penguin, 2010), 11.

241 Steven Hyman, Categorising Mental Disorders,Philosophy Bites, 2016, http://philosophybites.com/2016/01/steven-hyman-on-categorising-mental-disorders.html

242 Steve Hyman, e-mail to the author, March 26, 2017.

243 Morris West, the Devil's Advocate, (William Heinemann Ltd, 1959).

244 Glass, Deserters, xv -xvi.

245 Glass Deserters, xvii-xviii.

246 Hastings, All Hell Let Loose, Loc 2760.

247 Hastings, All Hell Let Loose, Loc 2765.

248 Shephard, War of Nerves, 239.

249 Neal Ascherson, review of "Deserter: The Untold Story of WWII by Charles Glass" The Guardian, March 28, 2013 www.theguardian.com/books/2013/mar/28/deserter-untold-story-glass-review

250 Hamner, inside cover of Enduring Battle.

251 Hamner, Enduring Battle, 4.

252 Stouffer, The American Soldier

253 Hamner, Enduring Battle, 173.

254 Hamner, Enduring Battle. 17-18.

255 S L A Marshall, Men Against Fire: The problem of Battle Command in Future War (New York: William Morrow, 1947).

256 Hamner, Enduring Battle, 3.

257 Leonard Wong et al, Why They Fight: Combat Motivation in the Iraq War (Carlisle Barracks, PA: Strategic Studies Institute, US Army War College, 2003).

258 Hamner, Enduring Battle, 173.

259 Koenig, "Hindsight Part Two," Serial

[260] Seth Lazar, "The Associative Account of Killing in War," in Global Political Theory, ed. David Held and Pietro Maffettone (Polity Press, 2016), Chapter 8, 169.

[261] Lazar, Killing in War, 159

[262] Lazar, Killing in War, 158.

[263] Lazar, Killing in War, 158.

[264] Lazar. Killing in War, 161

[265] Hamner, Enduring Battle, 174.

[266] Hamner, Enduring Battle, 174

[267] Hamner, Enduring Battle, 175.

[268] Hamner, Enduring Battle, 176.

[269] Cecile Fabre, "Internecine War Killings," Utilitas 24 (2) (2012): 214-236.

[270] Hamner, Enduring Battle, 176.

[271] Hamner, Enduring Battle, 177.

[272] Hamner, Enduring Battle, 177.

[273] Hamner, Enduring Battle, 84.

[274] Hamner, Enduring Battle, 95.

[275] Shephard, War of Nerves, 187-189.

[276] Hastings, All Hell Let Loose, Loc 2595.

[277] Martin E. P. Seligman and Michael D. Matthews, guest editors, Comprehensive Soldier Fitness Special issue of American Psychologist Vol. 66, No. 1, January 2011

[278] Hamner, Enduring Battle, 177.

[279] Hamner, Enduring Battle, 177-178.

[280] Hamner, Enduring Battle, 136.

[281] Adam Nicolson, The Mighty Dead: Why Homer Matters (William Collins, 2014), 125-126.

[282] Yuval Noah Harari, Homo Deus: A Brief History of Tomorrow (Harper, 2017), 288

[283] Harari, Homo Deus, 286.

[284] Harari, Homo Deus, 289.

[285] Alfred Lord Tennyson, The Charge of The Light Brigade (1854), Tennyson Poems (Letchworth, UK: The Temple Press, Everyman's Library, 1949) 394

[286] Approved Judgment, Regina and Alexander Wayne Blackman

[287] Gov.UK, "Policy paper, 2010 to 2015 government policy: armed forces covenant,"

Updated May 8, 2015 www.gov.uk/government/publications/2010-to-2015-government-policy-armed-forces-covenant/2010-to-2015-government-policy-armed-forces-covenant

[288] The Iraq Inquiry, July 6, 2016 www.iraqinquiry.org.uk/the-report/

[289] Harari, Homo Deus

[290] Hastings, All Hell Let Loose, Loc 9345.

[291] Omar Bartov, Hitler's Army: Soldiers, Nazis, and War in the Third Reich (Oxford University Press, 1992).

[292] Jon Cooksey, Operation Chariot: The Raid on St. Nazaire (Leo Cooper Ltd, 2004).

[293] Immanuel Kant, Critique of Pure Reason (Penguin Classics; Rev Ed edition, 2007).

[294] Collins. www.collinsdictionary.com/dictionary/english/im-all-right-jack

[295] Hamner, Enduring Battle, 188-189.

[296] Hamner, Enduring Battle, 190.

[297] Alex Bowlby, The Recollections of Rifleman Bowlby (Arrow Books Ltd, 1991) 23.

[298] Samuel Scheffler, Death and the Afterlife (Oxford University Press; Reprint edition, 2016)

[299] Haidt, Righteous Mind

[300] Koenig, "Hindsight Part Two," Serial.

[301] Koenig, "Present for Duty," Serial.

[302] Walter Purdy was the traitor of Colditz, a British fascist placed by the Germans in Colditz to report on escape attempts. Tom King, "Quiet man of Thundersley was the Colditz traitor," *Basildon, Canvey and Southend Echo*, Jan 3, 2008 www.echo-news.co.uk/news/1941694.quiet_man_of_thundersley_was_the_colditz_traitor/

[303] Stephen J. Dubner, "Who Serves in the Military Today?" Freakonomics, September 22, 2008 http://freakonomics.com/2008/09/22/who-serves-in-the-military-today/

[304] Sandel, Justice, 77.

[305] Aristotle, Politics (Oxford University Press; Revised ed. Edition, 2009)

[306] Glass, Deserters, xi.

[307] Gov.uk. "Rights and responsibilities: developing our constitutional framework" March 23, 2009, www.gov.uk/government/publications/rights-and-responsibilities-developing-our-constitutional-framework

[308] John Stuart Mill, On Liberty, (Penguin Classics; 1 edition, 2007), Chapter 1, 11.

[309] Thomas Paine, Rights of Man, Observations on the Rights of Man (Dover Publications; Thrift edition, 1999) 121.

[310] Jean-Jacques Rousseau, The Social Contract (Penguin Classics, 1968).

[311] Gov.uk. "Rights and responsibilities"

[312] Naval Marine Archive: The Canadian Collection. "England expects that every man will do his duty," http://navalmarinearchive.com/research/england_expects_signalflags.html

[313] History Today. "The Execution of Admiral Byng" March, 2007. www.historytoday.com/richard-cavendish/execution-admiral-byng

[314] National Museum of the Royal Navy, "Information sheet no 099 John Byng" Retrieved 7 September 2017. www.nmrn-portsmouth.org.uk/sites/default/files/John%20Byng.pdf

[315] Voltaire, Candide and Other Stories (Dover Publications; Reprint edition, 1991)

[316] Voltaire, Candide, 65.

[317] Stephen Bates and Richard Norton-Taylor, "No pardon for Admiral Byng. The MoD don't want to encourage any others," *The Guardian*, 15 March 2007.

[318] Paul Stilwell, Assault on Normandy: First-Person Accounts from the Sea Services (Naval Institute Press, 1994) 228.

[319] Roger Scruton, England: An Elegy (Continuum, 2006), 7.

[320] William Shakespeare, The Life and Death of Richard the Second, Act II, Scene I, 50 (Oxford University Press; Critical ed. Edition, 2011).

[321] William Blake, Jerusalem (Forgotten Books, 2017).

[322] Lazar, Killing in War, 167.

[323] Sandel, Justice, 235.

[324] Sandel, Justice, 218.

[325] Sandel, Justice, 218.

[326] The United Nations. Charter of The United Nations. www.un.org/en/charter-united-nations/

[327] John Tasioulas, "Are human rights anything more than legal conventions?" Aeon, April 11, 2017. https://aeon.co/ideas/are-human-rights-anything-more-than-legal-conventions?utm_source=Aeon+Newsletter&utm_campaign=23565fc383-EMAIL_CAMPAIGN_2017_04_11&utm_medium=email&utm_term=0_411a82e59d-23565fc383-69428181

[328] Sarah Bakewell, How To Live: A Life of Montaigne in one question and twenty attempts at an answer (Vintage, 2011), 181.

[329] Bakewell, How To Live, 181.

[330] Sandel, Justice, 220-225.

[331] Sandel, Justice, 221-223.

[332] Alasdair MacIntyre, After Virtue (University of Notre Dame Press, 1981), 204-205.

[333] Sandel, Justice, 235.

[334] Lazar, Killing in War, 162.

[335] Shipton, Western Desert.

336 Garrath Williams, "Praise and Blame," Internet Encyclopaedia of Philosophy, retrieved May 3, 2017, www.iep.utm.edu/praise/#H4

337 Williams, "Praise and Blame"

338 Green, Aftershock, 60.

339 Hamner, Enduring Battle, 219.

340 Crimp, The Diary of a Desert Rat, 38.

341 Koenig, "Escaping," Serial.

342 Glass, Deserters, 235.

343 Glass, Deserters, 241.

344 Lester Pearce, Regimental Secretary Military Provost Staff, e-mail to the author, January 5, 2016.

345 West Side Detroit Polish American Historical Society. "Pvt. Eddie D. Slovik." November 1, 2007. http://detroitpolonia.org/pvt-eddie-d-slovik

346 Benedict B. Kimmelman, "The Example of Private Slovik." American Heritage (September/October 1987) 38 (6). Retrieved January, 2016.

347 Kimmelman, "The Example of Private Slovik."

348 Kimmelman, "The Example of Private Slovik."

349 Kimmelman, "The Example of Private Slovik."

350 Kimmelman, "The Example of Private Slovik."

351 Kimmelman, "The Example of Private Slovik."

352 Kimmelman, "The Example of Private Slovik."

353 The Execution of Private Slovik." The Army Lawyer: A History of the Judge Advocate General's Corps, 1775-1975 (reprint of the US Army edition) (Honolulu: University Press of the Pacific, 2011).

354 Kimmelman, "The Example of Private Slovik."

355 Saul David, Mutiny at Salerno 1943: An Injustice Exposed (Conway, 2005), 182.

356 R L Crimp, Volume 3, ff. 96 and 100, 16 March and 26th April 1944, IWM (D) 96/50/1

357 Lester Pearce, Regimental Secretary Military Provost Staff, e-mail to the author, January 5, 2016.

358 The Hill, (1965) Director: Sidney Lumet, Writer: Ray Rigby (screenplay), Distributed by Metro-Goldwyn-Mayer

359 Glass, Deserters, 46.

360 Glass Deserters, 73.

361 Glass Deserters, 75.

362 Albert Camus, Myth of Sisyphus, Great Ideas 39 (Penguin, 2005), 119.

363 A Shales Detailed Fighting Account, 802.

364 Strawson, The Battle for North Africa, 127.

[365] Strawson, The Battle for North Africa, 124.

[366] Strawson, The Battle for North Africa, 125.

[367] Strawson, The Battle for North Africa, 130.

[368] Strawson, The Battle for North Africa, 132.

[369] Montgomery Personal Message, October 1942, Documents 12838, Catalogue date 2003-07-29, Imperial War Museum.

[370] Glass, Deserters, 80.

[371] Henry R. Ritchie, The Fusing of the Ploughshare: The Story of a Yeoman at War (Henry Ritchie; 2nd Edition edition, 1989).

[372] Hastings, The Rifle Brigade, 165.

[373] Major R D Cassidy, A Brief History of the Rifle Brigade. "World War Two 1939-1945." www.greenjackets-net.org.uk/rb/ww2.htm

[374] Cassidy, A Brief History.

[375] Cassidy, A Brief History.

[376] Cassidy, A Brief History.

[377] Cassidy, A Brief History.

[378] Hastings, The Rifle Brigade, 416-417.

[379] Cassidy, A Brief History.

[380] Cassidy, A Brief History.

[381] Hastings, The Rifle Brigade, 230.

[382] Hastings, The Rifle Brigade, 236.

[383] Hastings, The Rifle Brigade, 237.

[384] 2 Rifle Brigade (Prince Consort's Own), War Diary 1944 Apr-Dec, WO 170/1468, The National Archives, Kew.

[385] Leften S Stavrianos, 'The Mutiny in the Greek Armed Forces, April 1944,' American Slavic and East European Review, vol. IX (1950).

[386] 2 Rifle Brigade, War Diary.

[387] Hastings, All Hell Let Loose, Loc. 8385.

[388] Hastings, All Hell Let Loose, Loc 8399.

[389] Ben Macintyre, Operation Mincemeat (London: Bloomsbury, 2010).

[390] Macintyre, Operation Mincemeat, 270.

[391] Macintyre, Operation Mincemeat, 299-300.

[392] Hastings, All Hell Let Loose, Loc. 8417.

[393] Hastings, All Hell Let Loose, Loc. 8435.

[394] Hastings, All Hell Let Loose, Loc. 8440.

[395] Hastings, All Hell Let Loose, Loc. 8449.

[396] Hastings, All Hell Let Loose, Loc. 8494.

[397] Hastings, All Hell Let Loose, Loc. 8546.

398 Hastings, All Hell Let Loose, Loc. 8555.

399 Hastings, All Hell Let Loose, Loc. 8560.

400 Hastings, All Hell Let Loose, Loc. 8577.

401 Hastings, All Hell Let Loose, Loc. 8598.

402 Norman Lewis, Naples '44: An Intelligence Officer in the Italian Labyrinth (Eland Publishing Ltd, 2002), 49.

403 Matthew Parker, Monte Cassino (Headline, 2004), xvii.

404 "Getting MAD: Nuclear Mutual Assured Destruction, Its Origins and Practice," Strategic Studies Institute, (November, 2004),36.

405 Fredrick Taylor, Dresden: Tuesday 13 February 1945 (New York: HarperCollins, 2004), 432.

406 UNESCO. "Discours de la Directrice générale de l'UNESCO Irina Bokova, à l'occasion de la Réunion de haut niveau pour la protection du patrimoine culturel syrien, (August, 2013), 4. www.unesco.org/new/fileadmin/MULTIMEDIA/HQ/ERI/pdf/ReunionPatrim oineSyrie.pdf

407 Monuments Men Blog. "70th Anniversary of Ike's Orders - "We are bound to respect those monuments so far as war allows." December 29, 2013. www.monumentsmen.com/blog/2013/12/29/3661/3661/

408 The Monuments Men (2014), Directed by George Clooney, Screenplay by George Clooney, Grant Heslov, Distributed by Columbia Pictures (United States), 20th Century Fox (International).

409 Hastings, All Hell let Loose, Loc. 8616.

410 Ian Carter, "Anzio - The Invasion That Almost Failed," Imperial War Museum, accessed January 2016. www.iwm.org.uk/history/anzio-the-invasion-that-almost-failed

411 Carter, Anzio.

412 2 Rifle Brigade, War Diary.

413 R L Crimp, The overseas tour of a conscripted rifleman - Italy 29th April to 17th March 1945, Documents.5659, Catalogue date 1996-10-03, Imperial War Museum, London.

414 Crimp, Overseas Tour.

415 Crimp, Overseas Tour.

416 Camus, Sisyphus, 88.

417 2 Rifle Brigade, War Diary.

418 Crimp, Overseas Tour.

419 Alex Bowlby, The Recollections of Rifleman Bowlby (Leo Cooper, 1989).

420 Benjamin Harris, The Recollections of Rifleman Harris (CreateSpace Independent Publishing Platform, 2015).

421 "Alex Bowlby Obituary," *The Daily Telegraph,* August 16, 2005, accessed January 28, 2016, www.telegraph.co.uk/news/obituaries/1496268/Alex-Bowlby.html

422 Bowlby, Recollections, 8.

423 Hastings, The Rifle Brigade, 260.

424 Crimp, Overseas Tour.

425 Crimp, Overseas Tour.

426 Bowlby, Recollections, 12.

427 Crimp, Overseas Tour.

428 2 Rifle Brigade, War Diary.

429 Carter, Anzio.

430 2 Rifle Brigade, War Diary.

431 Crimp, Overseas Tour.

432 Hastings, The Rifle Brigade, 267.

433 Crimp, Overseas Tour.

434 2 Rifle Brigade, War Diary.

435 Crimp, Overseas Tour.

436 2 Rifle Brigade, War Diary.

437 Bowlby, Recollections, 2.

438 Bowlby, Recollections, 37.

439 The Commonwealth Graves Commission. Dereck Flowers Ware. www.cwgc.org/find-war-dead/casualty/2613311/WARE,%20DEREK%20FLOWERS

440 Bowlby, Recollections, 40.

441 Bowlby, Recollections, 41.

442 Crimp, Overseas Tour.

443 Crimp, Overseas Tour.

444 Crimp, Overseas Tour.

445 Bowlby, Recollections, 49.

446 Bowlby, Recollections, 50.

447 2 Rifle Brigade, War Diary.

448 Bowlby, Recollections, 51.

449 Bowlby, Recollections, 52.

450 2 Rifle Brigade, War Diary.

451 Hastings, The Rifle Brigade, 270.

452 2 Rifle Brigade, War Diary.

453 Crimp, Overseas Tour.

454 Bowlby, Recollections, 57.

455 Crimp, Overseas Tour.

456 Bowlby, Recollections, 59.

457 Bowlby, Recollections, 59.

458 Bowlby, Recollections, 59.

459 Bowlby, Recollections, 61.

460 Bowlby, Recollections, 64.

461 Hastings, All Hell Let Loose, Loc. 8741.

462 Bowlby, Recollections, 64.

463 Hastings, The Rifle Brigade, 272.

464 Crimp, Overseas Tour.

465 Hastings, The Rifle Brigade, 273.

466 2 Rifle Brigade, War Diary.

467 Hastings, The Rifle Brigade, 276.

468 Hastings, The Rifle Brigade, 276.

469 Crimp, Overseas Tour.

470 Crimp, Overseas Tour.

471 Crimp, Overseas Tour.

472 Crimp, Overseas Tour.

473 Bowlby, Recollections, 72-73.

474 Crimp, Overseas Tour.

475 Bowlby, Recollections, 76-77.

476 Crimp, Overseas Tour.

477 Bowlby, Recollections, 78-79.

478 Bowlby, Recollections, 79.

479 Bowlby, Recollections, 82.

480 Hastings, The Rifle Brigade, 278in.

481 2 Rifle Brigade, War Diary.

482 Bowlby, Recollections, 84.

483 Bowlby, Recollections, 88.

484 Bowlby, Recollections, 83.

485 Bowlby, 87.

486 Crimp, Overseas Tour.

487 Crimp, Overseas Tour.

488 Crimp, Overseas Tour.

489 Crimp, Overseas Tour.

490 Bowlby, Recollections, 101.

491 Hastings, All Hell Let Loose, Loc. 8755.

[492] Crimp, Overseas Tour.

[493] Hastings, The Rifle Brigade, 283.

[494] 2 Rifle Brigade, War Diary.

[495] 2 Rifle Brigade, War Diary.

[496] Bowlby, Recollections, 102.

[497] Alan Juniper Service Record.

[498] 2 Rifle Brigade, War Diary.

[499] Crimp, Overseas Tour.

[500] Alan Juniper Service Record.

[501] Corciano 44, The commune of Corciano, Futura Film, Published on April 21, 2015, www.youtube.com/watch?v=eD_N36OAl8M

[502] Filippo Tommaso Marinetti, "The Futurist Manifesto," Item 9, Page 3, *The Society for Asian Art*, www.societyforasianart.org/sites/default/files/manifesto_futurista.pdf

[503] Marinetti, The Futurist Manifesto, 4.

[504] Professor Jane Slaughter, review of Peasant Women and Politics in Fascist Italy: The Massaie Rurali, (review no. 339) www.history.ac.uk/reviews/review/339 Date accessed: 2 May, 2017

[505] Slaughter, review of Peasant Women and Politics.

[506] Jay Griffiths, "Fire, hatred and speed!" *Aeon*, February 8, 2017, https://aeon.co/essays/the-macho-violent-culture-of-italian-fascism-was-prophetic

[507] Rome, Open City (1945), Directed by Roberto Rossellini, Screenplay by Sergio Amidei and Federico Fellini, Minerva Film SPA (Italy) Joseph Burstyn & Arthur Maye.

[508] Lorenza Mazzetti, The Sky Falls (The Bodley Head, 1962).

[509] The Constantine Report. "Investigation Opened into the Nazi Murderers of Einstein's Family." Accessed April 8, 2016. www.constantinereport.com/search-for-nazi-murderers-of-einsteins-relatives/

[510] Corciano 44.

[511] Corciano 44.

[512] Corciano 44.

[513] Corciano 44.

[514] Tommy Livingstone, "British family hunt for Kiwi who helped deserting soldier," *The Dominion Post*, May 6, 2016. www.stuff.co.nz/dominion-post/news/79689177/british-family-hunt-for-kiwi-who-helped-deserted-soldier

[515] Maxine Rothwell, e-mail to the author, March 13, 2017.

[516] Poocs, May 6, comment on Tommy Livingstone, "British family hunt for Kiwi who helped deserting soldier," *The Dominion Post*, May 6, 2016.

www.stuff.co.nz/dominion-post/news/79689177/british-family-hunt-for-kiwi-who-helped-deserted-soldier

[517] Alan Juniper Service Record.

[518] Stephenie Stockley, e-mail to the author, October 14, 2016.

[519] Bowlby, Recollections, 264.

[520] Alex Bowlby, Obituary, *The Daily Telegraph*

Selected Bibliography

Aristotle, *Politics* (Oxford, rev. ed.). R. F. Stalley, ed. Ernest Barker, trans. Oxford University Press, 2009.

Barr, Niall. *Pendulum of war: The three battles of El Alamein* (New ed.). Vintage, 2010.

Bartov, Omer. *Hitler's army: Soldiers, Nazis, and war in the Third Reich*. Oxford University Press, 1992.

Blake, William. *Jerusalem* (Classic rep. ed). Forgotten Books, 2017.

Bowlby, Alex. *Recollections of Rifleman Bowlby*. Pen and Sword, 1969.

Camus, Albert. *Myth of Sisyphus* (Intl. ed.). Penguin, 2005.

Clifford, Alexander G. *Three against Rommel: The campaigns of Wavell, Auchinleck and Alexander*. GG Harrap, 1943.

Cooksey, Jon. *Operation chariot: The raid on St. Nazaire*. Leo Cooper Ltd., 2004.

Crimp, R. L. *Diary of a desert rat*. Pan Books, Ltd. 1974.

David, Saul. *Mutiny at Salerno, 1943: An injustice exposed*. Conway, 2005.

Fabre, Cécile. "Cosmopolitanism, just war theory and legitimate authority." *International Affairs* 84, no. 5 (2008): 963-976.

Fabre, Cécile. "Internecine war killings." *Utilitas* 24, no. 2 (2012): 214-236.

Fabre, Cécile. *Cosmopolitan war*. Oxford University Press, 2012.

Fagg, John Edwin. *History of the second world war* (United Kingdom Military Series). Sir James Butler, ed. British Information Services, 1961.

Green, Matthew. *Aftershock: Fighting war, surviving trauma and finding peace.* Portobello Books, 2015.

Haidt, Jonathan. *The righteous mind: Why are good people divided by politics and religion.* Penguin, 2012.

Hamner, Christopher H. *Enduring battle: American soldiers in three wars, 1776-1945.* University Press of Kansas, 2011.

Harari, Yuval Noah. *Homo Deus: A brief history of tomorrow.* Random House, 2016.

Hastings, Max. *All Hell let loose: The world at war 1939-1945.* Harper Press, 2012.

Hastings, Robin Hood William Stuart. *The Rifle Brigade in the second world war 1939-1945.* Gale & Polden Ltd., 1950.

Hogg, Ian. *Armour in conflict.* Jane's Publishing, 1989.

Humble, Richard. *Crusader: Eighth Army's forgotten victory, November 1941-January 1942.* Leo Cooper Books, 1987.

Hume, David. *A treatise of human nature: Being an attempt to introduce the experimental method of reasoning into moral subjects* (Penguin Classics, New ed.). Penguin, 1985.

Hunt, Sir David. *A Don at War.* Frank Cass, 1990.

Jackson, General Sir William. *The north African campaign, 1940-43.* Batsford, 1975.

Joyce, James. *A Portrait of the artist as a young man.* Penguin, 1965.

Kant, Immanuel. *Critique of pure reason* (Penguin Classics, rev. ed.) Marcus Weigelt, ed. Max Muller, trans. Penguin, 2008.

Koestler, Arthur, Cynthia Koestler, and Harold Harris. *Stranger on the square.* Vintage, 1984.

Krakauer, Jon. *Where men win glory: The odyssey of Pat Tillman.* Anchor, 2010.

Lazar, Seth. "Just war theory: Revisionists versus traditionalists." *Annual Review of Political Science* 20 (2017): 37-54.

Lewin, Ronald. *Rommel as military commander.* No. 28. Pen and Sword, 1990.

MacIntyre, Alasdair. *After virtue.* University of Notre Dame Press, 1981.

Marshall, Samuel Lyman Atwood. *Men against fire: The problem of battle command.* University of Oklahoma Press, 2000.

McMahan, Jeff. *Killing in war.* Oxford University Press, 2009.

Mead, Richard. *Churchill's lions: A biographical guide to the key British generals of World War II.* Spellmount, 2007.

Mill, John Stuart. *On Liberty* (Penguin Classics, rev. ed.). Gertrude Himmelfarb, ed. Penguin, 2007.

Mitcham Jr, Samuel W. *Rommel's lieutenants: The men who served the Desert Fox, France, 1940.* Stackpole Books, 2008.

Paine, Thomas. *Rights of man* (Dover Thrift ed.). Dover, 1999.

Remarque, Erich Maria. *All quiet on the western front.* Vintage, 1996.

Ritchie, Henry R. The fusing of the ploughshare: The story of a yeoman at war (2nd ed.). Henry Ritchie, 1989.

Rousseau, Jean-Jacques. *The social contract* (Penguin Classics). Maurice Cranston, trans. Penguin, 1968.

Sandel, Michael J. *Justice: What's the right thing to do?* Macmillan, 2010.

Sartre, Jean Paul. *The wall* (3rd Rev. ed.). New Directions, 1981.

Scammell, Michael. *Koestler: The indispensable intellectual.* Faber & Faber, 2011.

Scannell, Vernon. *Of love and war: New & selected poems*. Robson Book Ltd., 2002.

Scheffler, Samuel. *Death and the afterlife* (Oxford, rep. ed.). Niko, Kolodny, ed. Oxford University Press, 2016.

Scruton, Roger. *England: An elegy*. A & C Black, 2006.

Shakespeare, William. *The Life and Death of Richard II* (Oxford critical ed.). Anthony B. Dawson and Paul Yachnin, eds. Oxford University Press, 2011.

Shales, Julian. *A detailed fighting account of: 2nd Armoured Division, 9th Australian Division, 3rd Indian Motor Brigade, 7th Support Group, and 22nd Guards Brigade in contact with the Afrika Korps and units from the February to May 1941 Infantry, Artillery, and Tank Combat in Libya and Egypt* (Vol. 1). Armour Publishing, 2015.

Sharp, Marie-Louise, Nicola T. Fear, Roberto J. Rona, Simon Wessely, Neil Greenberg, Norman Jones, and Laura Goodwin. "Stigma as a barrier to seeking health care among military personnel with mental health problems." *Epidemiologic Reviews* 37, no. 1 (2015): 144-162.

Stavrianos, Leften S. "The mutiny in the Greek Armed Forces, April, 1944." *American Slavic and East European Review* 9, no. 4 (1950): 302-311.

Stewart, Adrian. *The early battles of Eighth Army: Crusader to the alamein line, 1941-42*. Stackpole Books, 2010.

Strawson, Jon. *The battle for north Africa* (No. 41). Pen and Sword, 2004.

Thalassis, Nafsika. "Treating and preventing trauma: British military psychiatry during the Second World War." PhD diss., University of Salford, UK, 2004.

Toye, Richard. *The roar of the lion: The untold story of Churchill's World War II speeches*. Oxford University Press, 2013.

Voltaire. *Candide* (Dover Thrift ed.). Francois-Marie Arouet, trans. Dover, 1991.

West, Morris. *The devil's advocate*. William Heinemann, Ltd. 1959.

About Lammi Publishing, Inc.

Incorporated in 2014, Lammi Publishing is dedicated to publishing Canadian military history from the wars before confederation to the mission in Afghanistan. Our philosophy is that we cannot forget. Our mission is to be a method of remembrance. Canadian military history has shaped not only our politics and government, but our society as well. Canadians naturally take pride in our famous victories in Western Europe, Afghanistan and South Africa. From the oceans to the air, Canadians have done their duty with skill and valor. Peacekeeping operations have taken our forces far and wide bringing hope and security to so many. Canadian uniforms have been seen around the world as harbingers of liberation, from Belgium in WWI to the Netherlands in WWII to Yugoslavia in the 1990s.

It is only by having easy access to material on these events that we can understand them, put them in context and remember. Information, analysis, and the memoires of those who served should be readily available instead of being locked away in a desk or a long-forgotten bookcase in the back of a library.

The rise of electronic books means that it is now possible for anyone to easily compile a library that would rival the best that our public libraries or universities can offer, with no more worries about short print runs and the vagaries of the antiquarian market.

To learn more about us and what we are doing, check out our website. http://lammipublishing.ca

Lightning Source UK Ltd.
Milton Keynes UK
UKHW021619260319
339925UK00005B/53/P